0 yards 750

Eixample

Catalonia
Pages 110–131

Further Afield
Pages 94–101

Catalonia

Barcelona

0 km 50
0 miles 50

EYEWITNESS TRAVEL

BARCELONA
& CATALONIA

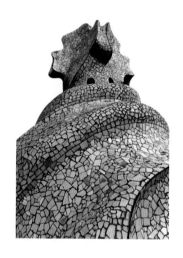

EYEWITNESS TRAVEL

BARCELONA
& CATALONIA

Main Contributor **Roger Williams**

DK

LONDON, NEW YORK,
MELBOURNE, MUNICH AND DELHI
www.dk.com

Project Editor Catherine Day
Art Editors Carolyn Hewitson, Marisa Renzullo
Editors Elizabeth Atherton, Felicity Crowe
Designer Suzanne Metcalfe-Megginson
Map Co-ordinator David Pugh
Picture Research Monica Allende
DTP Designers Samantha Borland, Lee Redmond, Pamela Shiels

Main Contributor
Roger Williams

Maps
Jane Hanson, Phil Rose, Jennifer Skelley (Lovell Jones Ltd),
Gary Bowes, Richard Toomey (ERA-Maptec Ltd)

Photographers
Max Alexander, Mike Dunning, Heidi Grassley, Alan Keohane

Illustrators
Stephen Conlin, Isidoro González-Adalid Cabezas (Acanto Arquitectura y Urbanismo S.L.),
Claire Littlejohn, Maltings Partnership, John Woodcock

Printed and bound in China by South China Printing Co. Ltd.

14 15 16 17 10 9 8 7 6 5 4 3 2 1

First published in the UK in 1999 by Dorling Kindersley Limited
80 Strand, London WC2R 0RL

**Reprinted with revisions 2000, 2001, 2002, 2003, 2004, 2005,
2006, 2008, 2009, 2010, 2011, 2013, 2014**

Copyright 1999, 2014 © Dorling Kindersley Limited, London
A Penguin Company

MIX
Paper from
responsible sources
FSC™ C018179

The information in this DK Eyewitness Travel Guide is checked regularly.
Every effort has been made to ensure that this book is as up-to-date as possible
at the time of going to press. Some details, however, such as telephone
numbers, opening hours, prices, gallery hanging arrangements and
travel information are liable to change. The publishers cannot accept responsibility
for any consequences arising from the use of this book, nor for any material
on third party websites, and cannot guarantee that any website address in
this book will be a suitable source of travel information. We value the views and
suggestions of our readers very highly. Please write to: Publisher, DK Eyewitness
Travel Guides, Dorling Kindersley, 80 Strand, London WC2R 0RL, UK
or email travelguides@dk.com.

Front cover main image: Sagrada Família by architect Antonio Gaudi, Barcelona

◀ Previous pages: The quayside at Cadaqués, on the Costa Brava

Contents

Jaume I, "El Conquistador", ruler of
Catalonia 1213–76

Introducing Barcelona and Catalonia

One of the many popular cafés in
Barcelona's redeveloped Old Port

Barcelona Area by Area

The small, whitewashed town of Cadaqués on the Costa Brava

Pa amb tomàquet – bread rubbed with
tomato, garlic and olive oil

Barcelona Metro and
Train Routes
Inside back cover

Spectacular stained-glass roof of
the Palau de la Música Catalana

Catalonia

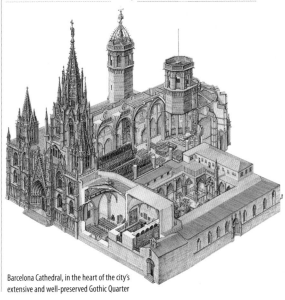

Barcelona Cathedral, in the heart of the city's
extensive and well-preserved Gothic Quarter

HOW TO USE THIS GUIDE

This guide has expert recommendations and detailed practical information that will enrich any visit to Barcelona and Catalonia. *Introducing Barcelona and Catalonia* puts the area in geographical, historical and cultural context. *Barcelona and Catalonia* is a six-chapter guide to important sights: *Barcelona at a Glance* highlights the city's

top attractions; *Old Town, Eixample* and *Montjuïc* explore Barcelona's central districts in more detail; *Further Afield* profiles sights that are outside the city centre; and *Catalonia* delves into the surrounding region's four provinces. *Travellers' Needs* covers hotels, restaurants and entertainment. The *Survival Guide* provides vital practical information.

Barcelona and Catalonia

The region is divided into five sightseeing areas – the central districts of Barcelona, sights outside the centre, and those beyond the city. Each area chapter opens with an introduction and a list of sights covered. Central districts have a Street-by-Street map of a particularly interesting part of the area. The sights further afield have a regional map.

Each chapter of *Barcelona and Catalonia* has a different colour-coded thumb tab.

Sights at a Glance lists the area's key sights (great buildings, art galleries, museums and churches) by category.

1 Area Map of the City
Sights are numbered and located on a map, with Metro stations where helpful. The sights are also shown on the *Barcelona Street Finder* on pp188–97.

Locator maps show where you are in relation to other parts of Barcelona or Spain.

2 Street-by-Street Map
The area shaded pink on the *Area Map* is shown here in greater detail with accurate drawings of all the buildings.

A suggested route for a walk covers the more interesting streets in the area.

3 Detailed Information on each Sight The sights listed at the start of the section are described individually and follow the numbering on the *Area Map*. A key to symbols summarizing practical information is shown on the back flap.

CATALONIA

Lleida · Andorra · Girona · Barcelona Province · Tarragona

There is a wealth of natural beauty in Catalonia's four provinces, plus the small Catalan-speaking country of Andorra. They offer rocky coasts and mountains, fertile plains and sandy shores. Many who visit don't stray far from the coast, but the rewards for venturing further afield are immense.

4 Introduction to Catalonia The chapter on *Catalonia* has its own introduction, providing an overview of the history and character of the region. The area covered is highlighted on the map of Spain shown on pages 112–13. The chapter explores Catalonia's rich historical, cultural and natural heritage, from the monasteries of Montserrat and Poblet to Tarragona's *casteller* festivals, from the sandy beaches of the Costa Daurada to the snowy peaks of the Pyrenees.

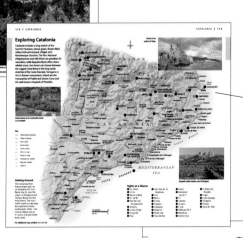

Exploring Catalonia

5 Pictorial Map This gives an illustrated overview of the whole region. All the sights covered in this chapter are numbered, and the network of major roads is marked. There are also useful tips on getting around the region by bus and train.

6 Detailed Information on each Sight All the important cities, towns and other places to visit are described individually. They are listed in order following the numbering given on the *Pictorial Map*. Within each town or city there is detailed information on important buildings and other sights.

Stars indicate the best features and works of art.

Monestir de Poblet

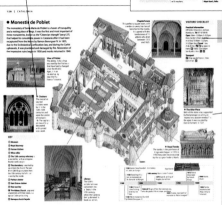

The Visitors' Checklist provides a summary of the practical information you will need to plan your visit.

7 The Top Sights These are given two or more full pages. Historic buildings are dissected to reveal their interiors. For larger historic sites, all the important buildings are labelled to help you locate those that most interest you.

INTRODUCING BARCELONA AND CATALONIA

GREAT DAYS IN BARCELONA

Days are long in Barcelona. The morning extends until well after midday, with lunch often starting around 2pm, and the late opening hours mean that afternoon merges into evening. With so much time at your disposal you'll want to make the most of your visit with a bit of planning. Each of these four itineraries follows a theme and all of the sights are reachable using public transport. Prices include travel, food and admission. Family prices are for two adults and two children.

La Rambla, an exciting avenue for a stroll at any time

Gaudí Greats

Two adults allow at least €120

- **Casa Batlló's organic forms**
- **Gaudí's extraordinary church, Sagrada Família**
- **An evening's shopping in style in Passeig de Gràcia**

Morning
For many visitors, Barcelona is synonymous with the unique architecture of Antoni Gaudí. He created many great buildings, all of which are worth visiting, but here are two places to make a start. Begin your day with a visit to Gaudí's most colourful and eccentric house, **Casa Batlló** *(see pp78–9)*. Discover its fantastic organic forms and be sure to make your way up to the roof terrace to see the remarkable chimneys and "dragon's back". A little further up the road is the equally renowned **La Pedrera**, also known as *Casa Milà (see p81)*. This can also be visited, but if you're short of time its remarkable façade can be admired from the outside. For lunch, you'll find there are several budget-priced restaurants in the streets near and parallel to Passeig de Gràcia.

Afternoon/Evening
Visit Gaudí's greatest, unfinished work, the **Sagrada Família** *(see pp82–5)*. Allow plenty of time to make sense of the dense detail on the two façades of this extraordinary church – the Passion façade and the Nativity façade – and also to explore the vertigo-inducing fantasy towers (you

Historic Treasures

Two adults allow at least €100

- **A stroll round the Gothic quarter and museums**
- **A Modernista concert hall**
- **Non-stop life on Spain's most famous street**

Morning
Barcelona's preserved medieval centre is the **Barri Gòtic** *(see pp56–7)*, a warren of streets where it is easy to get lost. You can happily spend the morning here without walking great distances. The focal point is the **Cathedral** *(see pp60–61)*. Next to it is the **Palau Reial** (Royal Palace), part of which is now the **Museu d'Història de la Ciutat** *(see pp58–9)*, where you can take a fascinating subterranean stroll over the excavated ruins of Roman Barcelona. The palace also houses what is perhaps Barcelona's most fascinating museum, the eclectic **Museu Frederic Marès** *(see p58)*. There are plenty of places for a budget lunch in this area.

Afternoon
After lunch, take a guided tour of the **Palau de la Música Catalana** *(see pp64–5)* and its dazzling Modernista interior. After that, plunge into the atmospheric **El Born district** *(see pp104–5)*, with its trendy shops. Take a look in the **Museu Picasso** *(see pp66–7)*, then wander to **La Rambla**, a busy street where there is always plenty of activity.

Richly ornamental interior of Palau de la Musica Catalana

Casa Batlló, a house in an alternative architectural universe

go up by lift and return to ground level by stairs). Coming back down to reality, return to the **Passeig de Gràcia** and browse in its stylish shops. Look out for the design emporium, **Vinçon** *(see p155)*.

Museu d'Art Contemporani façade

Art for Art's Sake

Two adults allow at least €70
- Romanesque marvels on Montjuïc hill
- Contemporary works of art
- Collection of Old Masters

Morning
The number of great galleries you can cram into a day depends on your appetite and stamina but here are five to give you a taster. Start at 10am when the **Museu Nacional d'Art de Catalunya (MNAC)** *(see p91)* opens on Montjuïc hill. Here, you'll see arguably the best collection of Romanesque art in any museum. Close by is the city's latest contemporary art gallery, **CaixaForum** *(see p92)*, situated in a Modernista factory. Lunch in a local café.

Afternoon
For a change of pace, head to the **Monestir de Pedralbes** *(see p97)*, a lovely 14th-century monastery with numerous religious objects and works of art on display. Back in the city centre, visit the **Museu d'Art Contemporani** *(see pp64–5)*, where you can be sure of something surprising, or visit the temporary exhibitions at the adjacent **Centre de Cultura Contemprània de Barcelona (CCCB)** *(see p164)*.

Morning
Tibidabo Amusement Park *(see p100)*, on the highest hill behind Barcelona, is a family day out in itself, with getting there by tram and funicular half the fun. But if you don't want to go that far, stroll down La Rambla and take the lift up the **Monument a Colom** *(see p71)* for a good view of this part of the city. From the nearby quayside, board a **Golondrina** *(see p71)* for a cruise round the harbour. Then cross the wavy footbridge for the Maremagnum shopping centre, also the best place to grab a bite to eat.

Afternoon/Evening
Attractions that are specifically for children can, if you want to extend the day, be saved until after dark. The **Aquarium** *(see p70)* offers several activities for kids, as well as tanks full of sharks and other fascinating creatures. Next to it, watch the hugely realistic (and stomach-churning) show at the **IMAX Cinema** *(see p164)*. A short walk away is the relaxing, child-friendly **Museu d'Historia de Catalunya** *(see pp70–71)* with exhibits on daily life in earlier times.

Barcelona's Aquarium, a wonderful experience for children

2 Days in Barcelona

- Admire Gaudí's unfinished masterpiece, the Sagrada Família
- Get lost in the medieval warren of the Barri Gòtic (Gothic Quarter)
- Tuck into a paella by the beach in Barceloneta

Day 1

Morning Explore one of the largest and best preserved medieval neighbourhoods in Europe, the **Barri Gòtic** *(see pp56–7)*. Admire the stunning **Cathedral** *(see pp60–61)*, particularly the enchanting cloister, and visit the remnants of the ancient Roman settlement in the **Museu d'Història de la Ciutat** (Barcelona History Museum) *(see pp58–9)*. Have lunch in one of the area's many restaurants and cafés.

Afternoon Stroll down **La Rambla** *(see pp62–3)* to **Port Vell** *(see p70)*, where yachts bob in the harbour. Then visit **Barceloneta** *(see p69)*, the fascinating fishing neighbourhood (perhaps grabbing some picnic supplies at the fantastic market on the Plaça de la Font), before hitting the beaches. Finish the day with paella on the seafront.

Day 2

Morning Jump on the Metro to reach Gaudí's extraordinary **Sagrada Família** *(see pp82–5)*, its towers visible across the city, yet still awaiting completion. There's another Modernista

A beautiful view of the city from the roof terraces of Gaudí's La Pedrera

masterpiece very close by in the fairytale **Hospital de la Santa Creu i Santa Pau** *(see p81)*. Head back to have lunch in the Eixample neighbourhood.

Afternoon Wander along the **Passeig de Gràcia** *(see p74)*, Barcelona's most fashionable street, perhaps doing a bit of shopping at one of the chic boutiques. This street is home to two of Gaudí's most spectacular domestic buildings: **La Pedrera** *(see p81)* and **Casa Batlló** *(see pp78–9)*. Both are open to visitors, or you could just admire the stunning façades. Go for tapas in the Eixample district.

3 Days in Barcelona

- Be amazed by Gaudí's "Dragon House", Casa Batlló
- Visit the fantastic Picasso Museum
- Admire the stunning Romanesque mosaics in MNAC

Day 1

Morning Amble down the famous promenade, **La Rambla** *(see pp62–3)*, then dive into the stone warren of the **Barri Gòtic** (Gothic Quarter) *(see pp56–7)*. Take a peek at the **Casa de la Ciutat** *(see p59)*, the **Palau de la Generalitat** *(see p59)*, and perhaps visit the fascinating **Museu d'Història de la Ciutat** (Barcelona History Museum) *(see pp58–9)*, and the sublime Gothic **Cathedral** *(see pp60–61)*. Tuck into lunch in one of

the neighbourhood's great old-fashioned taverns.

Afternoon Hang out in the trendy **Born** neighbourhood *(see pp104–105)*, where the narrow streets are lined with boho-chic boutiques. Visit the **Museu Picasso** *(see p66)* and the city's most beautiful Gothic church, the **Basílica de Santa Maria del Mar** *(see pp66–7)*, before enjoying a stroll around the **Parc de la Ciutadella** *(see p67)*. Enjoy some tapas at one of El Born's stylish eateries.

Day 2

Morning Devote the day to Gaudí. Spend the morning at the **Sagrada Família** *(see pp82–5)*, perhaps taking a lift up one of the enormous towers, and then wander up to the nearby **Hospital de la Santa Creu i Santa Pau** *(see p81)*, built by another Modernista master, Domènech i Montaner. Take the Metro to the Eixample neighbourhood for lunch.

Afternoon Visit **Casa Batlló** *(see pp78–9)*, one of Gaudí's most magical creations, and compare it with buildings by two other great Modernista architects which occupy the same block, known as the **Illa de la Discòrdia** *(see p80)*. If you've got time, perhaps also take in **La Pedrera** *(see p81)*, with its undulating roof terrace. You might also drop in to the **Fundació Antoni Tàpies** *(see p80)*, where contemporary artworks are displayed in an early Modernista building.

Barceloneta beach, one of the best urban beaches in the world

Day 3
Morning Spend the morning at the **Museu Nacional d'Art de Catalunya (MNAC)** *(see p91)*, admiring the superb medieval frescoes that once adorned isolated Pyrenean churches. Then amble up through lovely gardens to reach the **Castell de Montjuïc** *(see p93)* on top of the hill, to enjoy spectacular views. Sway across the harbour on the cable car to **Barceloneta** *(see p69)* and enjoy some freshly prepared seafood by the beach.

Afternoon Stroll through the salty old fishermen's *barrí* of Barceloneta up to **Port Vell** *(see p70)*, where fancy yachts have now taken the place of fishing boats. Say hello to Columbus, atop the **Monument a Colom** *(see p71)*, then tour the harbour in one of the pretty, old-fashioned "swallow boats" called *golindrinas (see p71)*, or visit the superb **Museu Marítim** *(see p71)*, set in medieval shipyards.

5 Days in Barcelona

- Picnic in Gaudí's Park Güell
- Tour the fabled Camp Nou stadium and visit the Museu del FC Barcelona
- Admire the opulence of the Modernista Palau de la Música Catalana

Day 1
Morning Wander down **La Rambla** *(see pp62–3)*, popping in to the Boqueria Market to be dazzled by the array of produce, before arriving at **Port Vell** *(see p70)*, the city's spruced-up harbour. Admire the **Monument a Colom** *(see p71)* or visit the **Maremagnum** shopping and entertainment centre *(see p70)*, also home to the city's wonderful **Aquarium** *(see p70)*.

Afternoon Get lost in the narrow lanes and squares of the atmospheric **Barri Gòtic** (Gothic Quarter) *(see pp56–7)*, dropping in at the **Museu d'Història de la Ciutat** (Barcelona History Museum) *(see pp58–9)* to admire the grand throne room where

Delicacies on display at the Boqueria market

Isabella and Ferdinand once greeted Columbus. Visit the beautiful Gothic **Cathedral** *(see pp60–61)*, before enjoying delicious tapas nearby.

Day 2
Morning Head into the multicultural **El Raval** neighbourhood *(see p64)*, beginning with a tour of Gaudí's **Palau Güell** *(see p64)*, one of his earliest commissions. Then head up to the dazzling, light-filled **Museu d'Art Contemporani** *(see p64)* for a shot of contemporary culture, and have lunch on the huge square in front of the museum.

Afternoon Wander along the **Passeig de Gràcia** *(see p106)*, where fancy shops rub shoulders with spectacular Modernista buildings, such as the trio of superb mansions including Gaudí's **Casa Batlló** in the Illa de la Discòrdia *(see pp78–9)*. Then head up to the **Park Güell** *(see pp98–9)* for spectacular, city-wide views.

Day 3
Morning Chic shops and arty cafés await you in the **Born** district *(see pp104–105)*, where you'll also find the **Museu Picasso** *(see p66)*, the **Basílica de Santa Maria** *(see p66–7)*, and the extraordinary **Palau de la Música Catalana** *(see p65)*, a lavish Modernista concert hall. Stop for lunch at Els Quatre Gats, once patronized by Picasso.

Afternoon Spend the afternoon in **Barceloneta** *(see p69)*, the old fishing district, which has a great market. Take a long

walk along the spectacular city beaches, and follow it up with a well-deserved seafood dinner.

Day 4
Morning Spend the morning at the **Sagrada Família** *(see pp82–5)*, Gaudí's vast and still unfinished temple, and the nearby **Hospital de la Santa Creu i Santa Pau** *(see p81)* designed by Domènech i Muntaner, another leading light of the Modernista movement.

Afternoon Make a pilgrimage to the Camp Nou stadium, which can be toured as part of a visit to the **FC Barcelona Museum** *(see p96)*. Walk out onto the pitch and imagine the crowds roaring. Then, go back in time at the **Monestir Maria de Pedralbes** *(see p97)*, an enchanting Gothic church and cloister, now part of the city's history museum.

Day 5
Morning Head to Montjuïc to visit the sublime Romanesque artworks in the **Museu Nacional d'Art de Catalunya (MNAC)** *(see p91)* and, if time allows, pop into the nearby **Archaeological Museum** *(see p91)*. Picnic in one of the lovely gardens nearby, or have lunch in the museum café.

Afternoon Visit the **Fundació Joan Miró** *(see p90)*, set in a stunning contemporary building with wonderful views over the city, then stroll back downhill to enjoy the enchanting spectacle of the **Font Màgica** fountain *(see p92)*.

Palau de la Música Catalana, a Modernista palace dedicated to local music

Portsmouth, ↑
Plymouth

Putting Barcelona and Catalonia on the Map

Catalonia lies in the northeastern corner of the Iberian Peninsula and occupies six per cent of Spain. Barcelona, its capital, lies almost exactly halfway along its coastline, which in turn stretches a quarter of the way down Spain's Mediterranean seaboard. Barcelona is the main bridging point to the Catalan-speaking Balearic Islands.

Key

━━ Motorway (highway)

── Major road

━━ International border

── Regional border

For map symbols *see back flap*

Barcelona City Centre

Set between the mountains and the sea, which still play an integral part in city life, Barcelona is a rare city, a patchwork of distinctive districts telling the story of its growth from a medieval core to the 19th-century expansion and today's ultra-modern showpieces. The three main sightseeing areas described in this guide illustrate this startling diversity. The hill of Montjuïc, abutting the sea, forms the southwestern end of an arc of steep hills that almost completely encloses the city. It is a district of monumental buildings and open spaces. The Old Town has a superb Gothic heart with a myriad of narrow streets twisting among ancient houses. The densely populated Eixample, in contrast, is a district of immensely long, straight streets and superb Modernista architecture.

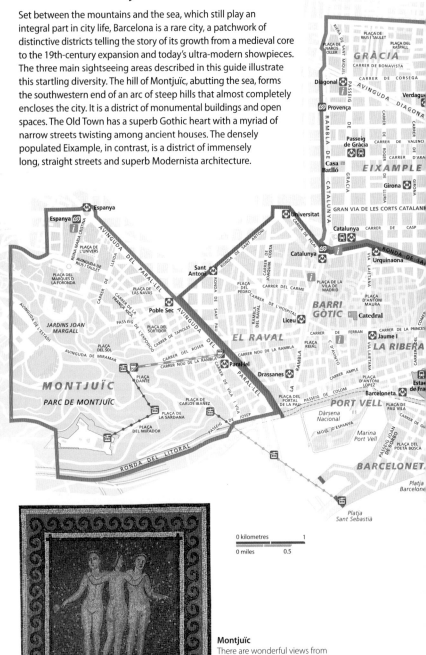

Montjuïc

There are wonderful views from the top of this large hill. Several of Barcelona's best museums are here, including the Archaeological Museum *(see p91)* which displays this Roman mosaic.

For keys to symbols *see back flap*

Eixample

This area covers the most interesting part of the city's 19th-century expansion. Walks along its streets will reveal countless details of the Modernista style, such as this ornate doorway of Casa Comalat *(see p29)* in Avinguda Diagonal.

Old Town

This area includes all the oldest districts of Barcelona and its port, the 18th-century fishing "village" of Barceloneta and the new waterside developments. This new swing bridge is in the Old Port *(see p69)*.

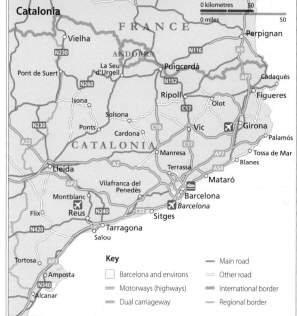

Catalonia

Much of Catalonia is mountainous, with Barcelona sited on a narrow coastal plain. The beaches of nearby Sitges (see p130) are popular with city-dwellers.

Key

☐ Barcelona and environs	━━ Main road
══ Motorways (highways)	⋯⋯ Other road
══ Dual carriageway	▦▦ International border
	━━ Regional border

A PORTRAIT
OF CATALONIA

Barcelona is one of the great Mediterranean cities. Few places are so redolent with history, few so boldly modern. Animated and inspired, it is a city that sparkles as much at night-time as in the full light of day. It is famous for its main avenue, La Rambla, for its bars, its museums and its enthusiasm for life.

Barcelona is the capital of the autonomous region of Catalonia, the most northeasterly corner of Spain, bordering France. The region is divided into four provinces, named after their provincial capitals: Barcelona, Girona, Lleida and Tarragona.

The city of Barcelona lies between two rivers, the Llobregat and the Besòs, and is backed by the Collserola hills which rise to a 512-m (1,680-ft) peak at the Tibidabo amusement park. The city grew up as the industrial sweatshop of Spain, though the shunting yards and seaside warehouses have now gone. Around four million people live in Barcelona and its suburbs – about half the population of Catalonia. It is Spain's second city after its old rival, Madrid.

Politics and Society

Catalonia is governed by the Generalitat, housed in the Palau de la Generalitat in the heart of the Old Town and on the site of the Roman forum. The region's parliament is located in the Parc de la Ciutadella. The city of Barcelona has a separate administration, and its town hall, the Casa de la Ciutat, faces the Generalitat across the Plaça de Sant Jaume. Catalonia has developed its own police force, which has now taken over from Spain's national police in most of Catalonia.

Catalans are progressive but, as in many other countries, people in rural areas are more conservative than those in the cities. For 23 years after Franco's death, the Generalitat was run by the conservative Convergència i Unió under Jordi Pujol, while the city council was run by socialists. In 2003, Catalans elected a socialist Generalitat to power under Pascual Maragall, who was replaced by José Montilla, also a socialist, in 2006, followed by Artur Mas, from Convergència i Unió, in 2011.

Strolling on La Rambla, Barcelona's tree-lined, traffic-free main avenue, is popular with locals and visitors

◄ Mask-like balconies ornament the façade of Antoni Gaudí's astonishing Casa Batlló

St George's Day in April – the day for giving books

Catalans, who banned bullfighting in 2012 and whose sedate national dance, the *sardana,* is unruffled by passion, are a serious, hardworking people. Some would rather be associated with northern Europeans than with other Spaniards, whom they regard as indolent. Part of their complaint against Madrid has been that, as one of the richest regions of Spain, they put more into the national coffers than they take out.

Two emotions are said to guide Catalans: *seny,* which means solid common sense, and *rauxa,* a creative chaos. A bourgeois, conservative element of Barcelona society can be seen at concerts and in pastry shops, but a certain surreal air is often evident, on La Rambla, for instance, where sometimes it seems that anything goes. The two elements are mixed in each person, and even the most staid may have the occasional *cop de rauxa,* or moment of chaotic ecstasy.

Catalans are not burdened with self-doubt. The vigour with which they have rebuilt parts of their capital since the early 1980s shows flair and a firm hand. Places of great sentimental value, such as Barceloneta's beach-side restaurant shacks,

were torn down. Stunning new buildings such as the Museu d'Art Contemporani were put up in the Old Town, and old buildings such as the Café Zurich, a famous rendezvous for writers, artists and intellectuals on La Rambla, were restored without hesitation.

Language and Culture

A Romance language similar to the old Langue d'Oc, or Provençal, once used in France, Catalan is Catalonia's official language, spoken by some eight million people. It has always been a living language and it continued to be spoken in the home even when it was banned by Franco. Catalans do not think it rude to talk to each other in Catalan in front of someone who speaks only Spanish. All public signs and official documents in Catalonia are in Spanish and Catalan.

Street performer on La Rambla

If *rauxa* fuels the creative spirit as claimed, then Catalonia has been blessed with an abundance. Modernisme, led by Antoni Gaudí, is the region's gift to world architecture. Painters Joan Miró,

Poster for a Pedro Almodóvar film

Beach at Tossa de Mar on the Costa Brava

Salvador Dalí and Antoni Tàpies were born here, while Pablo Picasso spent his formative years in Barcelona. Designs by Javier Mariscal, creator of the 1992 Olympic motifs and Cobi, the mascot, furniture by Oscar Tusquets and fashion by Toni Miró help make Barcelona a city of great style. Bigas Luna, locally-born director of *Jamón Jamón,* Pedro Almodóvar, whose film *All About My Mother* was shot in Barcelona and Woody Allen's *Vicky, Cristina, Barcelona* have raised the area's profile in the cinema.

Over the last 150 years, some outstanding musicians have emerged from Catalonia. Composers Isaac Albéniz (1860–1909), Enric Granados (1867–1916) and Frederic Mompou (1893–1987) brought music imbued with a true Iberian idiom into the classical mainstream. Pau Casals (1876–1973) ranked among the greatest of all cellists; Jordi Savall is an international figure in early music, and Montserrat Caballé and Josep Carreras can fill opera houses worldwide. New Catalan writing has burgeoned since the 1970s and there are many literary prizes; the most remarkable global success has been *The Shadow of the Wind* by Carlos Ruiz Zafón (English translation published in 2004).

Work and Leisure

Catalans stay true to their traditions and their families. Sunday lunch is a time to get together, although even during the week, most people who can do so return home for lunch. This creates a rush hour four times a day, with a lull in the early afternoon. Shops close around 8:30pm, and between 6pm and 8:30pm the streets are crowded. Dinner or entertainment starts around 9pm.

Allegiance to the local football team, Barça, is a matter of national pride for its supporters. Meals out, concerts and the cinema are popular activities. The week begins quietly but, as the weekend approaches, streets fill and visitors leaving La Rambla at midnight to go to bed may feel they are leaving a good party too soon.

Demonstration for Catalan independence

Flowers of the Matollar

The *matollar* is the distinctive landscape of Spain's eastern Mediterranean coast. This scrubland rich in wild flowers is the result of centuries of woodland clearance, during which the native holm oak was felled for timber and to provide land for grazing and cultivation. Many colourful plants have adapted to the extremes of climate here. Most flower in spring, when hillsides are daubed with yellow broom and pink and white cistuses, and the air is perfumed by aromatic herbs such as rosemary, lavender and thyme. Buzzing insects feed on the abundance of nectar and pollen.

Spanish broom is a small bush with yellow flowers on slender branches. The black seed pods split when dry, scattering the seeds on the ground.

The century plant's flower stalk can reach 10 m (32 ft).

Jerusalem sage, an attractive shrub which is often grown in gardens, has tall stems surrounded by bunches of showy yellow flowers. Its leaves are greyish-white and woolly.

Aleppo pine   Rosemary

Rose garlic has round clusters of violet or pink flowers at the end of a single stalk. It survives the summer as the bulb familiar to all cooks.

Foreign Invaders

Several plants from the New World have managed to colonize the bare ground of the *matollar*. The prickly pear, thought to have been brought back by Christopher Columbus, produces a delicious fruit which can be picked only with thickly gloved hands. The rapidly growing century plant, a native of Mexico which has tough, spiny leaves, sends up a tall flower shoot only when it is 10–15 years old, after which it dies.

Prickly pear in bloom

Flowering shoots of the century plant

Common thyme is a low-growing aromatic herb which is widely cultivated for use in the kitchen.

The mirror orchid, a small plant which grows on grassy sites, is easily distinguished from other orchids by the brilliant metallic blue patch inside the lip, fringed by brown hairs.

Climate Chart

Temp (°C) / **Rainfall (mm)**

J F M A M J J A S O N D

— Temperature　▪ Rainfall

Most plants found in the *matollar* come into bloom in the warm, moist spring. The plants protect themselves from losing water during the dry summer heat with thick leaves or waxy secretions, or by storing moisture in bulbs or tubers.

Wildlife of the Matollar

The animals which live in the *matollar* are most often seen early in the morning, before the temperature is high. Countless insects fly from flower to flower, providing a source of food for birds. Smaller mammals, such as mice and voles, are active only at night when it is cooler and there are few predators around.

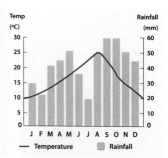

Holm oaks are very common in eastern Spain. The leaves are tough and rubbery to prevent water loss.

The strawberry tree is an evergreen shrub with glossy serrated leaves. Its inedible strawberry-like fruit turns red when ripe.

Ladder snakes feed on small mammals, birds and insects. The young are identified by a black pattern like the rungs of a ladder, but adults are marked with two simple stripes.

Tree heather

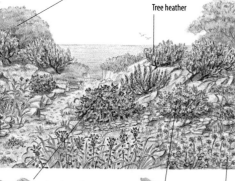

Scorpions hide under rocks or wood by day. When disturbed, the tail is curled quickly over the body in a threatening gesture. The sting, lethal to small animals, can cause some irritation to humans.

Grey-leaved cistus, growing on sunny sites, has crumpled petals and bright yellow anthers.

The Dartford warbler, a skulking bird which has dark plumage and a cocked tail, sings melodiously during its mating display. Males are more vividly coloured than females.

Narrow-leaved cistus exudes a sticky aromatic gum used in perfumes.

The swallow-tail butterfly is one of the most conspicuous of the great many insects living in the *matollar*. Bees, ants and grasshoppers are also extremely common.

Star clover is a low-growing annual whose fruit develops into a star-shaped seed head. Its flowers are often pale pink.

Romanesque Art and Architecture

Catalonia has an exceptional collection of medieval buildings constructed between the 11th and 13th centuries in a distinctive local Romanesque style. There are more than 2,000 examples, most of them churches. Those in the Pyrenees, which have largely escaped both attack and modernization, have survived particularly well. Churches had lofty bell towers, barrel-vaulted naves, rounded arches and imaginative sculpture, as well as remarkable wall paintings. Some frescoes and furniture have come to rest in the Museu Nacional d'Art de Catalunya *(see p91)* in Barcelona, which has the largest Romanesque collection in the world.

Sant Jaume de Frontanyà
(see p116) is a former Augustinian canonry with typical 11th-century features, such as the Lombard bands below the roofs of the three apses. The large octagonal central lantern is, however, unusual.

Vielha •   Artíes •

Esterri d'Àneu •

Boí •

Llavorsí •

Puigcerdà •

Sort •

Pont de Suert •   La Seu d'Urgell •

Martinet •

Ribes d Frese

La Pobla de Segur •

Bagà •

Coll de Nargó •

Rip

Tremp •

Berga •

Isona •

Gironella •

Solsona •

El Segre

Ponts •

Sant Climent de Taüll, an exemplary church in the Vall de Boí *(see p115)*, was consecrated in 1123. Its frescoes, including a *Christ in Majesty (see p91)*, are replicas, but the originals, which are now in Barcelona, are among the best in Catalonia.

Monestir de Santa Maria de Ripoll

The saints

The story of Solomon

The Old Testament

David and his musicians

The story of Moses

Christ with historical figures

The visions of Daniel

Plinth with patterns

The portal of the church of the former Benedictine monastery at Ripoll is known as "The Ripoll Bible" for its allegorical carvings. Although the church was founded in 879 and rebuilt under Abbot Oliva in 1032, the portal was added only in the late 12th century. In this fine piece of Romanesque decoration Christ sits above the doorway amid the beasts symbolizing the Apostles, and the monthly agricultural occupations are represented on the doorway pillars. There are seven biblical friezes running the length of the wall. The top frieze *(see p116)* over the tympanum represents the old men of the Apocalypse; the others are described in the captions above.

0 kilometres   30

0 miles   15

Sant Pere de Camprodon *(see p117)*, consecrated in 1169, is a monastery church in mature Romanesque style with five square apses. The slightly pointed barrel vault over the nave hints at the Gothic style to come.

Area of Major Romanesque Interest

Sant Cristòfol de Beget *(see p117)* is a beautiful church in a picturesque hamlet hidden deep in a valley. It has a uniquely preserved interior which includes a Romanesque baptismal font and this famous 12th-century crucifix – the *Majestat*.

Sant Pere de Rodes, situated at 600 m (1,968 ft) above sea level, was a Benedictine monastery. In its church's nave are the pillars of a Roman temple once on this site.

- Portbou
- La Jonquera
- Llançà
- Camprodon
- Figueres
- Roses
- Besalú
- *Golf de Roses*
- Olot
- Bàscara
- L'Escala
- Banyoles
- L'Estartit
- Parlavà
- Manlleu
- Anglès
- Girona
- 'ic
- Santa Coloma de Farners
- Palafrugell
- a
- Palamós
- Sant Feliu de Guíxols

Sant Pere de Besalú *(see p117)* is the 12th-century church of an earlier Benedictine monastery. Stone lions guard this window over the portal. Inside, the ambulatory has finely carved capitals.

The Museu Episcopal de Vic *(see p126)* adjacent to the cathedral has an exquisite collection of Romanesque art. It includes this richly coloured and moving portrayal of the Visitation, which was originally an altar decoration in Lluçà monastery.

Sant Pere de Galligants *(see p118)*, a former Benedictine abbey, captures the very essence of Romanesque style. It has an 11th-century portal with a rose window, three naves and an octagonal bell tower. The cloister capitals are carved with biblical scenes. It now houses Girona's archaeology museum.

Gaudí and Modernisme

Towards the end of the 19th century a new style of art and architecture, Modernisme, a variant of Art Nouveau, was born in Barcelona. It became a means of expression for Catalan nationalism and counted Josep Puig i Cadafalch, Lluís Domènech i Montaner and, above all, Antoni Gaudí i Cornet *(see p80)* among its major exponents. Barcelona's Eixample district *(see pp72–85)* is full of the highly original buildings that they created for their wealthy clients.

All aspects of decoration in a Modernista building, even interior design, were planned by the architect. This door and its tiled surround are in Gaudí's 1906 Casa Batlló *(see p80)*.

A dramatic cupola covers the central salon, which rises through three floors. It is pierced by small round holes, inspired by Islamic architecture, giving the illusion of stars.

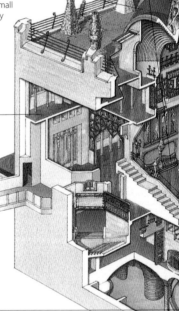

Upper galleries are richly decorated with carved wood and cofferwork.

The spiral carriage ramp is an early sign of Gaudí's predilection for curved lines. He would later exploit this to the full in the wavy façade of his masterpiece, La Pedrera *(see p81)*.

The Evolution of Modernisme

1850	1865	1880	1895	1910	1925

1859 Civil engineer Ildefons Cerdà i Sunyer submits proposals for expansion of Barcelona

1878 Gaudí graduates as an architect

1883 Gaudí takes over design of Neo-Gothic Sagrada Família *(see pp82–3)*

Detail of Sagrada Família

1888 Barcelona Universal Exhibition gives impetus to Modernisme

1900 Josep Puig i Cadafalch builds Casa Amatller *(see p80)*

1903 Lluís Domènech i Montaner builds Hospital de la Santa Creu i de Sant Pau *(see p81)*

1905 Domènech i Montaner builds Casa Lleó Morera *(see p80)*. Puig i Cadafalch builds Casa Terrades *(see p81)*

1910 La Pedrera completed

1926 Gaudí dies

Bizarrely decorated chimneys became one of the trademarks of Gaudí's later work. They reach a fantastic extreme on the gleaming, humpbacked roof of the Casa Batlló.

Elaborate wrought iron lamps light the grand hall.

Ceramic tiles decorate the chimneys.

Gaudí's Materials

Gaudí designed, or collaborated on designs, for almost every known medium. He combined bare, undecorated materials – wood, rough-hewn stone, rubble and brickwork – with meticulous craftwork in wrought iron and stained glass. Mosaics of ceramic tiles were used to cover his fluid, uneven forms.

Stained-glass window in the Sagrada Família

Mosaic of ceramic tiles, Park Güell *(see p98)*

Detail of iron gate, Casa Vicens *(see pp28–9)*

Tiles on El Capricho in Comillas, Cantabria

Parabolic arches, used extensively by Gaudí, beginning in the Palau Güell, show his interest in Gothic architecture. These arches form a corridor in his 1890 Col.legi de les Teresianes, a convent school in the west of Barcelona.

Escutcheon alludes to the Catalan coat of arms.

Palau Güell

Gaudí's first major building in the centre of the city, on La Rambla (see p62), established his international reputation for outstanding, original architecture. Built in 1889 for his life-long patron, the industrialist Eusebi Güell, the mansion stands on a small plot of land in a narrow street, making the façade difficult to see. Inside, Gaudí creates a sense of space by using carved screens, recesses and galleries.

Organic forms inspired the wrought iron around the gates to the palace. Gaudí's later work teems with wildlife, such as this dragon, covered with brightly coloured tiles, which guards the steps in the Park Güell.

La Ruta del Modernisme

The examples of Modernista architecture in Barcelona mapped here lie along a route designed by the city's tourist office. A *Guidebook*, available from Catalunya's tourist office *(see p175)*, the Hospital de Sant Pau, the Güell Pavillions on Avinguda Pedralbes *(see p81)* and some bookshops, provides up to 50 per cent discount on admission charges and gives you the freedom to plan your own itinerary. The Casa Batlló, Palau Güell and Palau de la Música Catalana all have guided tours, and entry is discounted at the selected museums. Many of the other premises, however, are privately owned houses, shops, cafés and hotels.

⑱ Casa Vicens

This bright, angular, turreted building by Antoni Gaudí, with ceramic mosaics and patterned brickwork, shows Moorish influence. The iron gate and fencing are hallmarks of his work.

㊶ Palau Baró de Quadras

Built in 1906, this handsome house is by Josep Puig i Cadafalch. The intricate, sculptured frieze above the first-floor windows has close affinities to Spanish early Renaissance Plateresque style.

⑲ Casa Lleó Morera

The first-floor dining room of this house is one of Barcelona's most stunning interiors. The stained-glass windows are by Lluís Rigalt and the eight ceramic mosaic wall panels, depicting idyllic country scenes, are by Gaspar Homar.

⑦ Antiga Casa Figueres

The mosaic, stained-glass and wrought-iron decoration of this, the most famous of the city's Modernista stores, was carried out in 1902 by Antoni Ros i Güell. It is today the elegant Pastisseria Escribà.

Key

···· Walking route

···· Bus route

···· Metro route

| 0 kilometres | 500 |
| 0 miles | 500 |

For map symbols *see back flap*

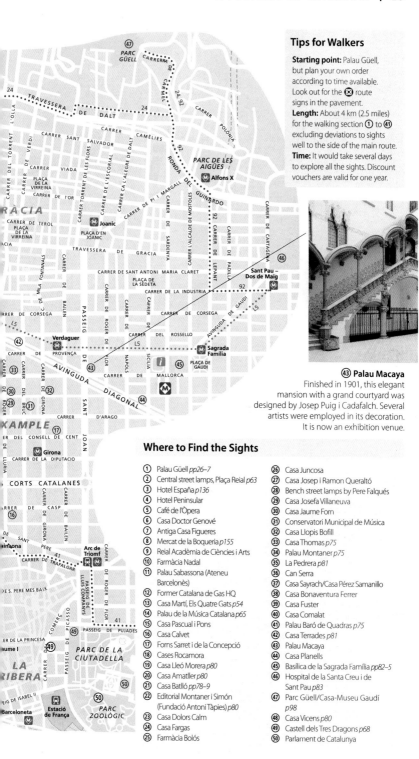

Tips for Walkers

Starting point: Palau Güell, but plan your own order according to time available. Look out for the ⊗ route signs in the pavement.

Length: About 4 km (2.5 miles) for the walking section ① to ㊶ excluding deviations to sights well to the side of the main route.

Time: It would take several days to explore all the sights. Discount vouchers are valid for one year.

㊸ **Palau Macaya**
Finished in 1901, this elegant mansion with a grand courtyard was designed by Josep Puig i Cadafalch. Several artists were employed in its decoration. It is now an exhibition venue.

Where to Find the Sights

Catalan Painting

Catalonia has a fine, if uneven, painterly tradition. It began where Spanish medieval painting was born – in the Pyrenees, where Romanesque churches were brightened by bold frescoes full of imagination *(see pp24–5)*. The subsequent Gothic period, which represented Catalonia at the height of its powers, was followed by a long period of lesser artistic achievement until the wealth of the 19th century revived the creative spirit. This fostered some of Europe's great 20th-century painters, all of whom, as Catalans, felt a close affinity to the spirit of Catalonia's incomparable Romanesque art.

St George and the Princess (late 15th century) by Jaume Huguet

Gothic

One of the first named artists in Catalonia was Ferrer Bassa (1285–1348), court painter to Jaume II. Bassa's exquisite decoration in the chapel of the Monastery of Pedralbes *(see p97)* constitutes the first known example of oil-painted murals, a style undoubtedly influenced by contemporary Italian painting.

In sculpture, Catalan Gothic begins with the work of Mestre Bartomeu (1250–1300), whose extraordinary, Oriental-looking *Calvary* is in the fine Gothic collection of Girona's Museu d'Art *(see p119)*.

There are also Gothic collections in Vic and Solsona *(see p126)* and particularly Barcelona, where the Museu Nacional d'Art de Catalunya *(see p91)* has the most impressive. Important works include those by Lluís Borrassà (1365–1425), who painted Tarragona cathedral's altarpiece, and Lluís Dalmau (d.1463), who visited Bruges and studied under Jan van Eyck. A feature of Catalan Gothic is *esgrafiat*, a process of gilding haloes, garments and backgrounds, which was favoured by one of the greatest Catalan Gothic artists, Jaume Huguet (1415–92). His *St George and the Princess* seems to capture the full majesty of a cultured and prosperous nation.

Renaissance to Neo-Classical

Artistically, Catalonia languished from the 16th to the 18th century, a period dominated by great masters from elsewhere in Spain: El Greco in Toledo, Murillo and Zurbarán in Seville, Ribera in Valencia, and Velázquez and later Goya in Madrid. A few of their works can be seen at the Museu Nacional d'Art de Catalunya *(see p91)* alongside Catalonia's only two distinguished artists of the period – Francesc Pla and Antoni Viladomat.

Procession outside Santa Maria del Mar (c.1898) by Ramon Casas

The 19th Century

Barcelona's art school opened above La Llotja *(see p65)* in 1849 and new patrons of the arts appeared with wealth generated by the industrial revolution. Industry had, however, already begun to train its own artists. In 1783 a school was founded in Olot *(see p117)* to train designers for local textile firms. An Olot School of artists developed; its main figures were Josep Berga i Boix (1837–1914) and Joaquim Vayreda i Vila (1843–94), who also founded the Art Cristià (Christian Art) workshops which today still produce church statuary.

The greens and browns of the Olot landscape artists were countered by the pale blues and pinks of the Sitges Luminists – Arcadi Mas i Font-devila (1852–1943) and Joan Roig i Soler (1852–1909).

The Gardens at Aranjuez (1907) by Santiago Rusiñol

They were influenced by Marià Fortuny, who was born in Reus in 1838 and had lived in Rome and Paris. He was commissioned by Barcelona's city council to paint a vast canvas of the Spanish victory at Tetuán, Spanish Morocco, in which 500 Catalan volunteers had taken part. It is now in the Museu d'Art Modern.

In 1892, 18 years after the first Impressionist exhibition in Paris, Mas i Fontdevila staged an exhibition in Sitges bringing together the Olot School and the Luminists. It was seen as the first Modernista event and featured two other artists: Santiago Rusiñol (1861–1931) and Ramon Casas (1866–1932), the towering figures of Modernista painting. Rusiñol, the son of a textile magnate, bought a house in Sitges, Cau Ferrat (see p130), which became a Modernista haunt. Casas, the first man in Barcelona to own a car, drew all the famous people of the day and also painted large, powerful canvases such as The Charge and Vile Garroting. Both Rusiñol and Casas were founding members of Els Quatre Gats café, which was modelled on Le Chat Noir in Paris.

The 20th and 21st Centuries

Although Pablo Ruiz Picasso (1881–1973) lived in Barcelona for only eight years (see p65), they were very formative. His early work was much influenced by the city and its environs, as can be seen

The Cathedral of the Poor (1897) by Joaquim Mir

Waiting for Soup (1899) by Isidre Nonell

in the Museu Picasso (see p66), as well as by the leading Catalan artists – landscape painter Isidre Nonell (1873–1911), Joaquim Mir (1873–1940), Rusiñol and Casas. He shared their view that Paris was vital to an artistic life and joined its Catalan fraternity. Despite a self-imposed exile during the Franco years, he kept in touch with Catalonia all his life.

Joan Miró (1893–1983) also attended the La Llotja art school. Thrown out for poor draughtsmanship, he went on to become one of the 20th-century's most original talents, remarkable for his playful abstracts.

A sense of play was also never far from Salvador Dalí (see p119), whom Miró encouraged in the way that he himself had been inspired by Picasso. Dalí joined both of them in Paris, where Miró introduced him to the Surrealists. Unlike his mentors, Dalí stayed in Catalonia after the Civil War. His house in Port Lligat (see p122) is his finest creation.

Also to remain was Josep-Maria Sert (1876–1945). A more traditional painter, he is best remembered for his vast murals in Barcelona's Casa de la Ciutat (see p59), and in the Rockefeller Center and the dining room of

the Waldorf Astoria in New York. His startling work in Vic cathedral (see p126) was burnt out in the Civil War, but he was able to repaint it before he died.

Today, Catalonia's best-known painter is Antoni Tàpies (1923–2012). A modest, uncompromising man, he was rooted in his own culture. Though an abstract painter, he often used the colours of the Catalan flag and admitted to being influenced by Romanesque art. Like Picasso and Miró, he has his own museum (see p80). A wide variety of work by other contemporary Catalan artists, such as Antoni Abad, can be seen at Barcelona's Museu d'Art Contemporani (see p64).

Lithograph (1948) in Catalan flag colours by Antoni Tàpies

The Flavours of Catalonia

Food is central to the Catalan soul, and it's no accident that Barcelona's most famous literary creation, detective Pepe Carvalho, is a discerning gourmet. Reflecting Barcelona's status as the undisputed style capital of the Mediterranean, the culinary scene in Catalonia is now one of the most exciting in Europe, with innovative chefs like Ferran Adrià, of the legendary El Bullí restaurant (now closed) and Tickets tapas bar, taking Catalonia's venerable gastronomic traditions and transforming them with spectacular flair. But the old ways survive in small, family-run restaurants, authentic, sawdust-strewn tapas bars, and particularly in the superb local markets.

Ceps *(bolets)*

Barcelona café serving traditional pastries and desserts

Visit any one of Barcelona's excellent markets to see the spectacular variety of fresh produce that is available in Catalonia: stalls are heaped high with glistening fish from the Mediterranean; superb-quality meat and game from the mountains; and a quite dazzling array of fruit and vegetables from the plains. Catalan cuisine, even at its most experimental, is essentially simple, and relies on the superb quality and range of the local produce. It is also very much a seasonal cuisine, and each time of the year has its specialities, from the onion-like *calçots* which appear in the spring, and the luscious plethora of summer fruit, to the wild mushrooms, roasted meats and hearty, warming stews of the autumn and winter.

Meat and Game

Catalan cured meats are justly famous throughout Spain, particularly the pungent cured sausage *fuet*. Pork finds its way onto almost every menu, with *peus de porc* (pigs' trotters) an old-fashioned favourite. Its mountain cousin, wild boar *(porc sanglar)* is popular in late autumn, along with game, especially partridge *(perdiu)*.

Xoriço picant · Fuet · Llonganissa · Xoriço · Pernil salat · Xoriço curat

Selection of Catalan cured meats, known as *embutits*

Local Dishes and Specialities

Some things are hallowed in Catalan cuisine, and none more so than the quartet of classic sauces which underpin almost everything. King of them all is *sofregit* (mentioned in the first Catalan cookbook of 1324), a reduction of caramelized onions, fresh tomatoes and herbs. *Samfaina* is made like *sofregit* but with the addition of roast aubergines (eggplant), courgettes (zucchini) and peppers. *Picada* is spicier, and ingredients vary but normally include breadcrumbs, garlic, almonds, saffron and pine nuts. *All i oli* is a garlicky, mayonnaise-like (but eggless) sauce, usually served with grilled meat and vegetables. But the classic Catalan dish is *pa amb tomàquet* – crusty bread rubbed with fresh tomatoes and garlic, then drizzled with olive oil. Simple, but utterly delicious.

Pa amb tomàquet

Escalivada is a salad made of marinated onions, peppers and aubergines (eggplant) that have been roasted until sweet.

Fruit and Vegetables

Spring is heralded by *calçots*, a cross between leeks and onions, tiny broad (fava) beans and delicate asparagus spears. In summer, market stalls blaze with the colours of cherries, strawberries, figs, peaches and melons, aubergines (eggplants), courgettes (zucchini), tomatoes and artichokes. In autumn, Catalans head for the hills to seek out wild mushrooms *(bolets)*, and classic Catalan bean dishes appear on menus as winter approaches.

Summer fruits and vegetables lovingly displayed at La Boquería market

Rabbit *(conill)* and snails *(cargols)* come into their own in hearty winter dishes. Meat and fish are sometimes combined in dishes known as *mar i muntanya* (sea and mountain).

Fish

Barcelona excels at seafood. Tapas bars commonly serve mouthwatering sardines, and rosy prawns grilled or tossed in garlic. Restaurants and markets offer a dizzying array of fresh fish, including monkfish, bass, hake, sole, squid, octopus, and every possible variety of shellfish. Fish is often served simply grilled *(a la brasa)*, or perhaps with a simple sauce. It's especially good cooked paella-style in *fideuà*, or in a stew such as *suquet de peix*. But humble dried, salted cod *(bacallà)* still reigns supreme in Catalan cuisine, and is at its most delicious when baked with tomatoes, garlic and wine *(a la llauna)*.

Locally caught sardines being grilled over charcoal

Best Food Shopping

La Boquería *(see p155).*

Bombones Blasi Alfons XII 26 and Còrsega 218 (93 414 26 38). Exquisite chocolates.

Olis Oliva Mercat de Santa Caterina (93 268 1472). A huge range of olive oils, plus salt.

La Pineda Carrer del Pi 16 (93 302 43 93). Delightful old grocer's, specializing in hams.

Tot Formatge Passeig del Born 13 (93 319 5375). Superb cheeses from Catalonia, Spain and elsewhere.

La Botifarrería de Santa María Carrer Santa María 4 (93 319 9123). Cured meats of all kinds.

La Llavor dels Orígens Carrer Vidreria 6–8 (93 310 7531). Catalan fare, organic where possible, including cheeses, hams, oils and conserves.

Conill amb cargols is a hearty country stew of rabbit and snails with tomatoes, spices and a splash of wine.

Suquet de peix is a rich stew of firm-fleshed fish (often hake), with tomatoes, garlic and toasted almonds.

Crema Catalana, the Catalan version of crème brûlée, is a rich, eggy custard with a caramelized sugar topping.

Cava Country

Cava is one of Catalonia's most appreciated exports. This relatively inexpensive sparkling wine is made in the same way as French champagne, undergoing a second fermentation in the bottle in which it is sold. It was made commercially from the mid-19th century and, in 1872, full-scale production was begun by Josep Raventós, head of Codorníu. This famous winery is still run by his descendants in Sant Sadurní d'Anoia, *cava* capital of the Penedès wine-producing region. Today *cava* continues to be made using local grape varieties – Macabeo, Xarel·lo and Parellada – and some pleasant pink *cava* is also produced. The literal meaning of *cava* is simply "cellar".

Codorníu, the first wine to be made using the *méthode champenoise*, brought *cava* international renown as one of the great sparkling wines.

Freixenet was established by the Sala family in 1914 and is now one of the leading *cava* brands. Their estate is in Sant Sadurní d'Anoia, heart of *cava* country, and Freixenet's distinctive black bottle is recognized throughout the world.

Raïmat, developed by the Raventós family using the Chardonnay grape, is considered by many to be the ultimate *cava*. Wrested from wasteland, the 3,000-hectare (7,410-acre) Raïmat estate, 14 km (9 miles) west of Lleida, has its own railway station and workers' village and has been declared a "model agricultural estate" by the Spanish government.

Segre
Bell-lloc
d'Urgell
Lleida   A2   Bellpuig
N240
Alcarràs
AP2   Juneda
Serós   Coste
del Se
Maials   La Granadella
La Bisbal de Falset
Flix
P r i o r a t   N420
Falset
Cambri
L'Hospitalet
de l'Infant
L'Ametlla
de Mar

The Other Wines of Catalonia

A porró for drinking wine

Wine *(vi)* in Catalonia is *negre* (red), *rosat* (pink) or *blanc* (white). *Garnatxa* is a dessert wine named after the grape it comes from; *ranci* is a matured white wine. A tradition, now only practised at local *festes* or old-style bars, is to pour wine into the mouth from a *porró* (long-spouted wine jug). There are nine official DO *(Denominació de Origen)* regions which include: **Empordà-Costa Brava:** light wines from the northeast. They include *vi de l'any*, drunk in the year it is produced. *Cava* is made in Peralada. **Alella:** a tiny region, just north of Barcelona, with good light whites. **Penedès:** great reds as well as some whites, with names such as Torres and Codorníu. Visit the wine museum in Vilafranca del Penedès *(see p127)*. **Conca de Barberà:** small quantities of both reds and whites. **Costers del Segre:** includes the delicious reds from the Raïmat estate. **Priorat:** characterful reds and good whites (Falset) from a pretty region of small villages west of Tarragona. **Tarragona and Terra Alta:** traditionally hefty wines, but getting lighter.

The Art Nouveau winery in Sant Sadurní d'Anoia is Codorníu's Modernista showpiece, designed by Josep Puig i Cadafalch in 1906. There are 26 km (16 miles) of cellars on five floors and visitors are taken round on a small train.

Key

Main *cava* districts

0 kilometres   20

0 miles   20

Gold medals were awarded to Codorníu for its *cava* as early as 1888. By 1897 it was being served at state functions instead of champagne.

Calaf   C25   Manresa

Tàrrega

Igualada   Castellolí   Granollers   AP7

Castellolí   Terrassa   Sabadell

Santa Coloma de Queralt   Masquefa ⑥   *Alella*   A54   Mataró

Conca de Barberà   *Penedès* ② ①   Rubí   Premià de Mar

Montblanc   ③ Sant Sadurní d'Anoia   Santa Coloma de Gramanet

Valls   ④   Barcelona

Vilafranca del Penedès   L'Hospitalet de Llobregat

El Prat de Llobregat

Tarragona   Sitges   Castelldefels

Reus   El Vendrell   Vilanova i la Geltrú

Torredembarra

Tarragona   *Mediterranean Sea*

Salou
Cap de Salou

Best Producers

① Codorníu
   Sant Sadurní d'Anoia
② Freixenet
   Sant Sadurní d'Anoia
③ Gramona
   Sant Sadurní d'Anoia
④ Mascaró
   Vilafranca del Penedès
⑤ Raïmat
   Costers del Segre
⑥ Raventós Rosell
   Masquefa

Cava Tips

What to buy
As with champagne, the drier the wine, the higher the price. The driest *cavas* are *brut de brut* and *brut nature*. *Brut* and *sec* are slightly less dry. Sweet *semiseco* and *dulce* are best with desserts. Although inexpensive compared with the French equivalent, costs do vary, with small, specialist producers commanding high prices.

Visiting a winery
The main *cava* producers are open to the public during office hours (but many close in August). Sant Sadurní d'Anoia is 45 minutes by train from Barcelona's Sants station and the most impressive cellars to visit here are Freixenet's and Codorníu's. Vilafranca del Penedès tourist office *(see p127)* has details of all *cava* winery visits.

A rewarding tour can be had by visiting the Freixenet cellars. The company sells more bottles of *cava* each year than the French sell champagne.

CATALONIA THROUGH THE YEAR

Each *barri* (district) in Barcelona and every town and village in Catalonia has a saint's day to be celebrated in an annual *festa major*. The *sardana (see p131)* is danced and, on the Costa Brava, *havaneres* (habaneras) are sung. Food is central to any event, and open-air feasts and special pastries and cakes feature strongly. Many towns, including Barcelona, have parades of giants *(gegants)*, bigheads *(capgrosses)* and dwarfs *(nans)* – papier-mâché caricatures of people once linked with local trade guilds. Demons and dragons provide drama. Catalans love pyrotechnics, and the fires at the midsummer *Revetlla de Sant Joan* are a lavish incendiary event. Many celebrations often start on the eve of the feast day proper.

Book stalls set up in Barcelona on Sant Jordi's Day, *el dia del llibre*

Spring

Almond blossom gives way to cherry and apple as the earth warms and the melting snows swell the rivers. The fishing season for trout and other freshwater fish starts in late March. At Easter, families get together, often going out of town to visit relatives, or to picnic and search for wild asparagus. May is the best month in which to see wild flowers, which are particularly spectacular in the Pyrenees.

March

Terrassa Jazz Festival *(two weeks in Mar)*. Concerts by musicians from all over the world.
Sant Medir *(3 Mar)*. In Barcelona processions distribute sweets in the district of Gràcia, and in Sants a week later.
Sant Josep *(19 Mar)*. Many Catalans are called Josep (often shortened to Pep). This is a holiday in Spain, although not in Catalonia. People celebrate their "name day" – the day

of the saint they are named after – more than they celebrate their birthday.
Setmana Santa (Holy Week) is the week before Easter and is filled with events.

April

Diumenge de Rams (Palm Sunday). Palm leaves are blessed in church, notably at the Sagrada Família in Barcelona. Processions of Roman soldiers turn out in Girona, and *via crucis* (passion plays) are put on in several places, notably the spa town of Sant Hilari Sacalm, Girona province.
Dijous Sant (Maundy Thu). Verges, Girona province. Men dressed as skeletons perform a death dance *(dansa de la mort)* thought to date back to times of plague in the 1300s.
Pasqua (Easter). On Good Friday *(Divendres Sant)* crucifixes are carried through the streets following the Stations of the Cross. On Easter Monday *(Dilluns de Pasqua)* godparents

buy godchildren *mona* (egg cake), and bakers compete to make the most elaborate confections.
Sant Jordi *(23 Apr)*. Feast of St George, patron saint of Catalonia, and a day devoted to the memory of Cervantes *(see p45)*, who died on this day in 1616. Men and boys give single red roses to wives, mothers and girlfriends, who give them books in return. The festival is also known as *el dia del llibre* (book day).

May

Fira de Sant Ponç *(11 May)*. Ancient celebration around the Carrer de l'Hospital in Barcelona, once the site of the city hospital. Aromatic and medicinal herbs and honey are sold.
Corpus Christi *(May/Jun)*. Flowers are laid in the streets of Sitges, and in Berga, Barcelona province, a monster dragon (la Patum) dances through the town's streets.

The feast of Corpus Christi, when carpets of flowers cover the streets

Average daily hours of sunshine

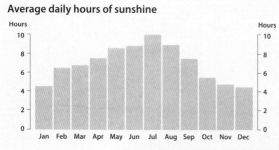

Sunshine Chart
Barcelona is a sunny city, enjoying clear blue skies for a large part of the year and often up to ten hours' sunshine a day in summer. In winter, even though it can be cold in the shade, the sun is high enough to give it warming power and it can be pleasant to sit outdoors on a sheltered, sunny terrace or patio.

Summer

The majority of Barcelona's inhabitants live in apartments, so they like to head out of town at weekends, either to the coast or the mountains. Motorways (highways) on Friday afternoons and Sunday evenings are best avoided. School holidays are long, starting at the end of June when the sea is warm enough for swimming. Crowds throng the marinas, the aroma of barbecued sardines fills the air, and a plethora of summer entertainment provides limitless options. Some shops and restaurants close in August.

June

Revetlla de Sant Joan *(23 & 24 Jun)*. St John's (Midsummer's) Eve is celebrated with fireworks, especially on Montjuïc in Barcelona. Bonfires are lit throughout Catalonia and lighted torches are brought down from the top of Mont Canigó, just over the border in France. *Cava* – a sparkling white wine *(see pp34–5)* – is drunk with a special *coca* (cake) sprinkled with pine nuts and crystallized fruit.
Castellers *(24 Jun)*. In Valls, Tarragona, a province famous for its *casteller* festivals, teams of men stand on each other's shoulders hoping to take the prize for building the highest human tower *(see p127)*.
Concert season *(Jun/Jul)*. Classical music concerts, held at different parks in Barcelona, are organized by the Institut Municipal de Parcs i Jardins. .
Grec Festival de Barcelona *(Jun/*

Holidaymakers at Platja d'Aro, a popular Costa Brava resort

Jul). National and international performances throughout Barcelona; the main venues are the Teatre Grec, Mercat de les Flors and Poble Espanyol.

July

Cantada d'havaneres *(first Sun in Jul)*. Drinking *cremat* (coffee and rum), musicians and singers belt out *havaneres* in towns along the coast, most famously at Calella de Palafrugell on the Costa Brava.

A team of *castellers* in action

Virgen del Carmen *(16 Jul)*. A maritime festival that takes place around Barcelona's port. As well as processions, there are bands playing *havaneres*.
Santa Cristina *(24 Jul)*. The biggest festival of Lloret de Mar, Costa Brava, when a statue of the Virgin is brought ashore by a decorated flotilla.

August

Festa major de Gràcia *(one week beginning around 15 Aug)*. Each district of Barcelona hosts its own *festa* in which streets try to outdo each other in the inventiveness of their decorations. The *festa* in the old district of Gràcia is the biggest and most spectacular and incorporates concerts, balls, music, competitions and street games.
Festa major de Vilafranca del Penedès *(mid-Aug)*. This town's annual festival is one of the best places to see *casteller* (human tower) competitions *(see p127)*.
Festa major de Sants *(around 24 Aug)*. The big annual *festa* takes place in the Sants district of Barcelona.

Average monthly rainfall (Barcelona)

Rainfall Chart
Barcelona experiences modest rainfall year-round – just sufficient to maintain the city's green spaces. However, rain tends to fall in sudden, but short-lived, torrential downpours and heavy thunderstorms are a feature of the summer months. Grey, drizzly weather lasting for days on end is very rare.

Autumn

The grape harvest *(verema)* is a highlight of the autumn, just before the vines turn red and gold. It is the season for seeking out mushrooms, which swell the market stalls. From October hunters set off to bag red-legged partridge, migrating ducks and wild boar. Hardier people can be seen swimming in the sea right up until November.

Cattle descending from the Pyrenees at the end of the summer

September
Diada de Catalunya *(11 Sep).* Catalonia's national day marks Barcelona's fall to Felipe V in 1714 *(see p47)* when the region lost its autonomy. Political demonstrations convey strong separatist sentiment. *Sardana (see p131)* bands and people singing *Els segadors (see p46)* can be heard and Catalan flags are everywhere.
La Mercè *(24 Sep).* This annual festival in Barcelona honours *Nostra Senyora de la Mercè* (Our Lady of Mercy) in a week of concerts, masses and dances. Look out for the *correfoc* – a

Harvesting grapes in autumn with high hopes for a successful crop

lively parade of fire-breathing dragons, giants and monsters; and the *piro musical* – fireworks set to music.
Sant Miquel *(29 Sep).* Celebrations for Barceloneta's patron saint recall Napoleon's occupation of Spain *(see p47).* Bum Bum, a Napoleonic general, parades through the streets to salvoes of gunfire. There is dancing on the beach.

October
Festes de Sarrià i de Les Corts *(first Sun in Oct).* Each of these Barcelona districts has a festival for its patron saint.
Día de la Hispanitat *(12 Oct)* National holiday to mark the discovery of America in 1492 *(see p46),* but most Catalans do not celebrate this anniversary.

November
Tots Sants (All Saints' Day) *(1 Nov).* Roast chestnuts and sweet potatoes are eaten and on the next day – *Dia dels difunts* (All Souls' Day) – people visit the graves of their relatives.

Public Holidays

Any Nou *(New Year's Day)* 1 Jan

Reis Mags *(Epiphany)* 6 Jan

Divendres Sant *(Good Friday)* Mar/Apr

Dilluns de Pasqua *(Easter Monday)* Mar/Apr

Festa del Treball *(Labour Day)* 1 May

Sant Joan *(Saint John's Day)* 24 Jun

Assumpció *(Assumption Day)* 15 Aug

Diada de Catalunya *(National Day)* 11 Sep

La Mercè 24 Sep

Dia de la Hispanitat *(Day of the Spanish-speaking nations)* 12 Oct

Tots Sants *(All Saints' Day)* 1 Nov

Dia de la Constitució *(Constitution Day)* 6 Dec

Immaculada Concepció *(Immaculate Conception)* 8 Dec

Nadal *(Christmas)* 25 Dec
Sant Esteve 26 Dec

Average daily temperature (Barcelona)

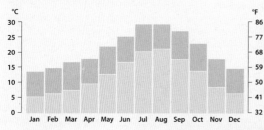

Temperature Chart
This chart shows the average minimum and maximum daily temperatures recorded in Barcelona. The sunshine in winter can be deceptive, as daytime temperatures can occasionally dip to near-freezing. Summer days are consistently hot. Hats and a high-factor sun screen are essential.

Winter

Ski resorts in the Pyrenees are a popular destination at weekends. Though days can be sunny and lunches still taken alfresco, the weather is unpredictable and the nights can be chilly. Christmas is a particularly delightful time to be in Barcelona, when the city vibrates with the spirit of celebration and sharing. Crafts and decorations are on sale in the Feria de Santa Llúcia in front of the Cathedral.

A ski resort in the Pyrenees, a popular destination for weekenders

December

Nadal and **Sant Esteve** *(25 & 26 Dec)*. Christmas is a time for people to come together. Traditional Christmas lunch consists of an *escudella* (meat stew) followed by turkey stuffed with apples, apricots, prunes, pine nuts and raisins.
Revellón *(31 Dec)*. All over Spain on New Year's Eve it has become a custom for people

to eat a grape between each chime of the midnight bell. To manage the feat brings good luck all year.

January

Reis Mags *(6 Jan)*. On the eve of the Epiphany the three kings arrive in various guises throughout Catalonia giving sweets to children. The main cavalcade in Barcelona is down by the port.
Santa Eulàlia *(12 Jan)*. The feast of the ancient patron saint of Barcelona is celebrated in the

old town. There is dancing and many people dress up as giants.
Els Tres Tombs *(17 Jan)*. Horsemen in top hats and tails ride three times through the city to honour St Anthony, patron saint of animals.
Pelegrí de Tossa *(20 & 21 Jan)*, Tossa de Mar. A 40-km (25-mile) pilgrimage marking the end of the plague is this town's biggest annual event.

February

De Cajón! Flamenco Festival *(early Feb–Mar)*. Concerts and classes are held in venues across Barcelona.
Carnestoltes (Carnival) *(Feb/ Mar)*. King Carnival presides over the pre-Lent celebrations, children dress up and every *barri* (district) in Barcelona puts on a party. Sausage omelettes are eaten on Shrove Tuesday *(Dijous gras)*, and on Ash Wednesday *(Dimecres de cendra)* a sardine is ceremoniously buried *(Enterrament de la sardina)*. There are major celebrations in Platja d'Aro on the Costa Brava and Vilanova on the Costa Daurada. Sitges is the place to go to see the full transvestite indulgence of the feast.

The winter festival of Els Tres Tombs in Vilanova i la Geltrú

Castellers build themselves into human towers during the September festival of La Mercè in Barcelona ▶

THE HISTORY OF CATALONIA

The Catalans have always been great seafarers, merchants and industrialists. Since they were united under the House of Barcelona, their nationhood has been threatened by marriages, alliances and conflicts with Madrid, and the road to their present status as a semi-autonomous region within Spain has been marked by times of power and wealth and troughs of weakness and despair.

Barcelona was not a natural site for human settlement. Its port was negligible and its heights, Montjuïc, had no water. The oldest evidence of man in Catalonia comes rather from other sites scattered across the region, notably the dolmens of the Alt (high) Empordà and passage graves of the Baix (low) Empordà and Alt Urgell.

In the first millennium BC the lands around Barcelona were settled by the agrarian Laeitani, while other parts of Catalonia were simultaneously colonized by the Iberians. The latter were great builders in stone and remains of one of their settlements are still visible at Ullastret on the Costa Brava. Greek traders arrived on the coast around 550 BC, founding their first trading post at Empúries (Emporion, *see p122*) near Ullastret.

It was the Carthaginians from New Carthage in southern Spain who put Barcelona on the map. They named the city after Hamil Barca, father of Hannibal who led his army of elephants from Catalonia over the Pyrenees and Alps to attack Rome.

In reprisal, the Romans arrived at Empúries and began the subjugation of the whole Iberian peninsula. They wiped out the Carthaginians as well as the Laeitani and established Tarraco (Tarragona, *see p130*) in the south of Catalonia as the imperial capital of Tarraconensis, one of the three administrative regions of the peninsula.

Roman Barcelona can be seen in the city gate beside the cathedral, while the 3rd-century walls that once encircled the town lie by the medieval Royal Palace (*see p58*). Foundations of the Roman city have been excavated in the basement of the Museu d'Història de la Ciutat (*see pp58–9*), and pillars from the Temple of Augustus can be glimpsed inside the Centre Excursionista de Catalunya (*see p57*) behind the cathedral.

When the Roman Empire collapsed, Visigoths based in Toulouse moved in to fill the vacuum. They had been vassals of Rome, practised Roman law, spoke a similar language and in 587 their Aryan king, Reccared, converted to the Christianity of Rome.

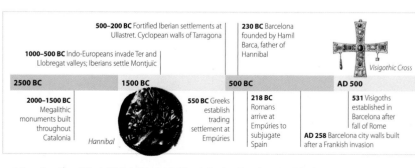

500–200 BC Fortified Iberian settlements at Ullastret. Cyclopean walls of Tarragona

230 BC Barcelona founded by Hamil Barca, father of Hannibal

1000–500 BC Indo-Europeans invade Ter and Llobregat valleys; Iberians settle Montjuïc

Visigothic Cross

| 2500 BC | 1500 BC | 500 BC | AD 500 |

2000–1500 BC Megalithic monuments built throughout Catalonia

Hannibal

550 BC Greeks establish trading settlement at Empúries

218 BC Romans arrive at Empúries to subjugate Spain

531 Visigoths established in Barcelona after fall of Rome

AD 258 Barcelona city walls built after a Frankish invasion

◀ Troops fraternizing with local militia in the Baixada de la Llibreteria, Barcelona, during the 1833–9 Carlist War

The Moors and Charlemagne

The Visigoths established their capital at Toledo, just south of modern Madrid. When King Wirtzia died in 710, his son, Akhila, is said to have called on the Saracens from north Africa for help in claiming the throne. In 711, with astonishing speed, Muslim and Berber tribes began to drive up through the Iberian peninsula, reaching Barcelona in 717, then Poitiers in France in 732, where they were finally stopped by the Frankish leader, Charles Martel.

Page from a 15th-century manuscript of the *Llibre del Consolat de Mar*

The Muslims made their capital the city of Córdoba in southern Spain, while the Visigothic nobles found hiding places in the Pyrenees, from which they conducted sorties against the invaders. They were aided by Charles Martel's grandson, Charles the Great (Charle-magne). In 801 Barcelona was retaken by the Franks, only to be lost and taken again. The shortness of the Muslim occupation left Catalonia, unlike the rest of Spain, unmarked by the culture and language of Islam.

Ramon Berenguer I of Barcelona (1035–76)

The Counts of Barcelona

Charlemagne created the Hispanic Marc, a buffer state along the Pyrenees, which he entrusted to local lords. The most powerful figure in the east was Guifré el Pelós (Wilfred the Hairy), who consolidated the counties of Barcelona, Cerdanya, Conflent, Osona Urgell and Girona and founded the monastery of Ripoll *(see p116)* – *el bressol de Catalunya* (the cradle of Catalonia). Guifré died in battle against the Moors in 897, but he had started a dynasty of Counts of Barcelona which was to last, unbroken, for 500 years.

Before the end of the 11th century, under Ramon Berenguer I, Catalonia had established the first constitutional government in Europe with a bill of rights, the *Usatges*. By the early 12th century, under Ramon Berenguer III, Catalonia's boundaries had pushed south past Tarragona. Catalan influence also spread north and east when he married Dolça of Provence, linking the two regions and, more lastingly, the principality of Barcelona was united with its neighbour Aragon in 1137 by the marriage of Ramon Berenguer IV and Petronila of Aragon. In 1196 the great monastery of Poblet *(see pp128–9)* in Tarragona province took the place of Ripoll as the pantheon of Catalan royalty.

717 Catalonia occupied by Muslims

801 Moors ejected. Charlemagne sets up buffer state

Charlemagne (742–814)

1060 Constitution, *Usatges*, is drawn up around the time that the word Catalan is first recorded

| 700 | 800 | 900 | 1000 |

711 North African Muslims invade Spanish mainland

Moorish sword

778 Charlemagne, leader of the Franks, begins campaign to drive Moors from Spain

878 Guifré el Pelós (Wilfred the Hairy), Count of Cerdanya-Urgell, consolidates eastern Pyrenees and gains virtual autonomy. He starts 500-year dynasty of Counts of Barcelona

1008–46 Abbot Oli builds church at Rip and oversees Benedictine buildin including Vic and Monserrat

Maritime Expansion

Under Jaume I the Conqueror (1213–76), Catalonia began a period of prosperity and expansion. By the end of the 13th century the Balearic islands and Sicily had been conquered; many of the ships used in the enterprise were built at the vast Drassanes shipyards in Barcelona *(see p71)*. Catalonia now ruled the seas and the *Llibre del Consolat de Mar* was a code of trading practice that held sway throughout the Mediterranean. Swashbuckling admirals included Roger de Llúria, who won a definitive victory over the French fleet in the Bay of Roses in 1285, and Roger de Flor, leader of a bunch of fierce Catalan and Aragonese mercenaries, the Almogàvers. These won battles for both the King of Sicily and the Byzantine emperor before Roger de Flor was murdered in 1305.

During Jaume I's long reign the *Corts* (parliament) was established, the city walls were rebuilt to enclose an area ten times larger than that enclosed by the old Roman walls, and noble houses arose down the new Carrer Montcada *(see p66)*.

La Llotja (the stock exchange) was sited by what was then the main port, and the church of Santa Maria del Mar *(see p66)* was built by grateful merchants. Under Pere IV (1336–87) two great halls were built: the Royal Palace's Saló del Tinell and the Casa de la Ciutat's Saló de Cent *(see pp56–7)*.

Ex voto in the form of a 15th-century ship

Prosperity brought a flowering of Catalan literature. Jaume I wrote his own *Llibre dels Feits (Book of Deeds)*, and Pere el Gran's conquest of Sicily in 1282 was described in glowing terms in a chronicle of Catalan history written by Bernat Desclot around 1285. The great Catalan poet Ramon Llull (1232–1315), born in Mallorca, was the first to use a vernacular language in religious writing. From 1395 an annual poetry competition, the Jocs Florals, was held in the city, attracting the region's troubadours. In 1450, Joanot Martorell began writing his Catalan chivalric epic narrative *Tirant lo Blanc*, though he died in 1468, 22 years before it was published. Miguel de Cervantes, author of *Don Quijote*, described it as simply "the best book in the world".

Wall painting showing Jaume I during his campaign to conquer Mallorca

1148 Frontier with Moors pushed back to Riu Ebre

1258–72 *Consolat de Mar*, a code of trading practice, holds sway throughout the Mediterranean

1282 Pere el Gran takes Sicily. His exploits are recorded in Desclot's *Chronicles*

1347–8 Black Death kills a quarter of the population

1359 Generalitat founded

1423 Conquest of Naples

1100

1200

1300

1400

1137 Barcelona united to neighbouring Aragon by royal marriage

1213–35 Jaume I (The Conqueror) takes Mallorca, Ibiza and Formentera

Jaume I (1213–76)

1302–5 Catalan mercenaries under Admiral Roger de Flor aid Byzantium against the Turks

1287 Conquest of Mallorca under Alfons III

Fernando and Isabel of Castile

Catholic Spain was united in 1479 when Fernando II of Catalonia-Aragon married Isabel of Castile, a region which by then had absorbed the rest of northern Spain. In 1492 they drove the last of the Moors from the peninsula, then, in a fever

Baptizing Jews during the era of the Catholic Monarchs

of righteousness, also drove out the Jews, who had large and commercially important populations in Barcelona *(see p58)* and Girona. This was the same year in which Columbus had set foot in America, returning in triumph to Barcelona with six Carib Indians *(see p60)*. However, the city lost out when the monopoly on New World trade was given to Seville and Cádiz. Though it still had great moments, such as its involvement in the victory over the Turks at Lepanto in 1571 *(see p71)*, Barcelona went into a period of decline.

Revolts and Sieges

During the Thirty Years War with France (1618–59), Felipe IV forced Barcelona's *Corts* to raise an army to fight the French, towards whom the Catalans bore no grudge. A viceroy was imposed on the city and unruly Spanish troops were billeted throughout the region. In June 1640 the population arose, and harvesters *(segadors)* murdered the viceroy. The *Song of the Harvesters* is still sung at Catalan gatherings.

Barcelona then allied itself with France, but was besieged and defeated by Felipe. The peace of 1659 ceded Catalan lands north of the Pyrenees to France.

Wall tile for a Catalan trade guild

A second confrontation with Madrid arose during the War of the Spanish Succession when Europe's two dominant royal houses, the Habsburgs and Bourbons, both laid claim to the throne. Barcelona, with England as an ally, found itself on the losing side, supporting the Habsburgs. As a result, it was heavily besieged by troops of

The great siege of Barcelona in 1714 during the War of the Spanish Succession

1450	1500	1550	1600	1650

1492 Columbus discovers Americas. Barcelona barred from trade with the New World. Jews expelled

1494 Supreme Council of Aragon brings Catalonia under Castilian control

The Spanish Inquisition, active from 1478

1619 Spanish capital established in Madrid

1659 Treaty of the Pyrenees at end of Thirty Years War draws new border with France; Roussillon ceded to France

1479 Fernando II of Catalonia-Aragon marries Isabel of Castile, uniting all the houses of Spain

1490 *Tirant lo Blanc*, epic tale of chivalry by Martorell *(see p45)*, published in Catalan

1571 Vast fleet sets sail from Barcelona to defeat the Ottomans at sea at Lepanto

1640 Revolt of the harvesters *(segadors)* against Spanish exploitation of Catalan resources during Thirty Years War with France

Women joining in the defence of Girona against the Napoleonic French in 1809

the incoming Bourbon king, Felipe V. The city fell on 11 September 1714, today commemorated as National Day *(see p38)*. Felipe then proceeded to annul all of Catalonia's privileges. Its language was banned, its universities closed and Lleida's Gothic cathedral became a barracks. Felipe tore down the Ribera district of Barcelona and, in what is now Ciutadella Park *(see p67)*, built a citadel to keep an eye on the population.

With the lifting of trade restrictions with the Americas, Catalonia began to recover economically. Progress, however, was interrupted by the 1793–95 war with France and then by the 1808–14 Peninsular War (known in Spain as the War of Independence) when Napoleon put his brother Joseph on the Spanish throne. Barcelona fell in early 1808, but Girona withstood a seven-month siege. Monasteries, including Montserrat *(see pp124–5)* were sacked and pillaged. They suffered further in 1835 under a

republican government when many were seen as too rich and powerful and were dissolved. This was a politically vigorous time, when a minority of largely rural reactionaries fought a rearguard action against the liberal spirit of the century in the Carlist Wars.

The Catalan Renaixença

Barcelona was the first city in Spain to industrialize, mainly around cotton manufacture, from imported raw material from the Americas. It brought immigrant workers and a burgeoning population, and in 1854 the city burst out of its medieval walls *(see p73)*. Inland, industrial centres such as Terrassa and Sabadell flourished and *colònies industrials* (industrial workhouses) grew up along the rivers where mills were powered by water.

Just as the wealth of the 14th century inspired Catalonia's first flowering, so the wealth from industry inspired the *Renaixença*, a renaissance of Catalan culture. Its literary rallying points were Bonaventura Aribau's *Oda a la patria* and the poems of a young monk, Jacint Verdaguer, who won poetry prizes in the revived Jocs Florals *(see p45)*.

Well-to-do *barcelonins* selecting from a wide range of locally produced calico in the early 19th century

Felipe V (1700–24)

1700	1750	1800	1850

1808–14 Peninsular War (War of Independence): Girona besieged, Barcelona occupied, Monastery of Montserrat sacked

1823–6 French occupy Catalonia

1835 Monasteries dissolved

1833–9 First Carlist War

1859 Revival of Jocs Florals poetry competition feeds renaissance of Catalan culture.

1714 Barcelona sacked by Felipe V, first Bourbon king. Catalan universities closed. Catalan language banned

1778 Catalonia allowed to trade with the Americas, bringing new wealth

1849 Spain's first railway built to link Barcelona and Mataró

1833 Aribau's *Oda a la patria* published

Poet Bonaventura Carles Aribau i Farriols

A hall of Spanish goods at the 1888 Universal Exhibition

Catalanism and Modernisme

The *Renaixença* produced a new pride in Catalonia, and "Catalanism" was at the heart of the region's accelerating move towards autonomy, a move echoed in Galicia and the Basque Country. Interruptions by the Carlist Wars came to an end in 1876 and resulted in the restoration of the Bourbon monarchy.

The first home-rule party, the *Lliga de Catalunya*, was founded in 1887, and disputes with the central government continued. It was blamed for the loss of the American colonies, and therefore lucrative transatlantic trade, and for involving Spain in unnecessary conflict in Morocco. *La setmana tràgica* (tragic week) of 1909 saw the worst of the violent protests: 116 people died and 300 were injured.

Meanwhile, on a more cultural and artistic level and in order to show off its increasing wealth, Barcelona held in 1888 a Universal Exhibition in the Parc de la Ciutadella where Felipe V's

Poster for 1929 Exhibition

citadel had recently been torn down. The urban expansion *(eixample)* inland was carefully ordered under a plan by Ildefons Cerdà *(see p73)* and industrial barons employed imaginative architects to show off their wealth, most successfully Eusebi Güell and Antoni Gaudí *(see pp26–7)*. The destruction of the monasteries had left spaces for sumptuous buildings such as the Palau de la Música Catalana *(see p65)*, the Liceu opera house and La Boqueria market *(see p155)*.

Spain's noninvolvement in World War I meant that Catalonia's Modernista architecture remained unscathed. Barcelona's place as a showcase city was confirmed with the 1929 International Exhibition on Montjuïc, many of whose buildings still remain.

Antoni Gaudí, Modernisme's most creative architect

Civil War

The *Mancomunitat*, a local council established in 1914, disappeared on the arrival in 1923 of the dictator Primo de Rivera, Barcelona's military governor. In 1931 Francesc Macià declared himself President of the Catalan Republic, which lasted three days. Three years later Lluís Companys was arrested and sentenced to 30 years' imprisonment for attempting to do the same.

Finally, on 16 July 1936, General Francisco Franco led

1888 Universal Exhibition held in Parc de la Ciutadella, showing off the new Modernista style

1872–6 Third and last Carlist War

1909 *Setmana tràgica*: violent protest against Moroccan Wars

Primo de Rivera (1870–1930)

1947 Spain declared a monarchy with Franco as regent

1931 Francesc Macià declares independence for Catalonia

| 1875 | 1900 | 1925 |

1893 Anarchist bombs in Liceu opera house kill 14

Carlist soldiers

1901 *Lliga Regionalista*, new Catalan party, wins elections

1929 International Exhibition on Montjuïc

1936–9 Spanish Civil War. Republican government retreats from Madrid to Valencia, then Barcelona

1939 50,000 go in exile in France. Catalan President Companys execut[ed]

Refugees on the march in 1939, fleeing towards the Pyrenees to seek asylum in France

an army revolt against the Republican government and the fledgling autonomous states. The government fled Madrid to Valencia, then Barcelona. City and coast were bombed by German aircraft, and shelled by Italian warships. When Barcelona fell three years later, thousands, including Companys, were executed in Franco's reprisals. Catalonia lost all it had gained, and its language was outlawed once more.

The *noche negra*, the dark night that followed Franco's victory, left Barcelona short of resources and largely neglected by Madrid. The 1960s, however, brought new economic opportunities, and between 1960 and 1975 two million Spaniards came to work in the city. The arrival of the first tourists to the coast during that time, to the Costa Brava and Costa Daurada, changed the face of Spain for ever.

Life after Franco

Champagne flowed freely in Barcelona's streets on the news of Franco's death in 1975. Democracy and the monarchy, under the Bourbon Juan Carlos, was restored.

Catalonia has since won a large degree of autonomy and in June 2006 a Statute of Autonomy of Catalonia was approved, providing a new legal framework for greater political independence.

Pasqual Maragall, Barcelona's mayor until 1997 and president of Catalonia from 2003 to 2006, steered the radical shake-up of the city for the 1992 Olympic Games. Barcelona changed dramatically, with a bold new waterfront, inspired urban spaces, and state-of-the-art museums and galleries. In 2011, after 32 years of socialist government, the centre-right Catalan nationalist party (CiU) rose to power in Barcelona. Parties supporting Catalonian independence continue to gain ground.

Opening ceremony, 1992 Barcelona Olympic Games

1953 US bases welcomed	**1975** Franco dies. King Juan Carlos restores Bourbon line
	1979 Partial autonomy granted to Catalonia
	1992 Olympic Games held in Barcelona
	2008 High Speed AVE train line between Barcelona and Madrid inaugurated

1950   **1975**   **2000**   **2025**

1960s Costa Brava leads package holiday boom

1985 Medes Islands become Spain's first marine nature reserve

1986 Spain enters European Union

Cobi, the Olympic mascot

2004 Universal Forum of Cultures held in Barcelona

2012 Large demonstrations are held in favour of Catalan independence.

BARCELONA & CATALONIA

Introducing Barcelona

Barcelona, one of the Mediterranean's busiest ports, is more than the capital of Catalonia. In culture, commerce and sports it not only rivals Madrid, but also considers itself on a par with the greatest European cities. The success of the 1992 Olympic Games, staged in the Parc de Montjuïc, confirmed this to the world. Although there are plenty of historical monuments in the Ciutat Vella (Old Town), Barcelona is best known for the scores of buildings in the Eixample left by the artistic explosion of Modernisme *(see pp26–7)* in the decades around 1900. Always open to outside influences because of its location on the coast, not too far from the French border, Barcelona continues to sizzle with creativity: its bars and the public parks speak more of bold contemporary design than of tradition.

Palau Nacional *(see p91)*, on the hill of Montjuïc, dominates the monumental halls and the fountain-filled avenue built for the 1929 International Exhibition. It now houses the Museu Nacional d'Art de Catalunya, with an exceptional collection of medieval art, rich in Romanesque frescoes.

Castell de Montjuïc *(see p93)* is a massive fortification dating from the 17th century. Sited on the crest of the hill of Montjuïc, it offers panoramic views of the city and port, and forms a sharp contrast to the ultra-modern sports halls built nearby for the 1992 Olympic Games.

Montjuïc
(see pp 86–93)

Christopher Columbus surveys the waterfront from the top of a 60-m (200-ft) column *(see p70)* in the heart of the Port Vell (Old Port). From the top, visitors can look out over the new promenades and quays that have revitalized the area.

0 kilometres		1
0 miles	0.5	

◀ The extraordinary façade of Casa Batlló, one of Barcelona's most distinctive Modernista buildings

La Pedrera *(see p81)* is the most avant-garde of all the works of Antoni Gaudí *(see p80)*. Barcelona has more Art Nouveau buildings than any other city in the world.

The Sagrada Família *(see pp82–5)*, Gaudí's unfinished masterpiece, begun in 1882, rises above the streets of the Eixample. Its polychrome ceramic mosaics and sculptural forms inspired by nature are typical of his work.

Eixample
(see pp72–85)

Barcelona Cathedral *(see pp60–61)* is a magnificent 14th-century building in the heart of the Barri Gòtic (Gothic Quarter). It has 28 side chapels which encircle the nave and contain some splendid Baroque altarpieces. The keeping of white geese in the cloisters is a centuries-old tradition.

Old Town
(see pp54–71)

Parc de la Ciutadella *(see p67)*, between the Old Town and the Vila Olímpica, has something for everyone. The gardens full of statuary offer relaxation, the boating lake and the zoo are fun, while the Museu Martorell is part of the Science Museum.

La Rambla *(see pp62–3)* is the most famous street in Spain, alive at all hours of the day and night. A stroll down its length to the seafront, taking in its palatial buildings, shops, cafés and street vendors, makes a perfect introduction to Barcelona life.

OLD TOWN

The old town, traversed by Barcelona's most famous avenue, La Rambla, is one of the most extensive medieval city centres in Europe. The Barri Gòtic contains the cathedral and a maze of streets and squares. Across from the Via Laietana, the El Born neighbourhood is dominated by the Santa Maria del Mar church and is replete with 14th-century mansions. This area is bounded by the leafy Parc de la Ciutadella, home to the city's zoo. The revitalized seafront is a stimulating mix of old and new. Trendy shops and restaurants make up the fashionable marina, contrasted with the old maritime neighbourhood of Barceloneta and the new Olympic port.

Sights at a Glance

Museums and Galleries
2 Museu Frederic Marès
10 Museu d'Art Contemporani
13 Museu Picasso
15 Museu de la Xocolata
18 Castell dels Tres Dragons
19 Museu d'Idees i Invents (MIBA)
20 Museu Martorell
25 Aquarium
26 Museu d'Historia de Catalunya
29 Museu Marítim and Drassanes

Parks and Gardens
17 Parc de la Ciutadella
21 Parc Zoològic

Harbour Sights
22 Port Olímpic
24 Port Vell
28 Golondrinas

Monuments
16 Arc del Triomf
27 Monument a Colom

Churches
6 Cathedral (pp60–61)
14 Basílica de Santa Maria del Mar

Historic Building
1 Casa de l'Ardiaca
3 Museu d'Història de la Ciutat –
   Plaça del Rei
4 Casa de la Ciutat
5 Palau de la Generalitat
8 Palau Güell
11 Palau de la Música Catalana
12 La Llotja

Streets and Districts
7 La Rambla
9 El Raval
23 Barceloneta

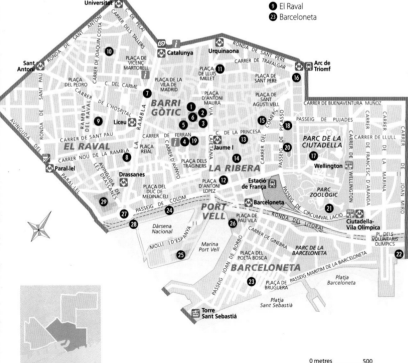

See also Street Finder
maps 2, 5 and 6

0 metres 500
0 yards 500

◀ The soaring Gothic vaulting of Barcelona's cathedral

For keys to symbols see back flap

Street-by-Street: Barri Gòtic

The Barri Gòtic (Gothic Quarter) is the true heart of Barcelona. The oldest part of the city, it was the site chosen by the Romans in the reign of Augustus (27 BC–AD 14) on which to found a new *colonia* (town), and has been the location of the city's administrative buildings ever since. The Roman forum was on the Plaça de Sant Jaume, where now stand the medieval Palau de la Generalitat, the seat of Catalonia's government, and the Casa de la Ciutat, the city's town hall. Close by are the Gothic cathedral and royal palace, where Columbus was received by Fernando and Isabel on his return from the New World in 1492 *(see p46)*.

❶ Casa de l'Ardiaca
Built on the Roman city wall, the Gothic-Renaissance archdeacon's residence now houses Barcelona's historical archives.

To Plaça de Catalunya

SANT SEVER

CARRER DEL BISBE

PIET

❻ ★ Cathedral
The façade and spire are 19th-century additions to the original Gothic building. Among the artistic treasures inside are medieval Catalan paintings.

SANT DOMÈNEC DEL CALL

SANT HONORAT

❺ Palau de la Generalitat
Catalonia's seat of government has superb Gothic features, such as the chapel and a staircase to an open-air, arcaded gallery.

PLAÇA DE SANT JAUME

CARRER DE FERRAN

To La Rambla

CARRER DE LA CIUTAT

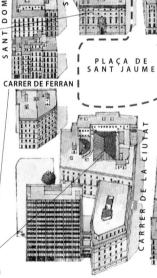

❹ Casa de la Ciutat (Ajuntament)
Barcelona's town hall was built in the 14th and 15th centuries. The façade is a Neo-Classical addition. In the entrance hall stands *Three Gypsy Boys* by Joan Rebull (1899–1981), a 1976 copy of a sculpture he originally created in 1946.

Key

— Suggested route

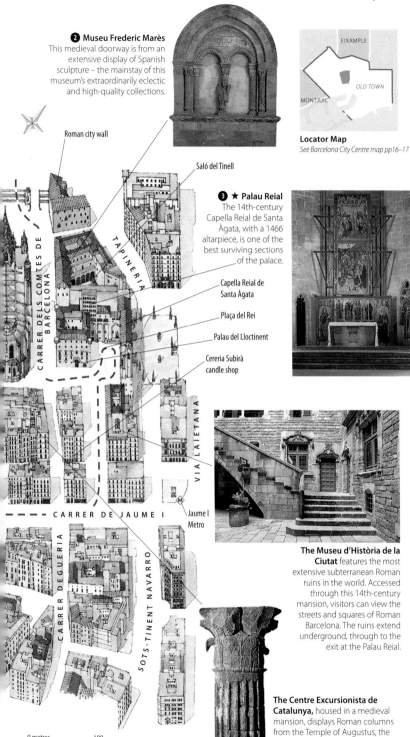

2 **Museu Frederic Marès**
This medieval doorway is from an extensive display of Spanish sculpture – the mainstay of this museum's extraordinarily eclectic and high-quality collections.

Roman city wall

Saló del Tinell

Locator Map
See Barcelona City Centre map pp16–17

EIXAMPLE

OLD TOWN

MONTJUIC

3 ★ **Palau Reial**
The 14th-century Capella Reial de Santa Àgata, with a 1466 altarpiece, is one of the best surviving sections of the palace.

Capella Reial de Santa Àgata

Plaça del Rei

Palau del Lloctinent

Cereria Subirà candle shop

CARRER DELS COMTES DE BARCELONA

TAPINERIA

VIA LAIETANA

CARRER DE JAUME I

Jaume I Metro

CARRER DEGUERIA

SOTS-TINENT NAVARRO

The Museu d'Història de la Ciutat features the most extensive subterranean Roman ruins in the world. Accessed through this 14th-century mansion, visitors can view the streets and squares of Roman Barcelona. The ruins extend underground, through to the exit at the Palau Reial.

The Centre Excursionista de Catalunya, housed in a medieval mansion, displays Roman columns from the Temple of Augustus, the site of which is marked by a millstone in the street outside.

0 metres 100
0 yards 100

For keys to symbols *see back flap*

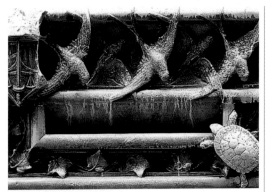

Decorated marble mailbox, Casa de l'Ardiaca

❶ Casa de l'Ardiaca

Carrer de Santa Llúcia 1. **Map** 5 B2.
Tel 93 256 22 55. 🚇 Jaume I. **Open**
9am–8:45pm Mon–Fri (to 7:30pm Jul
& Aug), 9am–1pm Sat. **Closed** public
hols, Sat in Jul–Sep.
🌐 bcn.cat/arxiu/arxiuhistoric

Standing beside what was
originally the Bishop's Gate in
the Roman wall is the Archdeacon's House. It was first built
in the 12th century, but in its
present form it dates from
around 1500 when it was
remodelled, including the
addition of a colonnade. In 1870
this was extended to form the
Flamboyant Gothic patio around
a fountain. The Modernista
architect Domènech i Montaner
(1850–1923) added the fanciful
marble mailbox, carved with
three swallows and a tortoise,
beside the Renaissance portal.
Upstairs is the Arxiu Històric de
la Ciutat (City Archives).

❷ Museu Frederic Marès

Plaça de Sant Iu 5. **Map** 5 B2. **Tel** 93
256 35 00. 🚇 Jaume I. **Open** 10am–
7pm Tue–Sat, 11am–8pm Sun &
public hols. **Closed** 1 Jan, 1 May, 24
Jun, 25 & 26 Dec. 🎟 free for under
16s, also Sun after 3pm & 1st Sun of
every month. 🏛 ♿
🌐 museumares.bcn.es

The sculptor Frederic Marès i
Deulovol (1893–1991) was also
a traveller and collector, and this
museum is a monument to his
eclectic taste. As part of the
Royal Palace, it was occupied by

13th-century bishops, 14th-
century counts of Barcelona,
15th-century judges and
18th-century nuns, who lived
here until they were expelled in
1936. Marès, who had a small
apartment in the building,
opened this museum in 1948.
It contains a fascinating
collection of works, including
some outstanding examples
of Romanesque and Gothic
religious art. In the crypt and
on the ground floor are stone
sculptures and two complete
Romanesque portals. The first
floor has Renaissance and
Baroque sculpture. Exhibits on
the second and third floors
range from children's toys,
clocks, crucifixes and costumes
to antique cameras, pipes
and postcards.

❸ Museu d'Història de la Ciutat – Plaça del Rei

Plaça del Rei. **Map** 5 B2. **Tel** 93 256
21 00. 🚇 Jaume I. **Open** 10am–7pm
Tue–Sat, 10am–8pm Sun, 10am–2pm
public hols. **Closed** 1 Jan, 1 May, 24
Jun, 25 Dec. 🎟 free for under 16s,
also Sun after 3pm & 1st Sun of the
month. 🏛 🌐 museuhistoria.bcn.es

The Royal Palace was the
residence of the count-kings of
Barcelona from its foundation in
the 13th century. The complex
includes the 14th-century
Gothic Saló del Tinell, a vast
room with arches spanning
17 m (56 ft). This is where Isabel
and Fernando *(see p46)* received
Columbus after his triumphal
return from America. It is also
where the Holy Inquisition sat,

Gothic nave of the Capella de Santa Àgata,
Palau Reial

Barcelona's Early Jewish Community

Hebrew tablet

From the 11th to the 13th centuries Jews
dominated Barcelona's commerce and culture,
providing doctors and founding the first seat of
learning. But in 1243, 354 years after they were
first documented in the city, violent anti-
Semitism led to the Jews being consigned to a
ghetto, El Call. Ostensibly to provide protection,
the ghetto had only one entrance, which led
into the Plaça de Sant Jaume. Jews were heavily
taxed by the monarch, who viewed them as "royal
serfs"; but in return they also received privileges,
as they handled most of Catalonia's lucrative trade with North
Africa. However, official and popular persecution finally led to the
disappearance of the ghetto in 1401, 91 years before Judaism was
fully outlawed in Spain *(see p46)*.

Originally there were three synagogues, the main one being in
Carrer Sant Domènec del Call, but only the foundations are left. A
14th-century Hebrew tablet is embedded in the wall at No. 5 Carrer
de Marlet, which reads: "Holy Foundation of Rabbi Samuel Hassardi.
His soul will rest in Heaven".

believing the walls would move if lies were told. On the right, built into the Roman city wall, is the royal chapel, the Capella de Santa Àgata, with a painted wood ceiling and an altarpiece (1466) by Jaume Huguet *(see p30)*. Its bell tower is formed by part of a watchtower on the Roman wall. Stairs on the right of the altar lead to the 16th-century tower of Martí the Humanist (who reigned from 1396 to 1410), the last ruler of the 500-year dynasty of the count-kings of Barcelona. From the top of the tower there are fine views.

The main attraction of the Museu d'Història lies below the ground. Entire streets and squares of old Barcino are accessible via a lift and walkways suspended over the ruins of Roman Barcelona. The site was discovered when the Casa Clariana-Padellàs, the Gothic building from which you enter, was moved here stone by stone in 1931, as demonstrated by an extraordinary photo of the original dig towards the end of the exhibit. The water and drainage systems, baths, homes with mosaic floors, dye works, laundries and even the old forum now make up the most extensive and complete subterranean Roman ruins in the world.

❹ Casa de la Ciutat

Plaça de Sant Jaume 1. **Map** 5 A2. **Tel** 93 402 73 00. 🚇 Jaume I or Liceu. **Open** 10am–1:30pm Sun (12 Feb and 23 Apr: 10am– 8pm), or by appointment (93 402 73 64). 📷 ♿

The magnificent 14th-century city hall *(ajuntament)* faces the Palau de la Generalitat. Flanking the entrance are statues of Jaume I *(see p45)*, who granted the city rights to elect councillors in 1249, and Joan Fiveller, who levied taxes on court members in the 1500s. Inside is the huge council chamber, the 14th-century Saló de Cent, built for the city's 100 councillors. The Saló de les Cròniques was commissioned for the 1929 International Exhibition and decorated by Josep-Maria Sert *(see p31)* with murals of events in Catalan history.

❺ Palau de la Generalitat

Plaça de Sant Jaume 4. **Map** 5 A2. 🚇 Jaume I. **Open** 23 Apr (St Jordi's Day), 11 & 24 Sep, 2nd & 4th Sat & Sun of month: 10:30am–1:30pm by appointment only through website. ♿ 📷 🌐 **gencat.cat**

Since 1403 the Generalitat has been the seat of the Catalonian Government. Above the

The Italianate façade of the Palau de la Generalitat

entrance, in its Renaissance façade, is a statue of Sant Jordi (St George) – the patron saint of Catalonia – and the Dragon. The late Catalan Gothic courtyard is by Marc Safont (1416).

Among the fine interiors are the Gothic chapel of Sant Jordi, also by Safont, and Pere Blai's Italianate Saló de Sant Jordi. The building is open to the public only on the saint's feast day. At the back, one floor above street level, lies the *Pati dels Tarongers*, the Orange Tree Patio, by Pau Mateu, which has a bell tower built by Pere Ferrer in 1568.

The Catalan president has offices here as well as in the Casa dels Canonges. The two buildings are connected across Carrer del Bisbe by a bridge built in 1928 and modelled on the Bridge of Sighs in Venice.

The magnificent council chamber, the Saló de Cent, in the Casa de la Ciutat

❻ Barcelona Cathedral

This compact Gothic cathedral, with a Romanesque chapel (the Capella de Santa Llúcia) and beautiful cloister, was begun in 1298 under Jaume II, on the foundations of a Roman temple and Moorish mosque. It was not finished until the early 20th century, when the central spire was completed. A white marble choir screen, sculpted in the 16th century, depicts the martyrdom of St Eulàlia, the city's patron. Next to the font, a plaque records the baptism of six native Caribbeans, brought back from the Americas by Columbus in 1493.

Nave Interior
The Catalan-style Gothic interior has a single wide nave with 28 side chapels. These are set between the columns supporting the vaulted ceiling, which rises to 26 m (85 ft).

KEY

① **The main façade** was not completed until 1889, and the central spire until 1913. It was based on the original 1408 plans of the French architect Charles Galters.

② **The twin octagonal bell towers** date from 1386–93. The bells were installed in this tower in 1545.

③ **Porta de Santa Eulàlia, entrance to cloisters**

④ **The Sacristy Museum** has a small treasury. Pieces include an 11th-century font, tapestries and liturgical artifacts.

⑤ **Capella de Santa Llúcia**

★ **Choir Stalls**
The top tier of the beautifully carved 15th-century stalls contains painted coats of arms (1518) of several European kings.

Capella del Santíssim Sagrament
This small chapel houses the 16th-century Christ of Lepanto crucifix.

Capella de Sant Benet
This chapel, dedicated to the founder of the Benedictine Order and patron saint of Europe, houses a magnificent altarpiece showing *The Transfiguration* by Bernat Martorell (1452).

VISITORS' CHECKLIST

Practical Information
Plaça de la Seu.
Map 5 A2.
Tel 93 342 82 62.
Open 8am–7:30pm daily, tours 1–5pm daily (2–5pm Sun).
🎧 (free 8am–12:45pm, 5:15–7:30pm daily). ♿ Sacristy Museum: **Open** 9am–1pm, 5–7pm daily. 📷 Choir and roof terrace: **Open** daily. 📷
✝ services daily.

Transport
🚇 Jaume I. 🚌 17, 19, 45.

★ Crypt
In the crypt, beneath the main altar, is the alabaster sarcophagus (1339) of St Eulàlia, martyred for her beliefs by the Romans during the 4th century AD.

★ Cloisters
The fountain, set in a corner of the Gothic cloisters and decorated with a statue of St George, provided fresh water.

400	700	1000	1300	1600	1900

559 Basilica dedicated to St Eulàlia and Holy Cross

877 St Eulàlia's remains brought here from Santa Maria del Mar

1339 St Eulàlia's relics transferred to alabaster sarcophagus

1046–58 Romanesque cathedral built under Ramon Berenguer I

1913 Central spire completed

1889 Main façade completed, based on plans dating from 1408 by architect Charles Galters

4th century Original Roman (paleo-Christian) basilica built

985 Building destroyed by the Moors

1257–68 Romanesque Capella de Santa Llúcia built

1298 Gothic cathedral begun under Jaume II

1493 Indians brought back from the Americas are baptized

Plaque of the Caribbeans' baptism

❼ La Rambla

The historic avenue of La Rambla, leading to the sea, is busy around the clock, especially in the evenings and at weekends. Newsstands, flower stalls, tarot readers, musicians and mime artists throng the wide, tree-shaded central walkway. Among its famous buildings are the Liceu Opera House, the huge Boqueria food market and some grand mansions.

Exploring La Rambla

The name of this long avenue, also known as Les Rambles, comes from the Arabic *ramla*, meaning the dried-up bed of a seasonal river. The 13th-century city wall followed the left bank of such a river that flowed from the Collserola hills to the sea. Convents, monasteries and the university were built on the other bank in the 16th century. As time passed, the riverbed was filled in and those buildings demolished, but they are remembered in the names of the five consecutive Rambles that make up the great avenue

between the Port Vell and Plaça de Catalunya.

Mercat de Sant Josep Plaza de la Boqueria. **Map** 2 F3. **Tel** 93 318 20 17. 🚇 Liceu. **Open** 8am–8:30pm Mon–Sat.

Palau de la Virreina La Rambla 99. **Map** 5 A2. **Tel** 93 316 10 00. 🚇 Liceu. **Open** noon–8pm Tue–Sun. **Closed** 1 Jan, 1 May, 25 & 26 Dec.

Museu de Cera Pg de la Banca 7. **Map** 2 F4. **Tel** 93 317 26 49. 🚇 Drassanes. **Open** 10am–1:30pm, 4–7:30pm Mon–Fri, 11am–2pm, 4:30–8:30pm Sat, Sun & public hols (Jul–Aug: 10am–10pm daily). 📷 ♿

The busy, tree-lined avenue of La Rambla

⑤ **Mercat de Sant Josep**
Popularly known as "La Boqueria", the Mercat de Sant Josep is Barcelona's most colourful food market.

⑦ **Gran Teatre del Liceu**
Barcelona's opera house has had to be restored twice following damage caused by fires in 1861 and 1994.

⑨ **Palau Güell**
This Neo-Gothic palace, completed in 1889, is considered to be one of Gaudí's most important works *(see p64)*.

The monument to Columbus at the bottom of the tree-lined Rambla

CARRE

C. NOU D LA RAMBL
⑨

CARRER LANCASTER

C. DE L'A DEL TEA

Drassanes 🚇

RAMBLA DE

RAMBLA

① Font de Canaletes
This 19th-century fountain has four taps from which to drink. Saying that someone "drinks the waters of Canaletes" indicates that he or she is from Barcelona.

② Reial Acadèmia de Ciències i Arts
Converted to a theatre in 1910, this building is the home of Barcelona's first official public clock.

③ Palau Moja
This Classical building dates back to 1790. The Baroque first-floor salon of Palau Moja is used for exhibitions.

④ Palau de la Virreina
The first person to live in this great palace in 1777, was the widowed *virreina* (viceroy's wife) of Spain in Peru.

⑥ Plaça de la Boqueria
This square features a colourful mosaic pavement by Joan Miró (1976) and a Modernista dragon designed for a former umbrella shop.

⑧ Plaça Reial
Barcelona's liveliest square was built in the 1850s and is adorned with palms. Its Neo-Classical carriage lamps were designed by Gaudí.

⑩ Museu de Cera
This waxwork museum is housed in an atmospheric, 19th-century stately home. The museum was established in 1973 and contains over 300 exhibits.

| 0 metres | 100 |
| 0 yards | 100 |

For keys to symbols *see back flap*

❽ Palau Güell

Nou de la Rambla 3–5. **Map** 2 F3.
Tel 93 472 57 75. 🚇 Liceu.
Open 10am– 8pm Tue–Sun (to 5:30pm Nov–Mar). **Closed** 1, 6 & 13 Jan, 25 & 26 Dec. 🎫 free for under 16s and 1st Sun of month. 🏛 📷 ♿ except roof terrace. 🆆 **palauguell.cat**

Gaudí's first major work in Barcelona's city centre was commissioned by his wealthy patron Eusebi Güell. Güell made it known that, even if he was investing in an inexperienced architect, there would be no limit to the budget at Gaudí's disposal.

Gaudí took his patron at his word as can be seen in the quality of the materials used for what was a disproportionately grand building raised on a small plot in a narrow street. The stonework is clad with marble and inside, high quality woods are employed throughout.

As in his other buildings, Gaudí designed furniture, lights, stained glass, and many other fittings, working closely with craftsmen to realise his ideas. The house was finished in 1889 and was used not only as a luxurious family home for a wealthy man but also a place to hold political meetings, chamber concerts and to put up important guests.

From the street there is little hint of the colour and playfulness to come in Gaudí's mature work, except in the spire-like chimneys behind the parapet on the roof. The austere façade of Palau Güell is symmetrical and characterised mostly by straight lines, both horizontal and vertical. The only indication of Gaudí's later preference for curves is in the two doorways, each formed by a parabolic arch – a geometric shape he would subsequently employ to great effect.

Inside, the most notable feature of the house is its very high central room on the main floor. Something between a sitting room and a covered courtyard, this central room rises fully three floors (of a six floor building) and is spanned by a cupola. The other rooms are grouped around it.

Palau Güell's spire-like roof chimneys

❾ El Raval

Map 2 F3. 🚇 Catalunya, Liceu.

The district of El Raval lies west of La Rambla and includes the old red-light area near the port, once known as Barri Xinès (Chinese quarter).

From the 14th century, the city hospital was located in Carrer de l'Hospital, which still has several herbal and medicinal shops today. Gaudí *(see p80)* was brought here after being fatally hit by a tram in 1926. The buildings now house the Biblioteca de Catalunya (Catalonian Library), but the elegant former dissecting room has been fully restored.

Towards the port in Carrer Nou de la Rambla is Gaudí's Palau Güell. At the end of Carrer

Sant Pau is the city's most complete Romanesque church, the 12th-century Sant Pau del Camp, with a charming cloister featuring exquisitely carved capitals.

❿ Museu d'Art Contemporani

Plaça dels Angels 1. **Map** 2 F2.
Tel 93 412 08 10. 🚇 Universitat, Catalunya. **Open** 25 Jun–24 Sep: 11am–8pm Mon, Wed, & Thu, 11am–10pm Fri, 10am–10pm Sat, 10am–3pm Sun; 25 Sep–23 Jun: 11am–7:30pm Mon & Wed–Fri, 10am–9pm Sat, 10am–3pm Sun. **Closed** 1 Jan, 25 Dec. 🎫 ♿ 📷 tours in English 4pm & 6pm Mon, 4pm Wed–Sat. 🆆 **macba.cat**
Centre de Cultura Contemporània: Montalegre 5. **Tel** 93 306 41 00.
🆆 **cccb.org**

This dramatic, glass-fronted building was designed by the American architect Richard Meier. Its light, airy galleries act as the city's contemporary art mecca. The permanent collection of mainly Spanish painting, sculpture and install-ations from the 1950s onwards is complemented by temporary exhibitions by foreign artists like South African photo-journalist David Goldblatt and US painter Susana Solano.

Next to the MACBA is the **Centre de Cultura Contem-porània de Barcelona** (CCCB), a lively arts centre.

Façade of the Museu d'Art Contemporani

Glorious stained-glass dome, Palau de la Música Catalana

⓫ Palau de la Música Catalana

Carrer de Sant Pere Més Alt, s/n. **Map** 5 B1. **Tel** 90 247 54 85. 🚇 Urquinaona. **Open** 10am–3:30pm daily (to 6pm Easter, to 8pm Aug); and for concerts. Buying tickets in advance online is recommended. 🛗 ♿ 🎧 on the hour in English. 🌐 **palaumusica.org**

This is a real palace of music, a Modernista celebration of tilework, sculpture and glorious stained glass. It is the only concert hall in Europe lit by natural light. Designed by Lluís Domènech i Montaner, it was completed in 1908. Although a few extensions have been added, the building still retains its original appearance. The elaborate red-brick façade is hard to appreciate fully in the confines of the narrow street. It is lined with mosaic-covered pillars topped by busts of the great composers Palestrina, Bach and Beethoven. The large stone sculpture of St George and other figures at the corner of the building portrays an allegory from Catalan folksong by Miquel Blay.

But it is the interior of the building that is truly inspiring. The auditorium is lit by a huge inverted dome of stained glass depicting angelic choristers. The sculptures of composers Wagner and Clavé on the proscenium arch that frames the stage area were designed by Domènech but finished by Pau Gargallo. The stunning "Muses of the Palau", the group of 18 highly stylized, instrument-playing maidens are the stage's backdrop. Made of terracotta and *trencadís* (broken pieces of ceramic) they have become the building's most admired feature.

The work of Josep Anselm Clavé (1824–74) in promoting Catalan song led to the creation of the Orfeó Català choral society in 1891, a focus of Catalan nationalism and the inspiration behind the Palau.

Although the Orfeó is now based at the more state-of-the-art L'Auditori in Plaça de les Glòries (*see p164*), there is a concert at the Palau nearly every night; it is the main venue for the city's jazz and guitar festivals and national and international symphony orchestras regularly grace its flamboyant stage.

The Palau's new era began with the completion of the work carried out by the top local architect Oscar Tusquets. An underground concert hall and an outdoor square for summer concerts were added, consolidating the Palau's reputation as Barcelona's most loved music venue.

⓬ La Llotja

Carrer del Consolat de Mar 2. **Map** 5 B3. **Tel** 93 547 88 49. 🚇 Barceloneta. **Closed** to public (except twice a year, days vary).

La Llotja (meaning commodity exchange) was built in the 1380s as the headquarters of the Consolat de Mar (*see p45*). It was remodelled in Neo-Classical style in 1771 and housed the city's stock exchange until 1994, the original Gothic hall acting as the main trading room. It can still be seen through the windows.

The upper floors housed the Barcelona School of Fine Arts from 1849 to 1970, attended by the young Picasso and Joan Miró (*see p29*). They are now occupied by local government offices.

Statue of Poseidon in the courtyard of La Llotja

A wedding service in the Gothic interior of Santa Maria del Mar

⓭ Museu Picasso

Carrer Montcada 15–23. **Map** 5 B2.
Tel 93 256 30 00. 🅜 Jaume I. **Open**
10am–8pm Tue–Sun. **Closed** 1 Jan,
1 May, 24 Jun, 25 & 26 Dec. 🏛 free
1st Sun of month, every Sun from
3pm. 🅐 🅒 email: museupicasso_
reserves@bcn.cat. Free tours in
English 11am Sun (not August). 🅐
🆆 **museupicasso.bcn.cat**

The popular Picasso Museum is
housed in five adjoining
medieval palaces on Carrer
Montcada: Berenguer d'Aguilar,
Baró de Castellet, Meca, Mauri
and Finestres. The museum
opened in 1963, showing works
donated by Jaime Sabartes, a
friend of Picasso. After Sabartes'
death in 1968, Picasso himself
donated paintings. He also left
graphic works in his will and
ceramics were donated by his
widow, Jacqueline.

The strength of the 3,000-piece
collection is Picasso's early works.
Even at the age of 15, he was
painting major works such as
The First Communion (1896) and
Science and Charity (1897). There
are a few works from his Blue
and Rose periods. Most famous
is his series of 44 paintings, *Las
Meninas*, which were inspired
by Velázquez's masterpiece.

⓮ Basílica de Santa Maria del Mar

Pl Sta Maria 1. **Map** 5 B3. **Tel** 93 310 23
90. 🅜 Jaume I. **Open** 9am– 1:30pm,
4:30–8:30pm (10:30am Sun). 🅐
🅒 guided visits to the roof terraces

This beautiful building, the city's
favourite church with superb
acoustics for concerts, is the
only example of a church
entirely in the Catalan Gothic
style. It took just 55 years to
build, with money donated by
merchants and shipbuilders. The
speed – unrivalled in the Middle
Ages – gave it a unity of style

Pablo Picasso in Barcelona

Picasso (1881–1973) was 13 when he arrived in Barcelona, where
his father, José Ruiz y Blasco, had found work teaching in the
city art school situated above the Llotja. The city was rich, but it
also possessed a large, poor working class which was becoming
organized and starting to rebel. Shortly after the family's arrival,
a bomb was thrown into a Corpus Christi procession.

The family settled at No 3 Carrer de la Mercè, a gloomy, five-
storeyed house not far from the Llotja. Picasso's precocious talent
gave him admittance to the upper school, where all the other
pupils were aged at least 20. Here he immediately made friends
with another artist, Manuel Pallarès Grau, and the two lost their
virginity to the whores of Carrer d'Avinyó, who were to inspire
Les Demoiselles d'Avignon (1906–7), considered by many art critics
to be the wellspring of modern art. Picasso travelled with Pallarès
to the Catalan's home town of Horta, where he painted some early
landscapes, now in the Museu Picasso. The two remained friends
for the rest of their lives.

Pablo Picasso, *Self-Portrait* in charcoal
(1899–1900)

both inside and out. The west front has a 15th-century rose window of the Coronation of the Virgin. More stained glass, dating from the 15th to the 18th centuries, lights the wide nave and high aisles. When the choir and furnishings were burned in the Civil War (see p48), it added to the sense of space and simplicity.

⑮ Museu de la Xocolata

Comerç 36. **Map** 5 C2. **Tel** 93 268 78 78. 🚇 Jaume I, Arc de Triomf. **Open** 10am–7pm Mon–Sat, 10am–3pm Sun & pub hols. **Closed** 1 Jan,1 May, 25 & 26 Dec. 🎫 free 1st Mon of month 🔲 by appointment. 🔲 **w** museuxocolata.com

Founded by Barcelona's pastry- and chocolate-makers' union, this museum takes you through the history of one of the most universally loved foodstuffs: from the discovery of cocoa in South America to the invention of the first chocolate machine in Barcelona. This is done using old posters, photographs and footage. The real thing is displayed in a homage to the art of the mona. A Catalan invention, this was a traditional Easter cake that over centuries evolved into an edible sculpture. Every year, pastissiers compete to create the finest piece, decorating their chocolate versions of well-known buildings or folk figures with jewels, feathers and other materials.

⑯ Arc del Triomf

Passeig Lluís Companys. **Map** 5 C1. 🚇 Arc de Triomf.

The main gateway to the 1888 Universal Exhibition, which filled the Parc de la Ciutadella, was designed by Josep Vilaseca i Casanovas. It is built of brick in Mudéjar (Spanish Moorish) style, with sculpted allegories of crafts, industry and business. The frieze by Josep Reynés on the main façade represents the city welcoming foreign visitors.

The pink brick façade of the late 19th-century Arc del Triomf

⑰ Parc de la Ciutadella

Passeig Picasso 1. **Map** 5 C3. 🚇 Barceloneta, Ciutadella-Vila Olímpica. **Open** 8am–sunset daily. 🔲

This popular park has a boating lake, orange groves and parrots living in the palm trees. It was once the site of a massive star-shaped citadel, built for Felipe V between 1715 and 1720 following a 13-month siege of

the city (see p47). The fortress was intended to house soldiers to keep law and order, but was never used for this purpose. Converted into a prison, the citadel became notorious during the Napoleonic occupation (see p47), and, during the 19th-century liberal repressions, was hated as a symbol of centralized power.

In 1878, under General Prim, whose statue stands in the middle of the park, the citadel was pulled down and the park given to the city, to become, in 1888, the venue of the Universal Exhibition (see p48). Three buildings survived: the Governor's Palace, now a school; the chapel; and the arsenal, which continues to be occupied by the Catalan parliament.

The park offers more cultural and leisure activities than any other in the city and is particularly popular on Sunday afternoons when people gather to play instruments, dance and relax, or visit the museum and zoo. A variety of works by Catalan sculptors, such as Marès, Arnau, Carbonell, Clarà, Llimona, Gargallo, Dunyach and Fuxà, can be seen in the park, alongside work by modern artists such as Tàpies and Botero.

The gardens in the Plaça de Armes boast a triumphal arch designed by architect Josep Fontseré, with the help of Antoni Gaudí, then still a young student.

Ornamental cascade in the Parc de la Ciutadella designed by Josep Fontseré and Antoni Gaudí

⓲ Castell dels Tres Dragons

Passeig de Picasso. **Map** 5 C2.
Tel 93 256 22 00. 🚇 Arc de Triomf,
Jaume I. **Closed** to the general public.

At the entrance to the Parc de la Ciutadella is the fortress-like Castell dels Tres Dragons (Castle of the Three Dragons), named after a play by Frederic Soler. A fine example of Modernista architecture, this crenellated brick edifice was built by Lluís Domènech i Montaner for the 1888 Universal Exhibition. He later used the building as a workshop for Modernista design, and it became a focus of the movement. Shortly afterwards it housed the History Museum and later on the Biology Museum. It is now a laboratory of the Science Museum and is open only to researchers.

Castell dels Tres Dragons, a prime example of Modernista architecture

⓳ Museu d'Idees i Invents (MIBA)

Carrer de la Ciutat 7. **Map** 5 A2.
Tel 93 332 79 30. 🚇 Jaume I.
Open 10am–7pm Tue–Fri, 10am–8pm Sat, 10am–2pm Sun. **Closed** 1 & 6 Jan, 25 & 26 Dec. 🅿 ♿
Ⓦ mibamuseum.com

Inventor, writer and local TV personality Pep Torres founded the Museum of Ideas and Inventions in 2011 to celebrate entrepreneurship, innovation and creativity. The museum has three sections: Limitless Society, a space for inventors to showcase their ideas; Corner of the Absurd,

Visitors peering into an animal enclosure at the Parc Zoològic

displaying humorous ideas intended to prompt a smile or a laugh; and Reflectionarium, which has inventions that provoke thought.

⓴ Museu Martorell

Parc de la Ciutadella. **Map** 5 C3.
Tel 93 256 60 02. 🚇 Arc de Triomf, Jaume I. **Closed** for renovation.

This landmark, Barcelona's oldest museum, opened in 1882, the same year the Parc de la Ciutadella became a public space. It was founded to house the natural science and archaeological collection bequeathed by Francesc Martorell i Peña to the city of Barcelona. This Neo-Classical building, designed by architect Antoni Rovira i Trias, was the city's first public museum. It is currently being renovated

as a branch of the Science Museum in the Fòrum area. It will house a permanent exhibition on the history of the natural sciences in Barcelona. Beside it is the Hivernacle, a glasshouse by Josep Amargós, and the Umbracle, a brick and wood conservatory by the park's architect, Josep Fontseré. Both date from 1884.

㉑ Parc Zoològic

Parc de la Ciutadella. **Map** 6 D3.
Tel 90 245 75 45. 🚇 Ciutadella–Vila Olímpica. **Open** Apr–Oct: 10am–7pm daily (to 8pm mid-May–mid-Sep); Nov–Mar: 10am–5:30pm daily. 🅿 ♿
Ⓦ zoobarcelona.com

This zoo was laid out in the 1940s to a relatively enlightened design – the animals are separated by

Hivernacle glasshouse, next to Museu Martorell in Parc de la Ciutadella

moats instead of bars. Roig i Soler's 1885 sculpture by the entrance, *The Lady with the Umbrella (see p19)*, has become a symbol of Barcelona. The zoo has pony rides, electric cars and a train for children. Dolphin and whale shows are currently held here but the marine animals will move to the Zoo Marí (Marine Zoo), not due for full completion until summer 2015.

Yachts at the Port Olímpic overlooked by Barcelona's tallest skyscrapers

㉒ Port Olímpic

Map 6 F4. 🚇 Ciutadella-Vila Olímpica.

The most dramatic rebuilding for the 1992 Olympics was the demolition of the old industrial waterfront and the laying out of 4 km (2 miles) of promenade and pristine sandy beaches. At the heart of the project was a 65-ha (160-acre) new estate of 2,000 apartments and parks called Nova Icària. The area is still popularly known as the Vila Olímpica because the buildings originally housed the Olympic athletes.

The sole building still standing of Barcelona's Old Port is the former General Stores building. The Stores were designed in 1881 by the engineer Maurici Garrán and were intended for use as trading depots. They were refurbished in 1992 and today house the Museu d'Història de Catalunya *(see pp70–71)*. On the sea

Sandy, palm-fringed beach at Barcelona's Port Olímpic

front there are twin 44-floor buildings, Spain's second and third tallest skyscrapers, one occupied by offices, the other by the Arts hotel *(see p137)*. They stand beside the Port Olímpic, which was also built for 1992. This has shops and nightclubs as well as two levels of restaurants around the marina which have made it a popular place to eat out. The wonderful outdoor setting attracts business people at lunchtime and pleasure seekers in the evenings and at weekends.

Lunch can be walked off along the string of beaches that is edged by a palm-fringed promenade with cafés. Behind the promenade, the coastal road heads around a park that is full of palm trees and lies beside the last three beaches, divided by rocky breakwaters. Swimming is safe on the gently sloping, sandy strands.

㉓ Barceloneta

Map 5 B5. 🚇 Barceloneta.

Barcelona's fishing "village", which lies on a triangular tongue of land jutting into the sea just below the city centre, is renowned for its little restaurants and cafés. Its beach is also the closest to the city centre and is well equipped with lifeguards, disabled access, showers and play areas for children.

The area was designed in 1753 by the architect and military engineer Juan Martín de Cermeño to rehouse people made homeless by the construction, just inland, of the Ciutadella fortress *(see p67)*. Since then it has housed largely workers and fishermen. Laid out in a grid system with narrow two- and three-storey houses, in which each room has a window on the street, the area has a friendly, intimate air.

In the small Plaça de la Barceloneta, at the centre of the district, is the Baroque church of Sant Miguel del Port, also by Cermeño. A market is often held in the square here.

Today, Barceloneta's fishing fleet is still based in the nearby Moll del Rellotge (the clock dock), by a small clock tower. On the opposite side of this harbour is the Torre de Sant Sebastià, terminus of the cable car that runs right across the port, via the World Trade Centre, to Montjuïc.

Fishing boat moored in Barceloneta harbour

Maremagnum shopping complex on the Moll d'Espanya, Port Vell

❷ Port Vell

Map 5 A4. ⬣ Barceloneta, Drassanes.

Barcelona's marina is located at the foot of La Rambla, just beyond the old customs house. This was built in 1902 at the Portal de la Pau, the city's former maritime entrance. To the south, the Moll de Barcelona, with a new World Trade Centre, serves as the passenger pier for visiting liners. In front of the customs house, La Rambla is connected to the yacht clubs on the Moll d'Espanya by a swing bridge and a pedestrian jetty, known as La Rambla de Mar. The Moll d'Espanya boasts a vast new shopping and restaurant complex known as the Maremagnum. Also on the Moll d'Espanya is an IMAX cinema and one of the largest aquariums in Europe.

On the shore, the Moll de Fusta (Timber Wharf), with terrace cafés, has red structures inspired by the bridge at Arles painted by Van Gogh. At the end of the wharf is *El Cap de Barcelona (Barcelona Head)*, a 20-m (66-ft) tall sculpture by Pop artist Roy Lichtenstein.

The attractive Sports Marina on the other side of the Moll d'Espanya was once lined with warehouses. The only one left, built by Elies Rogent in the 1880s, has been given a new lease of life as the Palau de Mar. Restaurants provide alfresco dining, but the building is otherwise given over to the Museu d'Història de Catalunya.

Spectacular glass viewing tunnel at the aquarium, Port Vell

❺ Aquarium

Moll d'Espanya. **Map** 5 B4. ⬣ Barceloneta, Drassanes. **Tel** 93 221 74 74. **Open** 9:30am–9pm daily (to 9:30pm Sat, Sun & Jun, Sep; to 11pm Jul–Aug). ⬣ ⬣ ⬣
🅦 **aquariumbcn.com**

Populated by over 11,000 organisms belonging to 450 different species, Barcelona's aquarium is one of the biggest in Europe. Occupying three levels of a glass building, the aquarium focuses particularly on the local Mediterranean coast. Two nature reserves, for instance, the Delta del Ebro and the Medes isles off the Costa Brava, are given a tank apiece. Tropical seas are also represented and moving platforms ferry visitors through a glass tunnel under an "ocean" of sharks, rays and sunfish. A large hall of activities for children includes an irregularly shaped tank of rays built around an island which is reached through crawl-through glass tunnels.

❻ Museu d'Història de Catalunya

Plaça Pau Vila 3. **Map** 5 A4. ⬣ Barceloneta, Drassanes. **Tel** 93 225 47 00. **Open** 10am–7pm Tue & Thu–Sat, 10am–8pm Wed, 10am–2:30pm Sun & public hols. **Closed** 1 & 6 Jan, 25 & 26 Dec. ⬣ except 1st Sun every month. ⬣ ⬣ noon & 1pm Sun & public hols. 🅦 **mhcat.cat**

This museum charts the history of Catalonia, from Lower Palaeolithic times through to

Café-lined façade of the Museu d'Història de Catalunya

the region's heydays as a maritime power and industrial pioneer. Second-floor exhibits include the Moorish invasion, Romanesque architecture, medieval monastic life and the rise of Catalan seafaring. Third floor exhibits cover the industrial revolution and the impact of steam power and electricity on the economy. There is also a glass floor laid over a relief map of Catalonia which visitors can walk over. The first floor is reserved for temporary exhibits. Some captions are in English; pick up a free guide for the rest.

A *golondrina* tour boat departing from the Portal de la Pau

The Columbus Monument lit by fireworks during La Mercè fiesta

㉗ Monument a Colom

Plaça del Portal de la Pau. **Map** 2 F4. **Tel** 93 302 52 24. Drassanes. **Open** 8:30am–8:30pm daily.

The Columbus monument at the bottom of La Rambla was designed by Gaietà Buigas for the 1888 Universal Exhibition *(see p48)*. At the time Catalans considered that the great explorer had been a Catalan rather than Italian.

The 60-m (200-ft) monument marks the spot where Columbus stepped ashore in 1493 after returning from his voyage to the Caribbean, bringing with him six Caribbean Indians. He was given a state welcome by the Catholic Monarchs in the Saló del Tinell of the Plaça del Rei *(see p58)*. The Indians' subsequent conversion to Christianity is

commemorated in the cathedral *(see pp60–61)*. A lift leads to a viewing platform at the top of the monument. The bronze statue was designed by Rafael Arché.

㉘ Golondrinas

Plaça del Portal de la Pau. **Map** 2 F5. **Tel** 93 442 31 06. Drassanes. Departures: variable (phone for details). Catamaran Orsom **Tel** 93 441 05 37. lasgolondrinas.com; barcelona-orsom.com

Sightseeing trips around Barcelona's harbour and to the Port Olímpic can be made on *golondrinas* ("swallows") – small double-decker boats that moor at Portal de la Pau in front of the Columbus Monument at the foot of La Rambla.

The half-hour harbour tours are on traditional wooden boats and go out beneath the castle-topped hill of Montjuïc towards the industrial port. There is also a one-and-a-half hour trip on modern catamarans that takes in Barcelona harbour, the local beaches and finally Port Olímpic.

㉙ Museu Marítim and Drassanes

Avinguda de les Drassanes. **Map** 2 F4. **Tel** 93 342 99 20. Drassanes. **Open** 10am–8pm daily. **Closed** 1 & 6 Jan, 25 & 26 Dec. free Sun from 3pm mmb.cat

The great galleys that were instrumental in making Barcelona a major seafaring power were built in the sheds of the Drassanes (shipyards) that now house the maritime

museum. These royal dry docks are the largest and most complete surviving medieval complex of their kind in the world. They were founded in the mid-13th century, when dynastic marriages uniting the kingdoms of Sicily and Aragón meant that better maritime communications between the two became a priority. Three of the yards' four original corner towers survive.

Among the vessels to slip from the Drassanes' vaulted halls was the *Real*, flagship of Don Juan of Austria, who led the Christian fleet to the famous victory against the Turks at Lepanto in 1571. The highlight of the museum's collection is a full-scale replica decorated in red and gold.

The *Llibre del Consolat de Mar*, a book of nautical codes and practice, is a reminder that Catalonia was once the arbiter of Mediterranean maritime law *(see p45)*. There are Pre-Columbian maps, including one from 1439 that was used by Amerigo Vespucci.

Stained-glass window in the Museu Marítim

EIXAMPLE

Barcelona claims to have the greatest collection of Art Nouveau buildings of any city in Europe. The style, known in Catalonia as Modernisme, flourished after 1854, when it was decided to tear down the medieval walls to allow the city to develop into what had previously been a construction-free military zone.

The designs of the civil engineer Ildefons Cerdà i Sunyer (1815–76) were chosen for the new expansion (eixample) inland. These plans called for a rigid grid system of streets, but at each intersection the corners were chamfered to allow the buildings there to overlook the junctions or squares. The few exceptions to this grid system include the

Diagonal, a main avenue running from the wealthy area of Pedralbes down to the sea, and the Hospital de la Santa Creu i de Sant Pau by Modernista architect Domènech i Montaner (1850–1923). He hated the grid system and deliberately angled the hospital to look down the diagonal Avinguda de Gaudí towards Antoni Gaudí's church of the Sagrada Família, the city's most spectacular Modernista building (see pp82–5). The wealth of Barcelona's commercial elite, and their passion for all things new, allowed them to give free rein to the age's most innovative architects in designing their residences as well as public buildings.

Sights at a Glance

Museums and Galleries
❸ Fundació Antoni Tàpies

Churches
❼ Sagrada Família pp82–5

Modernista Buildings
❶ Casa Batlló
❷ Illa de la Discòrdia

❹ La Pedrera
❺ Casa Terrades, "Casa de les Punxes"
❻ Hospital de la Santa Creu i de Sant Pau

See also Street Finder maps 3, 4 and 5

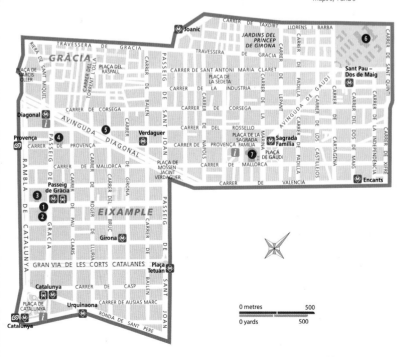

◀ A dizzying view into La Pedrera's interior courtyard

For keys to symbols see back flap

Street-by-Street: Quadrat d'Or

The hundred or so city blocks centering on the Passeig de Gràcia are known as the Quadrat d'Or, "Golden Square", because they contain so many of the best Modernista buildings *(see pp26–7)*. This was the area within the Eixample favoured by the wealthy bourgeoisie, who embraced the new artistic and architectural style with enthusiasm, not only for their residences, but also for commercial buildings. Most remarkable is the Mansana de la Discòrdia, a single block with houses by Modernisme's most illustrious exponents. Many interiors can be visited by the public, revealing a feast of stained glass, ceramics and ornamental ironwork.

Diagonal Metro

Vinçon home decor store
(see p155)

Passeig de Gràcia, the Eixample's main avenue, is a showcase of highly original buildings and smart shops. The graceful street lamps are by Pere Falqués (1850–1916).

RAMBLA DE CATALUNYA

PASSEIG DE GRÀCIA

❸ **Fundació Tàpies**
Topped by Antoni Tàpies' wire sculpture *Cloud and Chair*, this 1879 building by Domènech i Montaner houses a wide variety of Tàpies' paintings, graphics and sculptures.

Passeig de Gràcia Metro Ⓜ

❷ ★ **Illa de la Discòrdia**
In this city block, three of Barcelona's most famous Modernista houses vie for attention. All were created between 1900 and 1910. This ornate tower graces the Casa Lleó Morera by Domènech i Montaner.

To Plaça de Catalunya

Casa Lleó Morera

Casa Ramon Mulleras

Museu del Perfum

Casa Amatller

❶ **Casa Batlló**
(see pp78-79)

Palau Baró de Quadras was designed by Puig i Cadafalch in 1904 in a neo-Gothic style. The ornate façade is riddled with grotesque sculptures including this one, which adorns the doorway.

Locator Map
See Barcelona City Centre map pp16–17

EIXAMPLE

OLD TOWN

AVINGUDA DIAGONAL

CARRER DE PAU CLARIS

CARRER DE PROVENÇA

CARRER DE LLÙRIA

CARRER DE MALLORCA

CARRER DE ROUGER DE LLÙRIA

CARRER DEL BRUC

CARRER DE VALÈNCIA

CARRER DE

CARRER D' ARAGÓ

Casa Thomas

To Sagrada Família

Palau Ramon de Montaner

❺ **Casa Terrades "Les Punxes"**
Built in red brick with carved stone ornamentation, this 1905 house by Puig i Cadafalch echoes the Gothic buildings of northern Europe.

❹ ★ **La Pedrera**
Gaudí put all his architectural daring into this, his most famous house. The result is a remarkable wave-like façade and a roofscape of chimneys and vents resembling abstract sculptures.

0 metres 100
0 yards 100

Key

— Suggested route

For keys to symbols *see back flap*

❶ Casa Batlló

Unlike Gaudí's other works, this block of flats, which was commissioned by Josep Batlló i Casanovas on the prestigious Passeig de Gràcia, involved the conversion of an existing building. With its reworked façade in stunning organic forms and its fantastic chimneys and rooftop, it remains as bold and convention-defying today as it did when it was finished in 1906. The building has been said to symbolise the legend of St George killing the dragon, whose scaly back arches above the main façade. It was designated a UNESCO World Heritage Site in 2005.

View of façade and Dragon's Back

★ **The Chimneys**
Extraordinary chimneys, usually the unseen and functional parts of a building, have become Gaudí's trademark. These fine examples are tightly packed and covered in abstract patterns.

KEY

① **Stairs to main floor**

② **The Dining Room** ceiling ripples with bulbous forms which are thought to represent the splash caused by a drop of water.

③ **The light-well**, created by enlarging the orginal patio, provides maximum light to interior windows.

④ **The ceramic cross** was made in Mallorca but was damaged in transit. Gaudí liked the cracked effect and refused to send it back for repair. The arms point to the four cardinal points of the compass.

⑤ **Dragon's belly room**

⑥ **The iron balconies** have been likened to the masks worn in carnival processions.

⑦ *Trencadis* decorations

⑧ **Fireplace room** Josep Batlló's office has a mushroom-shaped fireplace tiled in earthy colours.

Patio and Rear Façade
This outdoor space at the back of the house allows a view of the rear façade which has cast-iron balconies and superbly colourful *trencadis* work at the top.

Attics
The closely packed brick arches supporting the roof are plastered and painted white giving the sensation of being inside the skeleton of a large animal.

Inspired by the sea, the extraodinary inner courtyard of Casa Batlló is decorated with thousands of blue azulejo titles

★ The Dragon's Back
One of the most extraordinary innovations to the house is this steep, narrow, colourfully tiled cap above the façade which it is difficult to see as anything other than the spine of a reptile. Inside it is a white domed room which was used as a water deposit.

VISITORS' CHECKLIST

Practical Information
Passeig de Gràcia 43.
Map 3 A4.
Tel 93 216 03 06.
Open 9am–9pm daily. 🚶 ♿ 📷 📷
W **casabatllo.cat**

Transport
🚇 Passeig de Gràcia.

Façade
Salvador Dalí saw the curving walls and windows as "representing waves on a stormy day". The spindly, individually shaped columns across the first floor windows were also compared to tibias, earning Casa Batlló the nickname "House of Bones".

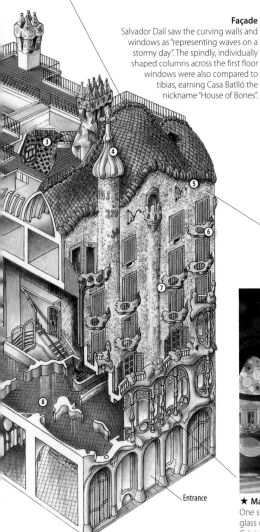

Entrance

★ Main Drawing Room
One side of this room is formed by stained-glass windows looking out over the Passeig de Gràcia. The ceiling plaster is moulded into a spiral and the doors and window frames undulate playfully.

Sumptuous interior of the Casa Lleó Morera, Illa de la Discòrdia

❷ Illa de la Discòrdia

Passeig de Gràcia, between Carrer d'Aragó and Carrer del Consell de Cent. **Map** 3 A4. 🚇 Passeig de Gràcia. Institut Amatller d'Art Hispànic: **Tel** 93 467 01 94. **Closed** for renovation until the end of 2014. 🗺

Barcelona's most famous group of Modernista *(see pp26–7)* buildings illustrates the wide range of styles used by the movement's architects. They lie in an area known as the Illa de la Discòrdia (Block of Discord), after the startling visual argument between them. The three finest were remodelled in the Modernista style from existing houses early in the 20th century. No. 35 Passeig de Gràcia is Casa Lleó Morera (1902–6), the first residential work of Lluís Domènech i Montaner. A shop was installed in the ground floor in 1943, but the Modernista interiors upstairs, with their magnificent stained-glass bay windows, still exist. The house is not open to the public, however if the door is open it is possible to see the painted ceiling of the hallway.

Beyond the next two houses is Casa Amatller, designed by Puig i Cadafalch in 1898. Its façade, under a stepped gable roof, features a harmonious blend of Moorish and Gothic windows. The ground floor of the house contains a shop. The entrance patio, with its spiral columns, and the staircase covered by a stained-glass skylight can be seen but

the rest of the building, including the beautiful wood-panelled library, is occupied by the Institut Amatller d'Art Hispànic, which is currently closed for renovation work. The third house in the block is Antoni Gaudí's Casa Batlló *(see pp78–9)* with its fluid façade evoking marine or natural forms. The bizarrely decorated chimneys became a trademark of Gaudí's later work.

❸ Fundació Antoni Tàpies

Carrer d'Aragó 255. **Map** 3 A4. **Tel** 93 487 03 15. 🚇 Passeig de Gràcia. **Open** 10am–7pm Tue–Sun & public hols. **Closed** 1 & 6 Jan, 25 Dec. 🗺 🕐 by appointment (93 207 58 62). ♿ 🌐 fundaciotapies.org

Antoni Tàpies *(see p31)*, who died in 2012, was one of Barcelona's best-known artists. Inspired by Surrealism, his abstract work is executed in a variety of materials, including concrete and metal *(see pp74–5)*. Although perhaps difficult to appreciate at first, the exhibits should help viewers obtain a clearer perspective of Tàpies' work. The collection is housed in Barcelona's first domestic building to be constructed with iron (1880), designed by Domènech i Montaner for his brother's publishing firm.

Antoni Gaudí (1852–1926)

Born in Reus (Tarragona) into an artisan family, Antoni Gaudí i Cornet was the leading exponent of Catalan Modernisme. After a blacksmith's apprenticeship, he studied at Barcelona's School of Architecture. Inspired by a nationalistic search for a romantic medieval past, his work was supremely original. His first major achievement was the Casa Vicens (1888) at No. 24 Carrer de les Carolines *(see p28)*. But his most celebrated building is the church of the Sagrada Família *(see pp82–5)*, to which he devoted his life from 1914. When he had put all his money into the project, he went from house to house begging for more. He was killed by a tram in 1926.

Decorated chimneypot, Casa Vicens

The rippled façade of Gaudí's apartment building, La Pedrera

❹ La Pedrera

Passeig de Gràcia 92. **Map** 3 B3. **Tel** 902 202 138. 🚇 Diagonal. **Open** Mar–Oct: 9am–8pm daily; Nov–Feb: 9am–6:30pm daily. **Closed** 7–13 Jan, 25 Dec. 🅿 🛗 📷 Night guided visits Wed–Sat. 🕸 **lapedrera.com**

Also known as Casa Milá (which translates as "The Stone Quarry"), La Pedrera is Gaudí's greatest contribution to Barcelona's civic architecture, and his last work before he devoted himself entirely to the Sagrada Família (see pp82–85).

Built between 1906 and 1910, La Pedrera departed from established principles of construction and, as a result, was ridiculed by Barcelona's intellectuals. Gaudí designed this eight-floor apartment block around two circular courtyards. The ironwork balconies, by Josep Maria Jujol, are like seaweed against the wave-like walls of white stone. There are no straight walls anywhere in the building.

The Milà family had an apartment on the fourth floor, which now features a typical Modernista interior. The museum, "El Espai Gaudí", on the top floor, includes models and explanations of Gaudí's work. From here, visitors can access the extraordinary roof. The sculptured ducts and chimneys have such a threatening appearance they are known as

espantabruixes, or witch-scarers. Free temporary exhibitions are held on the first floor.

❺ Casa Terrades

Avinguda Diagonal 416. **Map** 3 B3. 🚇 Diagonal. **Closed** to public.

This free-standing, six-sided apartment block by Modernista architect Josep Puig i Cadafalch gets its nickname, Casa de les Punxes (House of the Points), from the spires on its six corner turrets. It was built between 1903 and 1905 by converting three existing houses on the site and was Puig's largest work. It is an eclectic mixture of

Spire on the main tower, Casa Terrades

medieval and Renaissance styles. The towers and gables are influenced in particular by the Gothic architecture of northern Europe. However, the deeply carved, floral stone ornamentation of the exterior, in combination with red brick used as the principal building material, are typically Modernista.

❻ Hospital de la Santa Creu i de Sant Pau

Carrer de Sant Antoni Maria Claret 167, 08025 Barcelona. **Map** 4 F1. **Tel** 93 317 76 52. 🚇 Hospital de Sant Pau. Grounds: **Open** 9:30am–1:30pm daily. 🛗 📷 daily 10am, 11am, 12pm, 1pm in English, phone for other times. 🕸 **santpau.es**

Lluís Domènech i Montaner began designing a new city hospital in 1902. His innovative scheme consisted of 26 attractive Mudéjar-style pavilions set in large gardens, as he believed that patients would recover better among fresh air and trees. All the connecting corridors and service areas were hidden underground. Also believing art and colour to be therapeutic, he decorated the pavilions profusely. The roofs were tiled with ceramics, and the reception pavilion has mosaic murals and sculptures by Pau Gargallo. After his death, the project was completed in 1930 by his son, Pere.

Statue of the Virgin, Hospital de la Santa Creu i de Sant Pau

❼ Sagrada Família

Europe's most unconventional church, the Basílica de la Sagrada Família, is an emblem of a city that likes to think of itself as individualistic. Crammed with symbolism inspired by nature and striving for originality, it is the greatest work of Gaudí *(see pp26–7)*. In 1883, a year after work had begun on a Neo-Gothic church on the site, the task of completing it was given to Gaudí, who changed everything, extemporizing as he went along. It became his life's work and he lived like a recluse on the site for 14 years. He is buried in the crypt. At his death only one tower on the Nativity façade had been completed, but work resumed after the Civil War and several more have since been finished to his original plans. Work continues today, financed by public subscription.

Bell Towers
Eight of the 12 spires, one for each apostle, have been built. Each is topped by Venetian mosaics.

The Finished Church

Gaudí's initial ambitions have been kept over the years, using various new technologies to achieve his vision. Still to come is the central tower, which is to be encircled by four large towers representing the Evangelists. Four towers on the Glory (south) façade will match the existing four on the Passion (west) and Nativity (east) façades. An ambulatory – like an inside-out cloister – will run round the outside of the building.

★ Passion Façade
This bleak façade was completed between 1986 and 2000 by artist Josep Maria Subirachs. A controversial work, its sculpted figures are angular and often sinister.

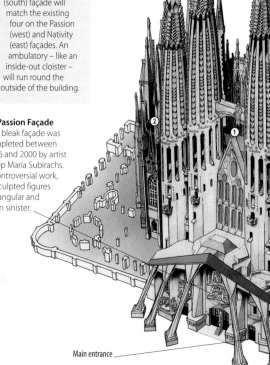

KEY

① **The altar canopy** was designed by Gaudí.

② **The apse**; stairs lead down from here to the crypt below.

③ **The bell tower** with a lift to reach the upper galleries.

Main entrance

Spiral Staircases
Steep stone steps – 370 in each staircase – are closed to the public, but visitors can reach the upper galleries by lift to enjoy the majestic views.

VISITORS' CHECKLIST

Practical Information
C/Mallorca 401
Map 4 E3.
Tel 93 513 20 60.
🔲 **sagradafamilia.org**
Open Apr–Sep: 9am–8pm; Oct–Mar: 9am–6pm daily (1 & 6 Jan, 25 & 26 Dec: 9am–2pm). Crypt: 9–10am & 6–9pm Mon–Sat, 9am–2pm & 6–9pm Sun services daily. except the towers. Tickets may be booked in advance online.

Transport
Sagrada Família. 19, 33, 34, 43, 44, 50, 51.

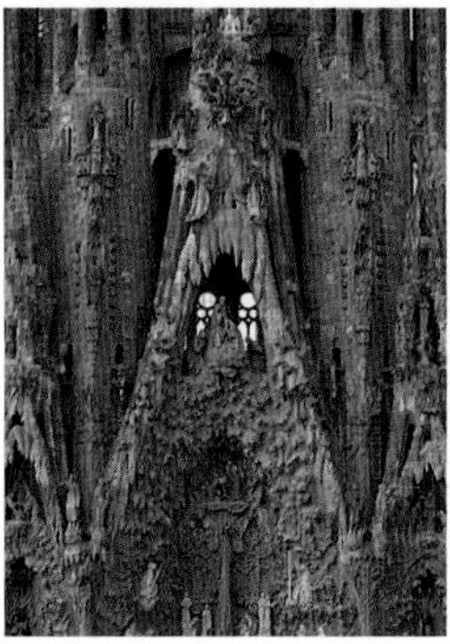

★ Nativity Façade
The most complete part of Gaudí's church, finished in 1930, has doorways representing Faith, Hope and Charity. Scenes of the Nativity and Christ's childhood are embellished with symbolism, such as doves representing the congregation.

★ Crypt
The crypt, where Gaudí is buried, was begun by the original architect, Francesc de Paula Villar i Lozano, in 1882. On the lower floor a museum traces the careers of both architects and the church's history.

Nave
In the nave, which was inaugurated in 2010, a forest of fluted pillars supports four galleries above the side aisles, while skylights let in natural light.

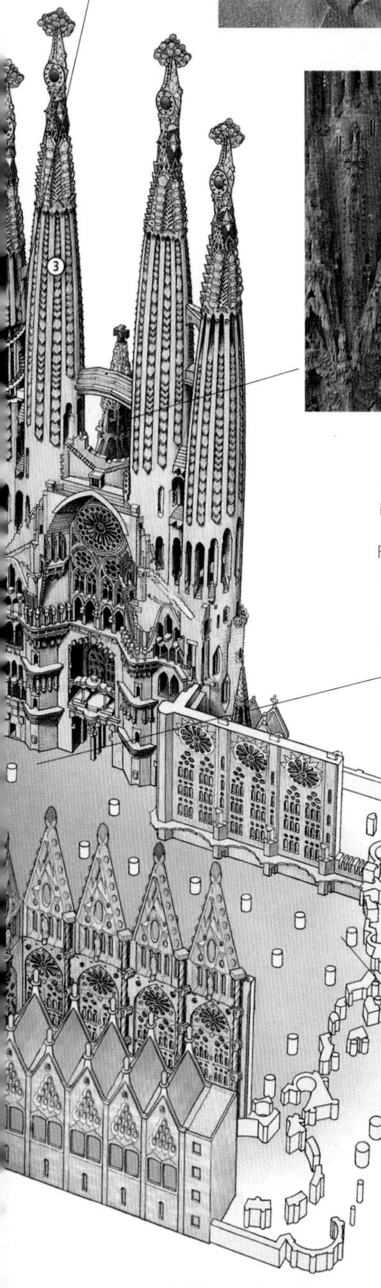

Passion Façade

It has been said that the Sagrada Família is like a book in stone: meant to be read in the same way as a medieval cathedral, with each element representing a Biblical event or aspect of Christian faith. This was certainly Gaudí's intent: his architecture was inseparable from the profound Catholicism which inspired it. The temple is dedicated to the Sagrada Família, the Holy Family. The two existing façades are detailed, visual accounts of two key Bible passages. The Glory façade (yet to be built) will address the theme of judgement of sinners.

Detail on brass door of the Passion façade

Main entrance to the Passion façade

Christ's Passion

The Passion façade depicts the sufferings and execution of Jesus, and its style reflects its subject matter. The statuary by Catalan sculptor Josep Maria Subirachs has attracted much criticism for its chunky, angular, "dehumanised" carving but Gaudí would probably have approved. He is known to have favoured an Expressionist style to give the story of Christ's Passion maximum impact.

A great porch whose roof is held up by six inclined buttress-like swamp tree roots shades the 12 groups of sculptures, arranged in three tiers and to be viewed from bottom to top, left to right in an inverted "S". The first scene, bottom left-hand corner, is the Last Supper at which Jesus (standing) announces his impending betrayal. Next to this is the arrest in the Garden of Gethsemane. An olive trunk's grain mimics the shape of the high priest's servant's ear that Peter cut off. The kiss of betrayal by Judas follows. The numbers of the cryptogram to the side of Jesus add up to 33 in every direction: his age at the time of his death.

The Flagellation

In the flagellation (between the central doors) Jesus is shown

Knights sculpture on the Passion façade

tied to a column at the top of a flight of three steps representing the three days of the Passion. Peter denying Christ is indicated by the cock that will crow three times in fulfilment of Jesus' prophecy. Behind this group of figures is a labyrinth, a metaphor for the loneliness of Jesus' path to the cross.

The sculptural group on the bottom right is in two parts. First is Ecce Homo (Christ bound with ropes and crowned with thorns). Pilate, overlooked by the Roman eagle, is shown washing his hands, freeing himself of responsibility for Jesus' death. Above, the "Three Marys" weep as Simon the Cyrene, a passer-by, is compelled by the Romans to pick up Christ's cross.

The Holy Shroud

The central sculpture depicts an event not described in the Bible but added to the story of the Passion by later tradition. A woman named Veronica holds up her head cloth which she has offered to Jesus to wipe the blood and sweat from his face. It has been returned impressed with his likeness.

Next comes the solitary figure of the Roman centurion on horseback piercing the side of Jesus with his sword. Above him, three soldiers beneath the cross cast lots for Jesus' tunic. The largest sculpture (top centre) shows Christ hanging from a horizontal cross. At his feet is a skull referring to the place of the Crucifixion, Golgotha. Above him is the veil of the Temple of Jerusalem. The final scene is the burial of Jesus. The figure of Nicodemus, who is anointing the body, is thought to be a self-portrait of the sculptor Subirachs.

Nativity Façade

The northern, Nativity façade (overlooking Carrer Marina), finished according to Gaudí's personal instructions before his death, is far more subdued than the Passion façade -- so much so that many of the sculptures barely rise out of the surface of the wall, making them difficult to identify. A great many natural forms are incorporated into the work, confusing interpretation further. Gaudí intended the whole work to be coloured but his wishes are unlikely ever to be carried out.

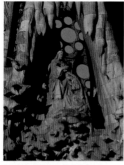

Detail of sculpture on Nativity façade

Faith, Hope and Charity

The lavish ornamentation of the façade is arranged around three doors dedicated to Hope (left), Faith (right) and Charity or Christian Love in the middle. The two columns between the doorways rest on a turtle and a tortoise, signifying the permanence and stability of Christianity. In contrast, the two chameleons on either extreme of the façade represent forces of change. The four angels on top of the columns are calling to the four winds and announcing the proximity of the end of the world.

Detail of a spire,
Nativity façade

Hope Doorway

The lowest carvings of the Hope Doorway show the Flight into Egypt (left) and the Slaughter of the Innocents (right). Above the door are Joseph and the child Jesus watched over by Mary's parents (Jesus' grandparents), St Ann and St Joachim. The lintel of the door is composed of a woodcutter's two-handled saw and various other tools such as a hammer, axe, square and mallet – all indicative of Joseph's profession as a craftsman. Further above is a triangular grouping showing the betrothal of Mary and Joseph. The spire above the doorway is in the form of an elongated boulder which is an allusion to the holy Catalan mountain of Montserrat (see pp124–5). At the base of this boulder sits Joseph in a boat; he bears a close resemblance to Gaudí himself and is very likely a posthumous homage by the masons who put the final touches to the façade after the master's death.

Faith Doorway

The Faith Doorway illustrates passages from the gospels and Christian theology. The heart of Jesus can be seen set into the lintel above the door. The scene on the lower left is the Visitation by Mary to Elizabeth, her cousin and mother of John the Baptist. On the right, Jesus wields a hammer and chisel in his father's workshop. Above the door is Jesus in the temple with John the Baptist (left) and John's father Zachariah (right). Higher up, the baby Jesus is presented in the temple, held by Simeon. As it rises, the stonework forms an intricate pinnacle recording the fundamentals of Catholicism, including a lamp with three wicks for the trinity, bunches of grapes and ears of wheat for the Eucharist, and a hand set with an eye, showing God's omniscience and infinite care.

Charity Doorway

The double doors of the central Charity Doorway are separated by a column recording Jesus' genealogy. The three Magi are on the lower left of the door with the shepherds opposite them. Out of the nativity emerges the spiky tail of a many-pointed star (or comet). Around it are a children's choir and musicians. Above the star is the Annunciation and the Coronation of the Virgin Mary by Jesus. Above is a pelican sitting on a crown next to a glass egg bearing the JHS monogram of Jesus.

The lavish Nativity façade entrance

MONTJUÏC

The hill of Montjuïc, rising to 213 m (699 ft) above the commercial port on the south side of the city, is Barcelona's biggest recreation area. Its museums, art galleries, gardens and nightclubs make it a popular place in the evenings as well as during the day.

There is likely to have been a CeltIberian settlement here before the Romans built a temple to Jupiter on their Mons Jovis, which may have given Montjuïc its name – though another theory suggests that a Jewish cemetery sited on the hill inspired the name Mount of the Jews.

The absence of a water supply meant that there were few buildings on Montjuïc until the castle was erected on the top in 1640. The hill finally came into its own as the site of the 1929 International Fair. With great energy and flair, buildings were erected all over the north side, with the grand Avinguda de la Reina Maria Cristina, lined with huge exhibition halls, leading into it from the Plaça d'Espanya. In the middle of the avenue is the Font Màgica (Magic Fountain), which is regularly illuminated in colour. Above it is the Palau Nacional, home of the city's historic art collections. The Poble Espanyol is a crafts centre housed in copies of buildings from all over Spain. The last great surge of building on Montjuïc was for the 1992 Olympic Games, which left Barcelona with international-class sports facilities.

Sights at a Glance

Museums and Galleries
1 Fundació Joan Miró
3 Museu Arqueològic
4 Museu Nacional d'Art de Catalunya (MNAC)
8 CaixaForum

Fountains
5 Font Màgica

Historic Buildings
10 Castell de Montjuïc

Modern Architecture
6 Pavelló Mies van der Rohe
11 Estadi Olímpic Lluís Companys

Squares
9 Plaça d'Espanya

Theatres
2 Teatre Grec

Theme Parks
7 Poble Espanyol

See also Street Finder maps 1 and 2

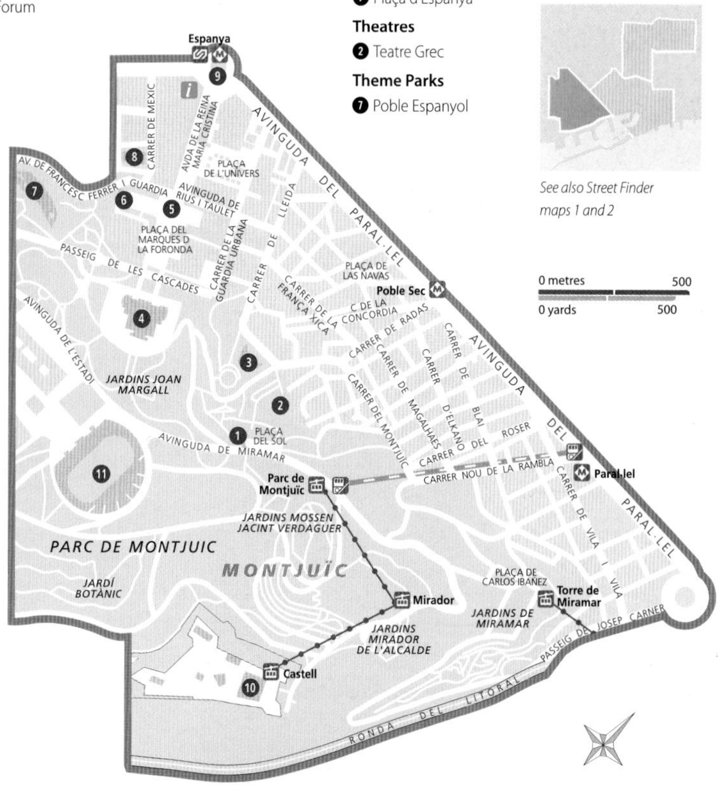

0 metres 500
0 yards 500

The Palau Nacional houses the outstanding Museu Nacional d'Art de Catalunya

For keys to symbols *see back flap*

Street-by-Street: Montjuïc

Montjuïc is a spectacular vantage point from which to view the city. It has a wealth of art galleries and museums, as well as theatres. Many of the buildings were designed for the 1929 International Exhibition, and the 1992 Olympics were held on its southern slopes. Montjuïc is approached from the Plaça d'Espanya between brick pillars based on the campanile of St Mark's in Venice. They give a foretaste of the eclecticism of building styles from the Palau Nacional, which houses magnificent Romanesque art, to the Poble Espanyol, which illustrates the architecture of Spain's regions.

❻ Pavelló Mies van der Rohe
This elegant statue by Georg Kolbe stands serenely in the steel, glass, stone and onyx pavilion built in the Bauhaus style as the German contribution to the 1929 International Exhibition.

AVINGUDA DE FRANCESC FERRER I GUARDIA

AVINGUDA DELS MONTANYANS

PASSEIG DE

❼ ★ Poble Espanyol
Containing replicas of buildings from many regions of Spain, this "village" provides a fascinating glimpse of vernacular styles.

AVINGUDA DE L'ESTADI

To Montjuïc castle and Olympic stadium

❹ ★ Museu Nacional d'Art de Catalunya (MNAC)
On show in the Palau Nacional (National Palace), the main building of the 1929 International Exhibition, is Europe's finest collection of Romanesque frescoes. These were a great source of inspiration for Joan Miró.

5 **Font Màgica**
Fountains and cascades descend in terraces from the Palau Nacional. Below is the Font Màgica (Magic Fountain), whose jets are programmed to "perform" to a music and light show as darkness falls. Sometimes the spectacle is accompanied by the twin columns of fountains which lead up the hill in a particularly fine display.

Locator Map
See Barcelona City Centre map
pp16–17

3 **Museu Arqueològic**
The museum displays important finds from prehistoric cultures in Catalonia and the Balearic Islands. The *Dama d'Evissa*, a 4th-century sculpture, was found in Ibiza's Carthaginian necropolis.

Museu Etnològic displays artifacts from Oceania, Africa, Asia and Latin America.

Mercat de les Flors
theatre *(see p162)*

Teatre Lliure is a prestigious Catalan theatre.

2 **Teatre Grec**
(see p90)

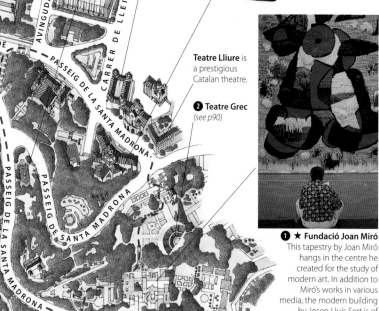

1 ★ **Fundació Joan Miró**
This tapestry by Joan Miró hangs in the centre he created for the study of modern art. In addition to Miró's works in various media, the modern building by Josep Lluís Sert is of architectural interest.

Plaça d'Espanya

RUIS I TAULET

AVINGUDA DE LA TÈCNICA

CARRER DE LLEIDA

PASSEIG DE LA SANTA MADRONA

PASSEIG DE SANTA MADRONA

PASSEIG DE LA SANTA MADRONA

AVINGUDA DE MIRAMAR

To Montjuïc castle and cable car

Key

— Suggested route

| 0 metres | | 100 |
| 0 yards | | 100 |

Flame in Space and Naked Woman (1932) by Joan Miró

❶ Fundació Joan Miró

Parc de Montjuïc. **Map** 1 B3. **Tel** 93 443 94 70. 🚇 Pl. Espanya, then bus 150 or 55; or Paral·lel, then funicular to Montjuïc. **Open** Jul–Sep: 10am–8pm Tue–Sat (to 9:30pm Thu); Oct– Jun: 10am–7pm Tue–Sat (to 9:30pm Thu), 10am–2:30pm Sun & public hols. **Closed** 1 Jan, 25 & 26 Dec. 🅿 🎧 ♿ 🌐 fundaciomiro-bcn.org

Joan Miró (1893–1983) went to La Llotja's art school *(see p65)*, but from 1919 spent much time in Paris. Though opposed to Franco, he returned to Spain in 1940 and lived mainly in Mallorca, where he died. An admirer of Catalan art *(see p31)* and Modernisme *(see p26–7)*, Miró remained a Catalan painter but invented and developed a Surrealistic style, with vivid colours and fantastical forms. Indefatigable and endlessly creative, he concentrated on ceramics in the 1950s, but also created remarkable tapestries, as well as book illustrations and works in a range of other media.

Miró began to consider establishing a museum in the late 1960s, but it was not until 1975, after the return of democracy to Spain, that the Miró Foundation became a reality. His friend, the architect Josep Lluís Sert, designed the stark, white building, a remarkable Rationalist construction arranged around courtyards and drenched with natural light which pours in through ingenious angled skylights. It houses an enormous permanent collection (which currently numbers more than 14,000 works). Miró himself donated the works and some of the best pieces on display include his Barcelona Series (1939–44), a set of 50 black-and-white lithographs. Other highlights include early works like the *Hermitage, Sant Joan d'Horta* (1917), painted in the beautiful Catalan town which would feature prominently in Miró's early work.

By the 1930s, Miró had found his own unique language, displayed in remarkable paintings like *Man and Woman in Front of a Pile of Excrement* (1935), Miro's reaction to the simmering violence which would erupt in the Spanish Civil War. Many of the later works are colourful and exuberant, such as *Caress of a Bird* (1967), one of the sculptures which adorn the Foundation's terrace.

The Foundation also has a small but exquisite collection of artworks by other celebrated artists. These include Alexander Calder's mesmerising *Mercury Fountain*, in which gleaming liquid mercury flows instead of water. There are also works by Basque sculptor Eduardo Chillida, and paintings by Mark Rothko and Antoni Tàpies.

When Miró first conceived of the museum, he wanted to create a space in which young artists could experiment, and the Espai 13 gallery showcases the work of emerging artists. The Foundation also hosts blockbuster exhibitions, which attract such huge crowds that the queues snake down the hill.

After your visit, you can relax in the small adjacent sculpture garden, with its wonderful panoramic views. This garden links into the neighbouring Jardins de Laribal, some of the oldest and most beautiful gardens on Montjuïc. The shady paths, dotted with fountains and tiled benches, wind gently down the hill towards a park information office which also contains a café-restaurant.

❷ Teatre Grec

Parc de Montjuïc. **Map** 1 C3. **Tel** 93 443 94 70. 🚇 Plaça Espanya, then bus 55, or bus 55 **Open** daily dawn to dusk, except during the Barcelona El Grec Festival in summer when opening is restricted to ticket-holders. 🌐 grec.bcn.cat/

This remarkable outdoor amphitheatre is hidden away amid greenery at the foot of Montjuïc. Originally a quarry, it was converted into an open-air theatre in 1929, when Montjuïc was remodelled as part of the International Exhibition. It is said to have been inspired by the ancient Greek theatre at Epidaurus, and it is also the epicentre of Barcelona's biggest performing arts festival – 'El Grec'.

This is easily one of the most atmospheric venues in the city, set amid extensive gardens, with groves of orange trees, pretty pavilions and a series of terraces and viewing points that frame beautiful views of the gardens themselves and the city beyond. During the Grec Festival, there is an open-air bar and a restaurant in the gardens.

The open-air Teatre Grec is modelled on ancient Greek amphitheatres

The Museu Nacional d'Art de Catalunya occupies the imposing National Palace

❸ Museu Arqueològic

Passeig Santa Madrona 39–41. **Map** 1 B3. **Tel** 93 423 21 49. 🚇 Espanya, Poble Sec. **Open** 9:30am–7pm Tue–Sat, 10am–2:30pm Sun & public hols. **Closed** 1 Jan, 25 & 26 Dec. 🗓 except last Sun of month; under 16s & over 65s free. 🚹 📷 🌐 mac.cat

Housed in the 1929 Palace of Graphic Arts, this fascinating archaeology museum contains artifacts from prehistory to the Visigothic period (AD 415–711). The mysterious Bronze Age megaliths called *talayots* from the Balearics are described here, and there are beautiful collections of Hellenic Mallorcan jewellery and Iberian silver treasures. Among the highlights of the collection is the Dama d'Eivissa ('The Lady of Ibiza'), a remarkable 4th-century sculpture in the form of an elaborately dressed goddess, and the startling Priapus of Hostafrancs, a 2nd-century Roman fertility symbol.

The museum boasts a superb collection of artefacts gathered from the Greco-Roman town of Empúries *(see p122)*, once the most important Greek colony on the entire Spanish peninsula. The displays include exquisite mosaics, coins, everyday items such as oil lamps and amphorae, and several statues, including a copy of the famous Asclepius (the original remains *in situ*). The collection concludes with ornate, gem-encrusted Visigothic jewellery, belt buckles, helmets and armour.

❹ Museu Nacional d'Art de Catalunya (MNAC)

Parc de Montjuïc, Palau Nacional. **Map** 1 A2. **Tel** 93 622 03 76. 🚇 Espanya. 🚌 150, 55. **Open** 10am–7pm Tue–Sat (until 8pm May–Sep), 10am–3pm Sun & public hols. **Closed** 1 Jan, 1 May, 25 Dec. 🗓 except Sun from 3pm and 1st Sun of month; under 16s & over 65s free. 🖼 🚹 📷 🌐 by appointment (93 622 03 75). 🌐 mnac.cat

The austere Palau Nacional was built for the 1929 International Exhibition, but since 1934 it has housed the city's most important art collection. The artworks span a thousand years, ranging from paintings and sculpture to furniture, photographs, drawings, prints and coins.

The museum has probably the world's greatest display of Romanesque items *(see pp24–5)*, centered around a series of magnificent 12th-century frescoes. The most remarkable are the wall paintings from Sant Climent de Taüll and La Seu d'Urgell *(see p146)*. These have been arranged in sets specially designed to recall the remote mountain churches high in the Pyrenees from which they came.

There is also a superb Gothic collection, which includes notable works by the 15th-century

Catalan artists Bernat Martorell, Lluís Dalmau and Jaume Huguet *(see p30)*. These impressive, often richly gilded works reflect Catalunya's growing wealth and power in this period.

The Cambó Bequest, a fine collection of paintings chosen to complement the medieval artworks, was donated by the collector and politician Francesc Cambó. This bequest, along with remarkable paintings on permanent loan from the Thyssen-Bornemisza collection in Madrid, ensures that the museum boasts an impressive Renaissance and Baroque collection, including works by El Greco, Zurbarán, Velázquez, Titian, Tiepolo, and Rubens.

The museum also boasts a good selection of 19th- and early 20th-century artworks and decorative objects, including beautiful curving furniture designs by Gaudí for the Casa Batlló. Also here is the famous painting by Ramon Casas of himself and Pere Romeu on a tandem, which once hung in the Els Quatre Gats tavern. The photography collection runs the gamut from early 19th-century portraits to gritty photo-journalism from the Spanish Civil War. The numismatic collection contains more than 100,000 coins, the earliest dating back to the 6th century BC.

12th-century *Christ in Majesty,* **Museu Nacional d'Art de Catalunya**

Part of the evening show put on by the Font Màgica, or "Magic Fountain"

❺ Font Màgica

Plaça Carles Buïgas **Map** 1 B2
🚇 Espanya **Shows** May–Sep: every 30 minutes 9–11pm Thu–Sun; Oct–Apr: every 30 minutes 7–8:30pm Fri & Sat. **Closed** 6 wks Jan and Feb ♿🖼 free.

This marvel of engineering was built by Carles Buigas (1898–1979) for the 1929 International Exhibition. The flamboyant Art Deco fountain shoots jets of multicoloured water to music in exuberant sound-and-light shows held every weekend. The musical themes vary but the show often culminates with Freddie Mercury and Montserrat Caballé's hugely popular duet *Barcelona*, performed at the 1992 Olympics.

The four columns just behind the Font Màgica were originally erected by Modernista architect Puig i Cadafalch at the turn of the 20th century. Designed to represent the stripes on the Catalan coat-of-arms, they were destroyed in 1928 as part of a ban on Catalan symbols. Now rebuilt, they are once again a potent symbol of Catalan pride.

❻ Pavelló Mies van der Rohe

Avinguda Francesc Ferrer i Guàrdia 7. **Map** 1 B2. **Tel** 93 423 40 16. 🚇 Espanya. 🚌 50. **Open** 10am–8pm daily. **Closed** 1 Jan, 25 Dec. 🖼 free to under 16s. 📷 10 am Sat (in English) or by appointment. 🌐 miesbcn.com

If the simple lines of this glass and polished stone pavilion look modern today, they must have shocked visitors to the 1929 International Exhibition.

Designed by Ludwig Mies van der Rohe (1886–1969), director of the Bauhaus school, it was an deemed an exhibit in its own right; its cool halls were left virtually empty, containing only one item – van de Rohe's world-famous Barcelona Chair. The building was torn down after the exhibition, but an exact replica was built for the centenary of the designer's birth.

Morning by Georg Kolbe (1877–1945), Pavelló Mies van der Rohe

❼ Poble Espanyol

Avinguda Francesc Ferrer i Guàrdia. **Map** 1 A2. **Tel** 93 508 63 30. 🚇 Espanya. **Open** 9am–8pm Mon, 9am–midnight Tue–Thu & Sun, 9am–3am Fri, 9am–4am Sat. ♿ 🖼 free 24th Sep for the Fiesta Mayor. 📷 📷 🌐 poble-espanyol.com

The idea behind the Poble Espanyol (Spanish Village) was to illustrate and display local Spanish architectural styles and crafts. It was laid out for the 1929 International Exhibition, but has proved to be enduringly popular and now attracts well over a million visitors a year. Over 100 buildings, streets and squares from across Spain have been recreated – from white-washed Andalusian homes to arcaded Castilian squares, and from Catalan villages to Basque farmhouses. Replicas of the towers in the walled city of Ávila in central Spain form the impressive main entrance.

Resident artisans produce crafts including hand-blown glass, sculpture, ceramics, Toledo damascene, leather goods and musical instruments. There is plenty more to entertain visitors, including shops, restaurants, bars, a flamenco show, a museum of modern art, a children's theatre and a varied programme of family-oriented craft and music workshops.

❽ CaixaForum

Avinguda de Francesc Ferrer i Guàrdia 6–8, Montjuïc. **Tel** 93 476 86 00. 🚇 Espanya. 🚌 13, 150. **Open** 10am–8pm daily (to 9pm Sat & Sun; Jul & Aug to 11pm Wed). **Closed** 1 & 6 Jan, 25 Dec. ♿🖼

Barcelona grows ever-stronger in the field of contemporary art and this exhibition centre can only enhance its reputation. The 'La Caixa' Foundation's collection of 700 works by Spanish and international artists is housed in the Antiga Fàbrica Casaramona, a restored textile mill in Modernista style.

The mill was built by Josep Puig i Cadafalch after he had completed the Casa de les Punxes. Opened in 1911, it was intended to be a model factory – light, clean and airy – but had only a short working life until the business closed down in 1920. The building became a storehouse and, after the Civil War, stables for police horses.

There are a series of galleries dedicated to temporary displays (often major international touring exhibitions), plus a permanent collection of contemporary art. Look out for family workshops, concerts, talks, film screenings and other cultural events – often free.

❾ Plaça d'Espanya

Avinguda de la Gran Via de les Corts Catalanes. **Map** 1 B1. 🚇 Espanya.

The fountain in the middle of this junction, the site of public gallows until 1715, is by Josep Maria Jujol, one of Gaudí's most faithful collaborators. The huge 1899 bullring to one side is by Font i Carreras, and boasts a dazzling red-brick façade. It has been converted into Las Arenas, a spectacular shopping and entertainment centre, with an observation deck on the roof where you can enjoy fantastic views of Montjuïc.

On the Montjuïc side is the Avinguda de la Reina Maria Cristina, flanked by two 47-m (154-ft) campaniles modelled on the bell towers of St Mark's in Venice and built as the entry to the 1929 International Exhibition. The avenue leads up to the Font Màgica *(see facing page)*.

❿ Castell de Montjuïc

Parc de Montjuïc. **Map** 1 B5. **Tel** 93 256 44 45. 🚇 Paral·lel, then funicular & cable car. 🚌 150 from Plaça Espanya. **Open** 9am–7pm daily (to 9pm Apr–Sep).

Crowning the very summit of Montjuïc is a huge, 18th-century castle, which enjoys spectacular views over the entire city, the port and a vast stretch of coastline. The first fortress here was built in 1640, and became the site of numerous battles during the War of the Spanish Succession in the early 1700s, when the Catalans fought the Bourbon king, Felipe V.

After Felipe V's success, the Bourbon rulers rebuilt the Montjuïc fortress in order to ensure that the local populace was kept under control. It became infamous as a prison and torture centre, a role it continued to play until after the Civil War. Notable Catalan leaders were imprisoned and executed here in the aftermath of the Civil War, including Lluís Companys *(see p48)*.

The castle contained a military museum for several decades, but when, in 2008, it was formally restored to the Catalan authorities by the Spanish government, it was decided to close the military museum and create a centre dedicated to peace. Renovation is still ongoing, but visitors can freely enter the complex, admire the vast Pati d'Armes where troops would once drill, and head up to the ramparts for the views. There's a café with a terrace on the Pati d'Armes, and in summer, outdoor cinema in the gardens.

Entrance to the Olympic Stadium, refurbished in 1992

⓫ Estadi Olímpic Lluís Companys

Passeig Olímpic. **Map** 1 A3. **Tel** 93 292 53 79. 🚇 Espanya, Poble Sec. 🚌 55. **Open** for concerts & football matches. Museum :**Open** 10am–6pm (to 8pm Apr–Sep) Tue–Sat, 10am–2pm Sun. **Closed** 1 Jan, 1 May, 25 & 26 Dec. ♿ 📷 🏛

The Estadi Olímpic Lluís Companys is the centrepiece of the so-called Anella Olímpica (Olympic Ring), the string of superb sports facilities erected for the 1992 Olympics. The stadium was built in 1929 for the International Exhibition, and was then remodelled in order to host the Olímpiad Popular in 1936. This event (conceived as a protest against the Olympics being held in Berlin under Hitler) was never took place because of the outbreak of the Spanish Civil War. However, the stadium got its chance to take a starring role in the 1992 Olympics, for which it was dramatically enlarged and modernised, although the original façade was preserved.

Next door is the glassy, modern Museu Olímpic i de l'Esport with interactive exhibits dedicated to sport. Nearby are the steel-and-glass Palau Sant Jordi stadium, Barcelona's biggest venue for concerts by the likes of Muse, Madonna and Bruce Springsteen; the Piscines Picornell, which includes a gym and fantastic indoor and outdoor swimming pools; and the diving pools used in the 1992 Olympics. These are open in summer to the delight of kids and they offer extraordinary views over the entire city.

Formally laid-out gardens carpet the former moat of the Castell de Montjuïc

FURTHER AFIELD

Radical redevelopments throughout the city in the late 1980s and 1990s gave Barcelona a wealth of new buildings, parks and squares. Sants, the city's main station, was rebuilt and the neighbouring Parc de l'Espanya Industrial and Parc de Joan Miró were created containing futuristic sculpture and architecture. In the east, close to the revitalized area of Poblenou, the city has a modern national theatre and concert hall. In the west, where the streets climb steeply, are the historic royal palace and monastery of Pedralbes, and Gaudí's Torre Bellesguard and Park Güell. Beyond, the Serra de Collserola, the city's closest rural area, is reached by two funicular railways. Tibidabo, the highest point, has an amusement park, the Neo-Gothic church of the Sagrat Cor and a nearby steel-and-glass communications tower. It is a popular place among *barcelonins* for a day out.

Sights at a Glance

Museums and Galleries
- ❸ Museu del Fútbol Club Barcelona
- ❹ CosmoCaixa
- ⓫ Museu Can Framis
- ⓬ Disseny Hub (DHUB)

Historic Buildings
- ❺ Monestir de Pedralbes
- ❾ Torre Bellesguard

Modern Buildings
- ❻ Torre de Collserola

Parks and Gardens
- ❶ Parc de Joan Miró

- ❷ Parc de l'Espanya Industrial
- ❼ Park Güell
- ❿ Parc del Laberint d'Horta

Squares and Districts
- ⓭ Estació del Nord
- ⓮ Museu de Ciències Naturals – Museu Blau
- ⓯ Poblenou

Theme Parks
- ❽ Tibidabo

Key
- ▨ Central city area
- ▭ Motorway (highway)
- ▬ Main road
- ═ Other road

0 km   1
0 miles   1

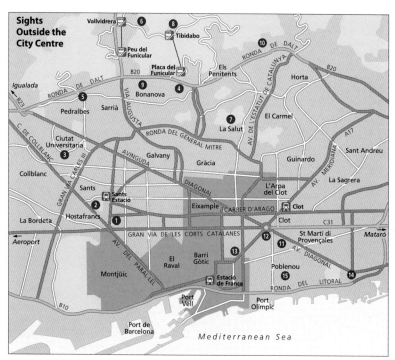

◀ The Neo-Gothic Temple Expiatori del Sagrat Cor dominates the summit of Tibidabo

Dona i Ocell (1983) by Joan Miró in the Parc de Joan Miró

❶ Parc de Joan Miró

Carrer d'Aragó 1. 🚇 Tarragona.
Open 10am until dusk daily.

Barcelona's 19th-century slaughterhouse *(escorxador)* became this unusual park in the 1980s, hence its alternative name, Parc de l'Escorxador.

It is constructed on two levels; the lower is devoted to football pitches interspersed with landscaped areas of palms, pines, eucalyptus trees and flowers; the upper is completely paved and dominated by a magnificent 1983 sculpture by the Catalan artist Joan Miró *(see p31)* entitled *Dona i Ocell (Woman and Bird)*. Standing 22 m (72 ft) high, its surface is covered with colourful glazed tiles. The park has several play areas for children.

❷ Parc de l'Espanya Industrial

Carrer Muntades 37. 🚇 Sants-Estació.
Open 10am until dusk daily.

This modern park, designed by Basque architect Luis Peña Ganchegui, owes its name to a textile mill that once stood on the 5-hectare (12-acre) site.

Laid out in 1986 as part of Barcelona's policy to provide more open spaces within the city, the park has canals and a rowing lake – with a Classical statue of Neptune at its centre. Tiers of steps rise around the lake like an amphitheatre and on one side a row of ten futuristic watchtowers dominates the entire area. Their only function is to serve as public viewing platforms and lamp standards.

Six contemporary sculptors are represented in the park, among them Andrés Nagel, whose enormous metal dragon incorporates a children's slide.

❸ Museu del Fútbol Club Barcelona

Avda de Arístides Maillol (7, 9). **Tel** 90 218 99 00. 🚇 Maria Cristina, Collblanc.
Open 10am–6:30pm Mon–Sat (to 8pm Apr–early Oct), 10am–2:30pm Sun & public hols. **Closed** 1 & 6 Jan, 25 Dec. 🚻 ♿ 🅿 of the stadium only (no tours on Champions League match days and museum closes at 3pm).
🌐 fcbarcelona.com/camp-nou/museo

Camp Nou, Europe's largest football stadium, is home to the city's famous football club, Barcelona FC (known as Barça).

Line of watchtowers in the Parc de l'Espanya Industrial

Founded in 1899, it is one of the world's richest soccer clubs, with some 100,000 members.

The stadium is a magnificent, sweeping structure, built in 1957 to a design by Francesc Mijans. An extension was added in 1982 and it can now comfortably seat 100,000 fans.

The club's museum displays memorabilia and trophies. The second floor has a multimedia presentation on the history of the club. There are also paintings and sculptures of famous club footballers commissioned for the Blaugrana Biennial, an exhibition held in 1985 and 1987. *Blaugrana* (blue-burgundy) are the colours of Barça's strip. The club's flags were used as an expression of nationalist feelings when the Catalan flag was banned during the Franco dictatorship.

As well as hosting its own high-profile matches (mainly at weekends), Camp Nou also accommodates affiliated local soccer clubs and promotes other sports in its sports centre, ice rink and mini-stadium.

View across Camp Nou stadium, prestigious home of Barcelona FC

❹ CosmoCaixa

Isaac Newton 26. **Tel** 93 212 60 50.
🔲 Avinguda del Tibidabo. 🚌 17, 22,
58, 73. **Open** 10am–8pm Tue–Sun
(daily Jul–Aug and bank holidays).
Closed 1 & 6 Jan, 25 Dec. ⬛ free 1st
Sun of month. 🔲 ♿

Barcelona's revamped science
museum is even more stimulating and interactive than its
popular predecessor, which
was housed in the Modernista
building that still stands on site.
Beside it now is a new glass-
and-steel building, with six of its
nine storeys set underground.
Exhibits covering the whole
history of science, from the
Big Bang to the computer age,
are housed in this modern
museum. One of its most
important pieces is a glasshouse
containing a recreated section
of flooded Amazon rainforest
inhabited by fish, amphibians,
insects, reptiles, mammals, birds
and plant species. Elsewhere, an
interactive tour through Earth's
geological history explains
processes such as erosion
and sedimentation, with a
Geological Wall that examines
different types of rock.

Other exhibits include the
Matter Room, taking a look at
Big Bang theory; "Tecnorevolució",
an interactive exploration of
cutting-edge technological
and scientific developments
such as nano-technology
and robot eyes; and a dazzling
3-D planetarium. There are
also innovative temporary
exhibitions on environmental
issues and family activities.

Madonna of Humility, Monestir
de Pedralbes

❺ Monestir de Pedralbes

Baixada del Monestir 9. **Tel** 93 256 34
34. 🔲 Reina Elisenda. **Open** Apr–Sep:
10am–5pm Tue–Fri, 10am–7pm Sat,
10am–8pm Sun; Oct–Mar: 10am–
2pm Tue–Fri, 10am–5pm Sat & Sun.
Closed 1 Jan, 1 May, 24 Jun, 25 Dec.
⬛ free under 16s, Sun from 3pm
and first Sun of month. 🔲 by
appointment (**Tel** 93 256 21 22).
🆆 **museuhistoria.bcn.es**

Approached through an arch
in its ancient walls, the lovely
monastery of Pedralbes
retains the air of an enclosed
community. This ambiance is
heightened by the good state
of preservation of its furnished
kitchens, cells, infirmary and
refectory. But the nuns of
the Order of St Clare moved
to an adjoining property in
1983, when the building was
opened to the public. The
monastery was founded in
1326 by Elisenda de Montcada
de Piños, fourth wife of
Jaume II of Catalonia and
Aragón. Her alabaster tomb
lies in the wall between church
and cloister. On the church
side her effigy is dressed in
royal robes; on the other, in a
nun's habit.

The monastery is built around
a three-storey cloister. The main
rooms include a dormitory, a
refectory, a chapterhouse, an
abbey and day cells. Numerous
works of art, as well as liturgical
ornaments, pottery, furniture,
altar cloths and gold and silver
work, are on display here.

The most important room
in the monastery is the Capella
(chapel) de Sant Miquel, with
murals of the *Passion* and the
Life of the Virgin, both painted
by Ferrer Bassa in 1346.

❻ Torre de Collserola

Carretera de Vallvidrera al Tibidabo.
Tel 93 211 79 42. 🔲 Peu del Funicular,
then Funicular de Vallvidrera & bus
211. **Open** check the website or
phone to confirm opening times.
Closed 1 & 6 Jan, 25, 26 & 31 Dec. ⬛
♿ 🆆 **torredecollserola.com**

In a city that enjoys thrills,
the ultimate ride is offered by
the communications tower
near Tibidabo mountain *(see
p100)*. A glass-sided lift swiftly
reaches the top of this 288-m-
(944-ft-) tall structure standing
on the summit of a 445-m
(1,460-ft) hill. The tower was
designed by English architect
Norman Foster for the 1992
Olympic Games. Needle-like
in form, it is a tubular steel
mast on a concrete pillar,
anchored by 12 huge steel
cables. There are 13 levels. The
top one has an observatory
with a telescope and a public
viewing platform with a 360°
view of the city, the sea and
the mountain chain on which
Tibidabo sits.

Barcelona v Real Madrid

FC Barcelona

Més que un club is the motto of Barcelona FC: "More
than a club". It has above all, however, been a symbol of
the struggle of Catalan nationalism against the central
government in Madrid. To fail to win the league is one
thing. To come in behind Real Madrid is a
complete disaster. Each season the big
question is which of the two teams
will win the title. Under the Franco
regime in a memorable episode in 1941, Barça
won 3–0 at home. At the return match in Madrid,
the crowd was so hostile that the police and
referee "advised" Barça to prevent trouble.
Demoralized by the intimidation, they lost 11–1.
Loyalty is paramount: one Barça player who left
to join Real Madrid received death threats.

Real Madrid

❼ Park Güell

In 1910 the industrialist Eusebio Güell commissioned Gaudí to lay out a private housing estate on a hillside above Barcelona. The plan was to create a mini-garden city with common amenities, leisure areas and decorative structures, but only two of the houses were ever built. What was left after the project fell through, however, was one of the most original public spaces ever conceived. The layout is loosely based on the Sanctuary of Apollo at Delphi and Gaudí makes ingenious use of the contours to create arcades and viaducts, all of natural stone. The most striking features of the park, however, are those covered with *trencadís* – mosaics made up of broken tiles – which are largely the work of the architect Josep Maria Jujol.

Hypostyle Hall
A total of 86 Classical columns – unusually conventional in style for Gaudí's work – support the weight of the square above. Set into the ceiling are four mosaic representations of the sun.

★ Entrance Pavilions
The two fairytale-like gatehouses have oval ground plans and intricately tiled *trencadís* exteriors. Inside are irregular rooms, odd-shaped windows and narrow staircases.

① ②

Entrance

KEY

① **Hill of the Crosses** is a stone tower reached by a serpentine path, from which there is a panoramic view over the city from the port to the heights of Tibidabo and Collserola.

② **Güell House**

③ **The Trias house** is one of only two houses to have been built in the would-be housing estate.

④ **The perimeter wall** follows the contours around the park. The Carretera El Carmel entry is formed by a swivelling section of wall executed in wrought iron.

★ Double Staircase
Water trickles from the mouth of the park's emblematic multicoloured dragon that presides over this monumental flight of steps. Above is an ornamental brown tripod and below another fountain, this time the head of a snake.

★ The Square
A serpentine bench covered in *trencadís* – the world's first collage – curves all the way around the edge of this square intended for markets and public events. From here are impressive views over Barcelona.

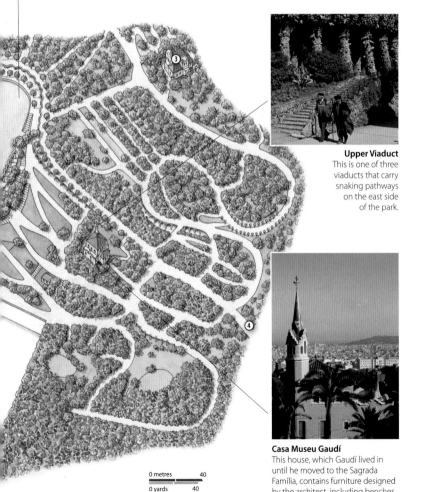

Upper Viaduct
This is one of three viaducts that carry snaking pathways on the east side of the park.

Casa Museu Gaudí
This house, which Gaudí lived in until he moved to the Sagrada Família, contains furniture designed by the architect, including benches and cupboards from La Pedrera.

0 metres	40
0 yards	40

Merry-go-round, Tibidabo

❽ Tibidabo

Plaça del Tibidabo 3–4. **Tel** 93 211 79
42. 🚇 Avda Tibidabo, then Tramvia
Blau & Funicular; or Peu del Funicular,
then Funicular & bus 111; or Bus T2A
from Plaça Catalunya. Amusement
Park: **Open** ring to confirm. **Closed**
Oct–Apr: Mon–Fri. 🚻 Temple Expiatori
del Sagrat Cor: **Tel** 93 417 56 86. **Open**
10am–8pm daily. 🚻 🖥 tibidabo.cat

The heights of Tibidabo can be
reached by Barcelona's last
surviving tram. The name,
inspired by Tibidabo's views of
the city, comes from the Latin
tibi dabo (I shall give you) –
a reference to the Temptation of
Christ when Satan took Him up
a mountain and offered Him the
world spread at His feet.
    The hugely popular Parc
d'Atraccions (Amusement Park,
see p163) first opened in 1908.
The rides were renovated in the
1980s. While the old ones retain
their charm, the newer ones
provide the latest in vertiginous
experiences. Their location at
517 m (1,696 ft) adds to the
thrill. Also in the park is the
Museu d'Autòmats, displaying
automated toys, juke boxes and
slot machines.
    Tibidabo is crowned by the
Temple Expiatori del Sagrat Cor
(Church of the Sacred Heart),
built with religious zeal but little
taste by Enric Sagnier between
1902 and 1911. A lift takes you
up to the feet of an enormous
figure of Christ.
    Just a short bus ride away is
another viewpoint – the Torre
de Collserola *(see p97)*.

❾ Torre Bellesguard

Carrer de Bellesguard 16. 🚇 Avda del
Tibidabo. **Closed** closed to public.

Bellesguard means "beautiful
spot" and here, halfway up the
Collserola hills, is the place
chosen by the medieval Catalan
kings as their summer home.
Their castle, built in 1408, was in
particular a favourite residence
of Barcelona's Martí the
Humanist *(see p59)*.
    The surrounding district of
Sant Gervasi was developed in
the 19th century after the
coming of the railway. In 1900
Gaudí built the present house
on the site of the castle, which
had fallen badly into ruin. Its
castellated look and the
elongated, Gothic-inspired
windows refer clearly to the
original castle. Gaudí kept the
vestiges of its walls in his
structure. The roof, with a
walkway behind the parapet, is
topped by a distinctive Gaudí
tower. Ceramic fish mosaics by
the main door symbolize
Catalonia's past sea power.

❿ Parc del Laberint d'Horta

Germans Desvalls, Passeig Castanyers.
Tel 010 (from Barcelona). 🚇 Mundet.
Open Mar & Oct: 10am–7pm; Apr:
10am–8pm; May–Sep: 10am–9pm;
Nov–Feb: 10am–6pm. 🏵 free Wed &
Sun. 🚻 🖥 bcn.es/parcsijardins

As its name suggests, the
centrepiece of the city's oldest
public park, created in the 18th
century for Joan Antoni
Desvalls, Marqués de Llúpia i

Wrought-iron entrance door at Antoni
Gaudí's Torre Bellesguard

d'Alfarràs, is a cypress maze.
The semi-wild garden slopes
steeply uphill from the
entrance beside the marquis'
semi-derelict palace which
now houses a gardening
school. It is a veritable
compendium of aristocratic
Baroque fantasies. Classical
temples dedicated to Ariadne
(who helped Theseus escape
from the Minotaur's labyrinth)
and Danae (mother of Perseus)
stand at either side of a broad
paseo, which oversees the
maze. From here a monumental
flight of steps leads up to a
Neo-Classical temple.
Elsewhere there is a "romantic
garden", a faux cemetery and, in
the woodland into which the
garden eventually leads, a
hermit's cave.

⓫ Museu Can Framis

Roc Boronat 116–126, Poblenou.
Tel 93 320 87 36. 🚇 Glòries,
Poblenou. 🚌 6, 7, 40, 42, 56, 141,
192. **Open** 11am–6pm Tue–Sat,
11am–2pm Sun. **Closed** 1 Aug–15
Sep. 🏵 🎫 noon Sat or by request.
🚻 🖥 fundaciovilacasas.com

The Can Framis museum
occupies a renovated
18th-century wool factory,
which is a monument to local
industry. It is managed by the
Vila Casa Foundation and holds
a permanent exhibition, called
The Existential Labyrinth, of
around 300 works dating from
the 1960s onwards. These works
are by a wide range of artists
born or living in Catalonia, like
Tàpies, Llimós, Zush and Culxart.
The Espai A0 gallery hosts good
temporary exhibitions by local
artists and photographers.

⓬ Disseny Hub Barcelona (DHUB)

Plaça de les Glòries Catalanes 37–38.
Tel 93 256 67 13. 🚇 Glòries. 🚌 7, 92,
192, H12. **Open** check website for
opening times. 🖥 dhub-bcn.cat

With more than 70,000
objects, the Design Museum
merges two museums that
were previously housed at

Catalonia's modern National Theatre near the Estació del Nord

different sites across the city. The new museum, opened in spring 2014, exhibits pieces from the Decorative Arts, Ceramics, Textile and Clothing Museum and the Graphic Arts Cabinet. The building, clad in glass and zinc, is a design statement in its own right, and was created by architects Josep Martorell, Oriol Bohigas and David Mackay.

The huge collection is organised on broadly historical lines, tracing the development of the objects that surround us in our everyday lives, from the decorative arts of past centuries (some artifacts date back to the Middle Ages) to contemporary design. The collections include furniture, clothing, jewellery, prints and posters, ceramics, glasswork and even vehicles. A varied programme of lectures and workshops is planned.

⑬ Estació del Nord

Avinguda de Vilanova. **Map** 6 D1.
Ⓜ Arc de Triomf.

Only the 1861 façade and the grand 1915 entrance remain of this former railway station, now remodelled as a sports centre, a police headquarters, and the city's bus station. Two elegant, blue-tiled sculptures, *Espiral arbrada (Branched Spiral)* and *Cel obert (Open Sky)* by Beverley Pepper (1992) sweep through the park. In front of the station, at Avinguda de Vilanova 12, is a carefully restored Modernista building constructed as a power station in 1897 by the architect Pere Falqués. Nearby, on Carrer de Zamora, is the Teatre Nacional de Catalunya, a vast temple to culture by the Barcelona architect Ricardo Bofill. The Museu de la Música is located here.

⑭ Museu de Ciències Naturals – Museu Blau

Plaça Leonardo da Vinci 4–5, Parc del Fòrum. **Tel** 93 256 60 02.
Ⓜ El Maresme i Fòrum (exit Rambla Prim). **Open** 10am–7pm Tue–Sat, 10am–8pm Sun. Register one day ahead for Science Nest (**Tel** 93 256 22 20) or at the box office on the day. **Closed** Mon; 1 Jan, 1 May, 24 Jun, 25 Dec. 🎟 free 1st Sun of month, Sun after 3pm and under 16s. ⬤ Ⓦ **museublau. bcn.cat**

The Natural Science Museum is a Barcelona institution that is over 100 years old and contains 3 million specimens in the fields of mineralogy, palaeontology, zoology and botany. Previously located in the Old Town, it is now housed in the Parc del Fòrum in a modern, innovative building designed by architects Herzog & de Meuron, who also conceived the Planet Life exhibition, a journey through the history of life and its evolution to the present day. The museum uses state-of-the-art interactive and audiovisual displays. There are also temporary exhibitions, a Media Library and a Science Nest for children up to age 6 at weekends, where images and sound effects recreate different natural surroundings.

La Rambla del Poblenou, a good place for a stroll and a cup of coffee

⑮ Poblenou

Rambla del Poblenou. Ⓜ Poblenou.

Poblenou is the trendy part of town where artists have built their studios in the defunct warehouses of the city's former industrial heartland. The area is centred on the Rambla del Poblenou, a quiet avenue, that extends from Avinguda Diagonal down to the sea. Here palm trees back a stretch of sandy beach. A walk around the quiet streets leading from the Rambla will reveal a few protected pieces of industrial architecture, legacies from the time Barcelona was known as "the Manchester of Spain".

Along the parallel Carrer del Ferrocarril is the Plaça de Prim with low, whitewashed houses reminiscent of a small country town. See pages 108–9 for a guided walk through Poblenou.

Blue-tiled sculpture by Beverley Pepper, Parc de l'Estació del Nord

THREE GUIDED WALKS

There is no shortage of good places to take a stroll in Barcelona. Each of the Street-by-Street maps in the book (the Old Town, the Eixample and Montjuïc) has a short walk marked on it which takes in the well-known sights in the area. Other classic walks are down La Rambla *(see pp62–3)* and around Park Güell *(see pp98–9)*. The walks described on the next six pages, however, take you to three less-explored districts, each with a distinct flavour.

The first walk is around El Born, once a run-down area to stay clear of but now an appealing quarter mixing old streets and fashionable shops. Next comes Gràcia, which could be thought of as "village Barcelona": a proud working-class area of low-rise houses, tiny boutiques and charming squares that host a busy nightlife. The final walk is around the post- industrial heartland of Poblenou whose buildings are being restored and put to new uses, and whose skyline is punctuated by a few surviving slender brick chimneys. Each route avoids heavy traffic as far as possible and makes the most of quiet or pedestrianized streets and squares. While there are monuments to be seen along the way, the appeal here is as much in the atmosphere of the areas and the unusual shops, characterful cafés and architectural oddities encountered. All three walks begin and end with a Metro station. As in any big city, care should be taken with personal belongings and although it is safe to walk at any time, be aware that the character of areas can change when the bars open.

Choosing a Walk

The Three Walks
This map shows the location of the three guided walks in relation to the main sightseeing areas of Barcelona.

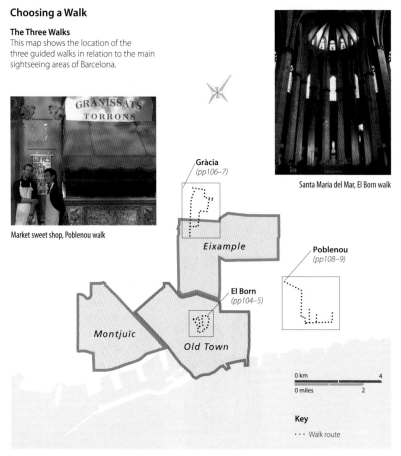

Market sweet shop, Poblenou walk

Santa Maria del Mar, El Born walk

Gràcia
(pp106–7)

Eixample

Poblenou
(pp108–9)

El Born
(pp104–5)

Montjuïc

Old Town

0 km			4
0 miles		2	

Key

· · · Walk route

◄ The early Gaudí façade of Casa Vicens on Carrer de les Carolines, Gràcia walk

A One-hour Walk around El Born

The tiny district of El Born, across the Via Laietana from the Barrí Gotic, has made a comeback after long years of neglect. Close to the waterfront, this area flourished in Catalonia's mercantile heyday from the 13th century. The narrow streets still bear the names of the craftsmen and guilds that set up here, for instance, hatters in Carrer dels Sombrerers, mirror-makers in Carrer dels Mirallers, and silversmiths in Carrer de la Argenteria. While it still has something of a medieval air, El Born has become the hip and arty place to be.

of Gothic mansions dating from the 14th century with later Renaissance refurbishments. Most of the buildings are now museums and galleries. The Casa Cervelló-Guidice at 25 ⑥ is the only building on the street still with its original façade. Opposite the Casa Cervelló-Guidice, at 20 ⑦, is the Palau Dalmases, whose patio has

⑮ Passeig del Born, the main street of El Born area

The Carrer de Montcada
From Jaume I Metro station in Plaça de l'Angel ① set off down Carrer de la Argenteria but turn left almost at once at the tobacconist's (marked "Tabac") into Carrer del Vigatans. After passing the youth hostel on your left, note the carved head protruding from the wall on the right at the corner of Carrer dels Mirallers ②. Before you reach the end of the street, turn right into Carrer dels Mirallers. On your left you will shortly see an old-fashioned bar called

El Nus ③, whose stone walls, chandeliers and dark wood furniture evoke the atmosphere of Barcelona in days gone by. At the end of the street you meet the side wall of the church of Santa Maria del Mar ④. Turn left along Carrer Sombrerers. On your left at 23 is Casa Gispert ⑤, a famous old shop selling coffee roasted on the premises, and local nuts and dried fruit. When you can go no further, turn left into Placeta de Montcada which becomes Carrer Montcada (see p66), an immaculate collection

an ornately carved staircase. It is now a some-what eccentric bar, hosting all manner of live artistic performances, including classical music and live opera some evenings. Its neighbour at 22 is El Xampanyet ⑧, the city's best known bar for *cava* (Catalan sparkling wine) and tapas. Much of the right-hand side of Montcada is taken up by five palaces including the Museu Picasso ⑨ (see p66). Opposite this are two important medieval palaces, the Palau Nadal at number 14 ⑩ and the Palau Marquès de Lliò at number 12, which from June 2014

Tips for Walkers

Starting point: Plaça de l'Angel.
Length: 1.5 km (1 mile).
Getting there: Go to Jaume I Metro station in the Plaça de l'Angel on Line 4.
Stopping off points: There are many bars and eateries along the route including the Café del Born (Plaça Comercial) and Origens 99,9% (Carrer Vidrieria 6–8), a Catalan restaurant and shop. You'll find lots on Carrer de la Argenteria, notably Xocolateria Xador (for hot chocolate; 61–3), and Taller de Tapas (51).

⑨ Visitors flocking to the popular Museu Picasso

⑯ Enjoying the café culture in Plaça de Comercial in front of Mercat del Born

hieroglyphic-like frieze. Carrer Triangle leads you into Carrer del Rec and before long you meet the Passeig del Born ⑮. It was the jousts held in this broad avenue from the 13th to 17th centuries that gave the name to the Born quarter of which it forms the heart. To the left, the Passeig opens out into the Plaça de Comercial, dominated by the Mercat del Born ⑯, the former wholesale market. This old iron and glass building, modelled on Les Halles in Paris, has now been converted into a cultural centre. Excavations on the site have helped archaeologists piece together a clear picture of life in 18th-century Barcelona. Continue on Carrer del Rec on the other side of the Passeig del Born and turn right at the next junction into Carrer de l'Esparteria. Turn left at Carrer de Vidriera to reach Plaça de les Olles. Turn right here and follow the wide pavement which skirts the Plaça del Palau. It also passes an old ironmonger's with giant paella pans. When you reach the corner with Carrer dels Canvis Vells, across the road from La Llotja (see p65) ⑰, turn right. Bear right into the Carrer de l'Anisadeta, which is so short that it is over almost as soon as it is begun, and you find yourself back in the charming Plaça de Santa Maria ⑱, facing the church of the same name (see pp66–7), a perfect place to stop for a coffee or a glass of wine on a café terrace. Pop inside to admire the beautiful Catalan Gothic interior. Bear left across the square to the start of Carrer de la Argenteria, the busiest street in El Born, lined with bars and shops. Follow this back to your starting point at the Metro in Plaça de l'Angel.

Catalanes (see pp100–101). At the end of Montcada turn right along Carrer de la Princesa, where you'll find tempting shops. First you pass the windows of Brunells pastry shop at 22 ⑫, then the turrón and sweet shop of La Campana (founded in 1890) at 36 ⑬.

The Passeig del Born
Take the next small street to the right, Carrer del Corretger, which turns a sharp corner. Turn right at the cake shop into Carrer Triangle. Look up into the arch at the start of Carrer de l'Hostal de Sant Antoni (on your right) ⑭ to see an unusual

⑫ Brunells chocolate shop

will house The World Culture Museum, offering a journey through the cultures of Asia, Africa, America and Oceania. Just after, the Palau del Marquès de Lli̇ó (or Mora) ⑪ was once part of Barcelona's Textiles and Costume Museum, with a fabulous collection now on show at the Disseny Hub (DHUB) building on Plaça de les Glóries

A 90-minute Walk through Gràcia

When you cross the Avinguda Diagonal and plunge into the maze of sinuous streets and small squares on the other side, it is easy to get the impression that you have left the city behind and entered a village. Since Gràcia became part of Barcelona in 1897 it has never lost its sense of independence and identity. During the day, it feels calmly removed from the pace of modern metropolitan life just a few blocks away. In August and in the evening, however, expect a hullabaloo as the district draws crowds to its exotic shops and nightlife.

quickly right down Carrer Domènech. Turn left at the end up Carrer de Francisco Giner and this will lead you into Plaça de la Vila de Gràcia ⑤, where a 33-m (108-ft) clock tower is overlooked by the sky blue façade of Gràcia's local government headquarters. A plaque on the wall

③ The façade of Casa Fuster, a Modernista building, now a hotel

The Passeig de Gràcia
From Plaça Joan Carles I ① the famous Passeig de Gràcia continues briefly as a modest, plane tree-shaded avenue. On your left, almost immediately, you come to Casa Bonaventura Ferrer ②, a Modernista building by Pere Falqués I Urpi, with stonework sculpted into swirling leaves and a façade finished off with an iron crown. A short way along, the road narrows to go round another Modernista building (although its inspiration is clearly Neo-Gothic).

The last work of architect Lluis Domènech i Montaner, Casa Fuster ③ has been converted into a hotel. The Café Vienés on the ground floor is open to non-residents.

The squares of Gràcia
A few steps beyond Casa Fuster up the Passeig de Gràcia's well-to-do continuation, Gran de Gràcia, you can see the handsome stained-glass *miradores* (upper-floor bay windows) above La Colmena *patisseria* at 15 ④. Then go back to Casa Fuster and turn down the road behind its rear façade, Carrer Gràcia. Turn left and

Tips for Walkers
Starting point: Plaça Joan Carles I.
Length: 2.5 km (1.5 miles).
Getting there: Diagonal Metro station in Plaça Joan Carles I is on Line 3 or reached by FCG train.
Stopping-off points: Most of Gràcia's squares have bars and restaurants. Try Bo Restaurant (tapas) in Plaça de la Vila de Gràcia; Café del Sol (drinks and music) or Mirasol (classic bar) in Plaça de Sol; Niu Toc (fish) on Plaça Revolució de Setembre de 1868 or Virreina Bar (sandwiches and beer) in Plaça de la Virreina.

⑤ A performance of *castellers* at fiesta time in Gràcia

⑥ Nightlife at the Plaça del Sol

Key

• • • Walk route

commemorates the achievements of Catalonia's *castellers*, teams of amateur gymnasts who can often be seen building human towers up to eight people high on fiesta days in Gràcia. Cross the square and leave by Carrer Mariana Pineda. Cross Travessera de Gràcia, one of the district's main shopping streets, and stroll along Carrer

Xiquets de Valls, named after a renowned team of *castellers*. This brings you into the Plaça del Sol **⑥**, a nightlife hub popularly known as Plaça dels Encants. Turn left to leave by Carrer Maspons. Straight ahead, on the other side of Carrer del Torrent l'Olla, is the Plaça Revolució de Setembre de 1868 **⑦**. The name commemorates the *coup d'état* led by General Prim, which unseated Spain's ruling Bourbon dynasty, who were so antagonistic to the Catalans they ushered in the first republican government in Spain's history. Turn left into the square and leave by Carrer de Verdi that sprouts from the top of it. This is a busy but pleasant street of modern shops. After passing Cinemes Verdi (on your right), which often shows original-version foreign films, turn right down Carrer de l'Or. You soon arrive in one of Gràcia's most agreeable squares, the Plaça Virreina **⑧**, where the church of Sant Joan faces downhill towards two fine buildings: one is a residence with a tower and the other a redbrick house in Modernista style with a graphic red and cream façade and wrought-iron balconies.

Casa Vincens

Leave Virreina by the shady Carrer de Astúries and stay on it across the top of Plaça Diamant

④ Stained-glass windows in *miradores*

⑨. This is where a civil war air-raid shelter has been discovered – open at weekends by appointment (call 93 219 61 34). Turn right up Carrer Torrent l'Olla and left down Santa Agata. When you reach Gran de Gràcia cross over it into Carrer de les Carolines. At the bottom of this street at 24 is one of Antoni Gaudí's early works, Casa Vicens **⑩**. It is privately owned but well worth admiring from the outside. Commissioned as a summer house by a brick- and tile- maker, it took the inexperienced Gaudí five years to build (1883–8). Inspired by Moorish architecture, the house was a bold break with tradition and the lavish use of colour and ornament clearly indicate where Gaudí's interests lay. The exterior of the house is a checkerboard of green and white tiles and other tiles with a marigold motif. The riotous ironwork shows off with extravagant loops and intriguing beasts. Now retrace your steps to Gran de Gràcia. If you are in the mood for more Gaudí, go uphill to Plaça Lesseps and from there follow the signs to Park Güell *(see pp98–9)*. If not, go downhill past pretty Plaça Trilla **⑪**. You can either finish the walk at Fontana Metro station or continue on back to your starting point.

⑩ The interior and stained-glass windows at Casa Vicens

For keys to symbols *see back flap*

A Two-hour Walk through Poblenou

It's hard to believe today but the trendy district of Poblenou once had the highest concentration of smoke-belching factories in Catalonia. By the 1960s these had gone out of business or moved to the outskirts, leaving their old buildings to decay. With the 1992 Olympic Games came an impetus for recovery and since then Poblenou's warehouses have been spruced up and converted into chic studios for artists and photographers. New developments brought hotels, discos and restaurants, creating a fascinating mix of industrial archaeology and contemporary culture.

③ The controversial Torre Agbar

The Avinguda Diagonal

Leave the Metro station in Plaça de les Glòries Catalanes ① (an area of ongoing redevelopment; see p101) by the Carrer Badajoz exit, which will lead you on to the wide seaward extension of Avinguda Diagonal ②. This takes you directly beneath a tall, unusual and much-criticised building that breaks up the city skyline, the Torre Agbar ③. A domed cylindrical tower of 33 floors, unkindly described as an

upended blue cigar, it was built by French architect Jean Nouvel for the local water company, Aigües de Barcelona.

Continue on down Diagonal, which has a wide *paseo* in the middle flanked by traffic lanes, tramways that link Glòries with Sant Adrià del Besòs as well as cycle tracks. About 700 m (half a mile) down Diagonal turn right into Rambla del Poblenou ④, the main street of Poblenou that leads eventually to the sea. After crossing Carrer de Pere IV, the Rambla narrows and becomes more attractive. In the middle is a memorial to Doctor Josep Trueta ⑤. This pioneering surgeon was born in Poblenou in 1897 and, after working to save lives during the bombardments of the Civil War, went into a 30-year exile in England on the fall of democracy in 1939.

right) ⑥, a handsome salmon-coloured building by Josep Masdeu dating from 1914, which is decorated with Modernista floral motifs.

At the next junction with Carrer Joncar, turn left between El Tio Che ⑦, a well-known shop founded in 1912, selling ice cream and *turrón* (a typical Spanish sweet made of almonds) and, opposite it, the Casino de l'Aliança de Poblenou ⑧, a concert hall (not a gambling enterprise as its name might suggest). Turn right

Rambla del Poblenou

Keep straight on down the Rambla over the next three circular road junctions. Along the way are several buildings worth stopping to look at, such as 51 (on the

⑤ Memorial to civil-war hero Dr Josep Trueta

Tips for Walkers

Starting point: Plaça de Les Glòries Catalanes.
Length: 3.5 km (2 miles).
Getting there: Glòries Metro station is on Line 1.
Stopping off points: There are bars on Rambla de Poble Nou, swish restaurants on Carrer Taulat and a few cheaper bars on Carrer Maria Aguilo. Go for an ice cream at El Tio Che.

⑦ El Tio Che, the renowned ice-cream and *turrón* parlour

at the first junction you come to down Carrer Maria Aguilo, a lively but humanly scaled pedestrianized shopping street. On the left, up a short street, is the district's market, the Mercat de la Unió ⑨. Beside it is a handsome building, 24 Plaça de la Unió, with Art Nouveau white and green ceramic festoons draped over the windows. Just north of the market is the district's public library ⑩ at Calle Joncar 35, housed

in a beautiful building dating from 1884 which used to be a textile factory. Cross over Carrer del Taulat (the junction is slightly staggered) into Carrer del Ferrocarril and turn left into the old square of Plaça del Prim ⑪. Here, you'll see gnarled, leaning, fat-rooted ombu trees (an Argentinian species) and low whitewashed houses. Now somewhat lost amid the modernity around it, this square is the original heart of Poblenou, from which all else grew. It is said that among the fishermen and workers who lived on this square there were many followers of the mid-19th century Icaria Utopian movement, which militated against capitalism and attempted to create a world of "universal brotherhood". Return to Carrer del Taulat and turn right. If you wish to end your walk here, turn left up Carrer de Bilbao to reach Poblenou Metro

station. Otherwise, continue along Taulat, a strip of gardens through modern residential developments.

A short detour to the corner of Carrer de Ramon Turró and Espronceda takes you to a garden ⑫ dedicated to the Indian social reformer and philosopher Mahatma Gandhi, with a sculpture of him by the Nobel Peace Prize winner Adolfo Pérez Esquivel.

Returning to Passeig del Taulat, ahead of you all the while rises the most characteristic surviving industrial building in Poblenou, the Torre de les Aigües ⑬. Turn left into Carrer de la Selva to get to the base of this structure, which stands in

⑬ Torre de les Aigües

the middle of Plaça Ramon Calsina. This round, red-brick tower, 63 m (207 ft) high, was built to raise and store water from the nearby Besos river. Near the top of it is a vertigo-inducing metal staircase that leads round the brickwork to a balcony. From

here continue up Carrer de la Selva to Selva de Mar Metro station on the corner of Carrer de Pujades. On the way you might like to wander a few steps to your left along Carrer de Llull. On the corner with Carrer de Provençals rises the highest chimney in Barcelona ⑭. This graceful flat-topped 65-m (213-ft) spire used to form part of the now-defunct Macosa steelworks. Return to Carrer de la Selva and end your walk at the Selva de Mar Metro stop.

⑪ The unusual ombu trees in the village-like Plaça del Prim

For keys to symbols *see back flap*

CATALONIA

Lleida · Andorra · Girona · Barcelona Province · Tarragona

There is a wealth of natural beauty in Catalonia's four provinces, plus the small Catalan-speaking country of Andorra. They offer rocky coasts and mountains, fertile plains and sandy shores. Many who visit don't stray far from the coast, but the rewards for venturing further afield are immense.

Lying beyond the constant bustle of Barcelona, Catalonia is essentially a rural region, with no large cities and few industrial blights. Of the four provinces, all named after their principal city, Lleida is the largest and least populated. Among its jewels are the Romanesque churches of the Boí valley and the Aigüestortes National Park.

The province of Girona is blessed with mountains and sea. This eastern end of the Pyrenees has the magical Cerdanya valley and the ancient monasteries of Ripoll and Sant Joan de les Abadesses, as well as medieval villages and a handsome and too-often overlooked capital city. Its coast, the Costa Brava, is rocky and full of delights.

Barcelona province has its own coasts; the Maresme to the north is rather spoiled by the railway running beside the sea, but the Garraf to the south is more exciting – Sitges is a highly fashionable spot. Inland are the Holy Mountain of Montserrat (Catalonia's spiritual heart), the Penedès winelands, and the country town of Vic.

Tarragona, the most southerly of the provinces, has one of the peninsula's former Roman capitals. Here the land rolls more gently, supporting fruit and nut orchards and the monastic communities of Poblet and Santes Creus, before falling away towards the rice lands of the Ebre. The coastline is more gentle, too, with long, sandy beaches.

Aigüestortes y E. Sant Maurici National Park in the central Pyrenees, in the province of Lleida

◀ Rocky outcrops surround the tranquil bay and golden beach of Tossa del Mar, on the Costa Brava

Exploring Catalonia

Catalonia includes a long stretch of the Spanish Pyrenees, whose green, flower-filled valleys hide picturesque villages with Romanesque churches. The Parc Nacional d'Aigüestortes and Vall d'Aran are paradises for naturalists, while Baqueira-Beret offers skiers reliable snow. Sun-lovers can choose between the rugged Costa Brava or the long sandy stretches of the Costa Daurada. Tarragona is rich in Roman monuments. Inland are the monasteries of Poblet and Santes Creus and the well-known vineyards of Penedès.

Isolated houses in the countryside around La Seu d'Urgell

Key

▭▭▭	Motorway (highway)
▭▭▭	Other highway
▬▬▬	Main road
⋯⋯⋯	Minor road
▬▬▬	Scenic route
┄┄┄	Main railway
───	Minor railway
▬▬▬	International border
▬▬▬	Regional border
△	Summit

Getting Around

The motorway from France enters Spain at La Jonquera and, from Barcelona, follows the coast via Tarragona and Tortosa. Buses connect most towns. The main north–south railway hugs the coast from Blanes southwards. Other lines connect Barcelona to Vic and Lleida (see inside back cover).

For additional map symbols see back flap

Pau
Toulouse

① VALL D'ARAN

③ BAQUEIRA-BERET

VIELHA ② Arties   Pica d'Estats 3115m

PARC NACIONAL D'AIGÜESTORTES   Esterri d'Àneu

N230   Boí   ⑤

Llavorsí

④ VALL DE BOÍ   Tossal de l'Orri 2457m

Pont de Suert   Sort   N14

LA SEU D'URGELL ⑦

N260   La Pobla de Segur

Coll de Nargó

Tremp   Embassament de Talarn   Embassament d'Oliana

N230   Isona

Embalse de Canelles   El Segre   Ponts   C14

Alfarràs   Artesa de Segre

Balaguer   Agramunt   C A T

Almacelles   Bellcaire d'Urgell   C25

A22   N230   Bell-lloc d'Urgell   A2   Tàrrega

LLEIDA ㉔   Bellpuig

Alcarràs   Juneda   Belianes   Santa Coloma de Queralt

A2   les Borges Blanques

AP2   AP2   N240

Seròs   MONTBLANC

Zaragoza   La Granadella   POBLET ㉕ ㉖   SANTES CREUS

N211   Maials   ㉗

La Bisbal de Falset   Alcover   Valls   AP2

Flix   C14

Ascó   Falset   N420   Reus ✈   Torredembarra

Batea   Móra d'Ebre   Móra la Nova   Cambrils   ㉛   TARRAGONA

Gandesa   Cap de Salou

Ebre   Rasquera   A7   L'Hospitalet de l'Infant   C O S T A

Xerta   N340   L'Ametlla de Mar

El Perelló   Golf de Sant Jordi

TORTOSA ㉜

L'Aldea   ㉝   Cap Tortosa

Amposta   DELTA DE L'EBRE

Sant Carles de la Ràpita

Ulldecona   AP7   La Banya

Alcanar

Valencia

0 kilometres		25
0 miles		15

Church on the seafront of Sitges

R A N C E
RRA
la Vella
P y r e n e e s
8 PUIGCERDÀ
Martinet
de Cadí
67m
N152
Bagà
La Pobla
de Lillet
Ribes de
Freser
C38
Camprodon
Perpignan
La Jonquera
Portbou
Llançà
Cap de
Creus
AP7
N260
FIGUERES
15 CADAQUÉS
Roses
Golf de Roses
14
SANT JOAN DE
LES ABADESSES
10
RIPOLL **9**
A26
11 OLOT
12 BESALÚ
Bàscara
16 EMPÚRIES
L'Escala
el Ter
Berga
el Llobregat
Prats de
Lluçanès
Gironella
C17
Sant Quirze
de Besora
Manlleu
Banyoles
C66
L'Estartit
Parlavà
Pantà de Sau
El Ter
13 GIRONA
17 PERATALLADA
NA
21 VIC
Anglès
Santa Coloma
de Farners
Cassà de la
Selva
C66
Palafrugell
22 CARDONA
C16
Tona
C25
Caldes de Malavella
Sils
S'Agaró
Palamós
Súria
Sallent
Moià
Arbúcies
Llagostera
Sant Feliu de Guíxols
L O N I A
Manresa
Montseny
AP7
Tordera
18 TOSSA DE MAR
La Garriga
Lloret de Mar
Costa
Brava
MONTSERRAT
Sant Celeni
Granollers
Calella
19
BLANES
20
C16
Terrassa
Castellolí
Sabadell
A54
Arenys de Mar
A2
Martorell
Rubí
Mataró
Premià de Mar
L'Anoia
Sant Feliu
de Llobregat
Santa Coloma
de Gramanet
Barcelona
AP7
28 VILAFRANCA
DEL PENEDÈS
L'Hospitalet de Llobregat
C32
El Prat de Llobregat
ell
29 SITGES
Castelldefels
Vilanova
i la Geltrú
MEDITERRANEAN
SEA
URADA
30

Vineyards outside Gandesa, west of Tarragona

Sights at a Glance

The Vall d'Aran, surrounded by the snow-capped mountains of the Pyrenees

Butterflies of the Vall d'Aran

A huge variety of butterflies and moths is found high in the valleys and mountains of the Pyrenees. The isolated Vall d'Aran is the home of several unique and rare subspecies. The best time of the year in which to see the butterflies is between May and July.

Chequered Skipper
(*Carterocephalus palemon*)

Clouded Apollo
(*Parnassins mnemosyne*)

Grizzled Skipper (underside)
(*Pyrgus malvae*)

❶ Vall d'Aran

Lleida N230. 🚌 Vielha. 🛈 Vielha (973 64 06 88).

This valley of valleys – *aran* means valley – is a lovely 600-sq-km (230-sq-mile) haven of forests and meadows filled with flowers, surrounded by towering mountain peaks.

The Vall d'Aran was formed by the Riu Garona, which rises in the area and flows out to France as the Garonne. With no proper link to the outside world until 1924, when a road was built over the Bonaigua Pass, the valley was cut off from the rest of Spain for most of the winter. Snow blocks the narrow pass from November to April, but today access is easy through the Túnel de Vielha from El Pont de Suert.

The fact that the Vall d'Aran faces north means that it has a climate similar to that on the Atlantic coast. Many rare wild flowers and butterflies flourish in the perfect conditions that are created by the shady slopes and damp breezes. It is also a famous habitat for many species of narcissus.

Tiny villages have grown up beside the Riu Garona, often around Romanesque churches, notably at **Bossòst**, **Salardú**, **Escunhau** and **Arties**. The valley is also ideal for outdoor sports such as skiing and is popular with walkers.

❷ Vielha

Lleida. 🏔 3,000. 🚌 🛈 Carrer Sarriulera 10 (973 64 01 10). 🛒 Thu. 🎭 Festa de Vielha (8 Sep), Feria de Vielha (8 Oct).

Now a modern ski resort, the capital of the Vall d'Aran retains its medieval past. The Romanesque church of **Sant Miquel** has an octagonal bell tower and a 12th-century crucifix, the *Mig Aran Christ*. It formed part of a larger carving representing the Descent from the Cross. The **Museu de la Vall d'Aran** is devoted to Aranese culture.

🏛 **Museu de la Vall d'Aran**
Carrer Major 26. **Tel** 973 64 18 15. **Open** 10am–1pm (mid-Jun–mid-Sep only), 5–8pm Tue–Sat, 10am–1pm Sun. **Closed** bank hols. 🐾

Mig Aran Christ (12th-century), Sant Miquel church, Vielha

❸ Baqueira-Beret

Lleida. 🚠 100. 🚌 *i* Baqueira-Beret
(902 41 54 15). 🎭 Romeria de Nostra
Senyora de Montgarri (2 Jul).

This extensive ski resort, one of
the best in Spain, is popular
with both the public and the
Spanish royal family. There is
reliable winter snow cover and
a choice of over 40 pistes at
altitudes from 1,520 m to 2,470 m
(4,987 ft to 8,104 ft).

Baqueira and Beret were
separate mountain villages
before skiing became popular,
but they have now merged
to form a single resort. The
Romans took full advantage of
the thermal springs located
here, which are nowadays
appreciated by tired skiers.

❹ Vall de Boí

Lleida N230. 🚉 La Pobla de Segur.
🚌 Pont de Suert. *i* Barruera (973 69
40 00). **W** vallboi.com

This small valley on the edge of
the Parc Nacional d'Aigüestortes
is dotted with tiny villages,
many of which are built around
magnificent Catalan
Romanesque churches.

Dating from the 11th and
12th centuries, these churches
are distinguished by their tall
belfries, such as the six-storey
bell tower of the **Església de
Santa Eulàlia** at Erill-la-Vall.

The two churches at Taüll,
Sant Climent *(see p24)* and
Santa Maria, have superb
frescoes. Between 1919 and
1923 the originals were taken
for safekeeping to the Museu
Nacional d'Art de Catalunya in
Barcelona, where their settings
have been recreated *(see p91)*.
Replicas now stand in their
place. You can climb the towers
of Sant Climent for superb views
of the surrounding countryside.

Other churches in the area
worth visiting include those at
Coll, for its fine ironwork;
Barruera; and **Durro**, which has
another massive bell tower.

At the head of the valley is the
hamlet of **Caldes de Boí**,
popular for its thermal springs
and ski facilities. It is also a good
base for exploring the Parc

The tall belfry of Sant Climent church at
Taüll in the Vall de Boí

Nacional d'Aigüestortes *(see
below)*, the entrance to which is
only 5 km (3 miles) from here.

❺ Parc Nacional d'Aigüestortes

Lleida. 🚉 La Pobla de Segur. 🚌 Pont
de Suert, La Pobla de Segur. *i* Boí
(973 69 61 89); Espot (973 62 40 36).

The pristine mountain scenery
of Catalonia's only national park
is among the most spectacular
to be seen in the Pyrenees.

Established in 1955, the park
covers an area of 102 sq km
(40 sq miles). Its full title is Parc
Nacional d'Aigüestortes i Estany
de Sant Maurici, named after
the lake *(estany)* of Sant Maurici
in the east and the Aigüestortes
(literally, twisted waters) area in
the west. The main village is the
mountain settlement of Espot,
on the park's eastern edge,
although you can access the
park from Boí in the west.
Around the park are waterfalls
and some 150 lakes and tarns
which, in an earlier era, were
scoured by glaciers to depths
of up to 50 m (164 ft).

The finest scenery is around
Sant Maurici lake, which lies
beneath the twin shards of the
Serra dels Encantats, (Mountains
of the Enchanted). From here,
there is a variety of walks,
particularly along the string
of lakes that leads north to the
towering peaks of Agulles
d'Amitges. To the south is the
dramatic vista of Estany Negre,
the highest and deepest tarn
in the park.

Early summer on the lower
valley slopes is marked by
rhododendrons, while later on
wild lilies bloom in the forests
of fir, beech and silver birch.

The park is also home to a
variety of wildlife. Chamois
(also known as izards) live on
the mountain screes and in the
meadows, while beavers and
otters can be spotted by the
lakes. Golden eagles nest on
mountain ledges, and grouse
and capercaillie are found in
the woods.

During the summer the park
is popular with walkers, while
in winter, the snow-covered
mountains are ideal for cross-
country skiing.

A crystal-clear stream, Parc Nacional d'Aigüestortes

Les Quatre Barres

Catalonia's national
emblem

The four red bars on the *senyera*, the Catalan flag, are said to represent the four provinces: Barcelona, Girona, Lleida and Tarragona. The design derives from a legend of Guifré el Pelós, first Count of Barcelona *(see p44)*. It relates how he received a call for help from Charles the Bald, who was King of the West Franks and grandson of Charlemagne. Guifré went to his aid and turned the tide of battle, but was mortally wounded. As he lay dying, Charles dipped his fingers in Guifré's blood and dragged them across his plain gold shield, giving him a grant of arms.

❻ Andorra

Principality of Andorra. 🏙 84,000.
🚌 Andorra la Vella. 𝒊 Plaça de la Rotonda, Andorra la Vella (376 87 31 03). 🆆 andorra.ad

Andorra occupies 464 sq km (179 sq miles) of the Pyrenees between France and Spain. In 1993, it became fully independent and held its first ever democratic elections. Since 1278, it had been an autonomous feudal state under the jurisdiction of the Spanish bishop of La Seu d'Urgell and the French Count of Foix (a title adopted by the President of France). These are still the ceremonial joint heads of state.

Andorra's official language is Catalan, though French and Castilian are also spoken by most residents.

For many years Andorra has been a tax-free paradise for shoppers, a fact reflected in the crowded shops and supermarkets of the capital **Andorra la Vella**. Les Escaldes (near the capital), as well as Sant Julià de Lòria and El Pas de la Casa (the towns nearest the Spanish and French borders), have also become shopping centres.

Most visitors never see Andorra's rural charms, which match those of other parts of the Pyrenees. The region is excellent for walkers. One of the main routes leads to the **Cercle de Pessons**, a bowl of lakes in the east, and past Romanesque chapels such as **Sant Martí** at La Cortinada. In the north is the picturesque Sorteny valley where traditional farmhouses have been converted into snug restaurants.

❼ La Seu d'Urgell

Lleida. 🏙 13,000. 🚌 𝒊 Carrer Major 8 (973 35 15 11). 🛍 Tue & Sat. 🎉 Festa major (last week of Aug). 🆆 turismeseu.com

This Pyrenean town became a bishopric in the 6th century. Feuds between the bishops of Urgell and the Counts of Foix over land, gave rise to Andorra in the 13th century. The **cathedral** has a Romanesque statue of Santa Maria d'Urgell. The **Museu Diocesà** contains a 10th-century copy of St Beatus of Liébana's *Commentary on the Apocalypse*.

Ⅲ Museu Diocesà
Plaça del Deganat. **Tel** 973 35 32 42.
Open 10am–1:30pm, 4–7:30pm Mon–Sat (to 6pm Oct & Mar–May), 10am–1:30pm Sun & Nov–Feb.
Closed 1 Jan, 25 Dec. 🧩 🛍

Carving, La Seu d'Urgell cathedral

❽ Puigcerdà

Girona. 🏙 9,000. 🚊 🚌 𝒊 Carrer Querol 1 (972 88 05 42). 🛍 Sun. 🎉 Festa de l'Estany (third Sun of Aug); Festa del Roser (mid-Jul). 🆆 puigcerda.com

Puig is Catalan for hill. Despite sitting on a relatively small hill compared with the encircling mountains, which rise to 2,900 m (9,500 ft), Puigcerdà nevertheless commands a fine view down the beautiful Cerdanya valley. The town of Puigcerdà was founded in 1177 by Alfons II as the capital of Cerdanya, an important agricultural region, which shares a past and its culture with the French Cerdagne. The Spanish enclave of **Llívia**, an attractive little town with a medieval pharmacy, lies 6 km (3.75 miles) inside France.

Cerdanya is the largest valley in the Pyrenees. At its edge is the **Cadí-Moixeró** nature reserve *(see p170)*, a place for ambitious walks.

Portal of Monestir de Santa Maria

❾ Ripoll

Girona. 🏙 11,000. 🚊 🚌 𝒊 Plaça del Abat Oliba (972 70 23 51). 🛍 Sat. 🎉 Festa major (11–12 May), La Llana y Casament a Pagès (Sun after Festa major). 🆆 elripolles.com

Once a tiny mountain base from which raids against the Moors were made, Ripoll is now best known for the **Monestir de Santa Maria** *(see p24)*, founded in 879. The town is called the "cradle of Catalonia" as the monastery was the power base of Guifré el Pelós (Wilfred the Hairy), founder of the House of Barcelona *(see p44)*. He is buried here. In the later 12th century, the west portal was decorated with what are regarded as the finest Romanesque carvings in Spain. This and the cloister are the only parts of the medieval monastery to have survived.

Environs
In the mountains to the west is **Sant Jaume de Frontanyà** *(see p24)*, another superb Romanesque church.

The medieval town of Besalú on the banks of the Riu Fluvià

⑩ Sant Joan de les Abadesses

Girona. 🚉 3,600. 🚌 **ℹ** Plaça de Abadia 9 (972 72 05 99). 🚆 Sun. 🎭 Festa major (second week of Sep). 📧 **W** santjoandelesabadesses.cat

A fine, 12th-century Gothic bridge arches over the Riu Ter to this unassuming market town, whose main attraction is its **monastery**.

Founded in 885, it was a gift from Guifré, first count of Barcelona, to his daughter, the first abbess. The church has little decoration except for a wooden calvary, *The Descent from the Cross*. Though made in 1150, it looks modern. The figure of a thief on the left was burnt in the Civil War and replaced so skilfully that it is hard to tell it is new. The museum has Baroque and Renaissance altarpieces.

12th-century calvary, Sant Joan de les Abadesses monastery

Environs

To the north are **Camprodon** and **Beget**, both with Romanesque churches (*see p25*). Camprodon also has some grand houses, and its region is noted for sausages.

⑪ Olot

Girona. 🚉 34,000. 🚌 **ℹ** Carrer Hospici 8 (972 26 01 41). 🚆 Mon. 🎭 Feria de Mayo (1 May), Corpus Christi (Jun), Festa del Tura (8 Sep), Feria de Sant Lluc (18 Oct). **W** turismeolot.cat

This small market town sits at the centre of a landscape that is pockmarked with extinct volcanoes. But it was an earthquake in 1474 that destroyed its medieval past.

During the 18th century the town's textile industry spawned the "Olot School" of art (*see p30*): cotton fabrics were printed with drawings. In 1783 the Public School of Drawing was founded. Much of the school's work, which includes paintings such as Joaquim Vayreda's *Les Falgueres*, is in the **Museu Comarcal de la Garrotxa**. Modernista sculptor Miquel Blay's damsels support the balcony at No. 38 Passeig Miquel Blay.

🏛 Museu Comarcal de la Garrotxa

Carrer Hospici 8. **Tel** 972 27 11 66. **Open** Jul–Sep: 11am–2pm, 4–7pm Tue–Fri; Oct–Jun: 10am–1pm, 3–6pm Tue–Fri; all year: 11am–2pm, 4–7pm Sat, 11am–2pm Sun. 🎭 🚻

⑫ Besalú

Girona. 🚉 2,000. 🚌 **ℹ** Plaça de la Llibertat 1 (972 59 12 40). 🚆 Tue. 🎭 Sant Vicenç (22 Jan), Festa major (weekend closest to 25 Sep), Music Festival (Aug–Sep). 📧 **W** besalu.cat

A magnificent medieval town, with a striking approach across a fortified bridge over the Riu Fluvià, Besalú has two fine Romanesque churches: **Sant Vicenç** and **Sant Pere** (*see p25*). The latter is the sole remnant of a Benedictine monastery founded in 977, but pulled down in 1835.

In 1964 a **mikvah**, a Jewish ritual bath, was discovered by chance. It was built in 1264 and is one of only three of that period to survive in Europe. The tourist office has the keys to all the town's attractions.

To the south, the sky-blue lake of **Banyoles**, where the 1992 Olympic rowing contests were held, is ideal for picnics.

Shop selling *llonganisses* in the mountain town of Camprodon

Girona Town Centre

① Església de Sant Pere
     de Galligants
② Banys Àrabs
③ Església de Sant Feliu
④ Catedral
⑤ Museu d'Art
⑥ Museu d'Història
     de la Ciutat
⑦ Museu d'Història dels Jueus

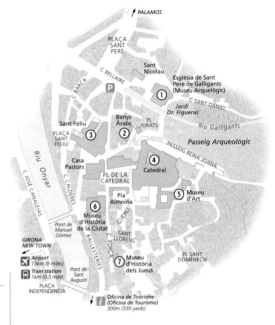

0 metres   250
0 yards   250

❸ Girona

Girona. 🅰 96,000. ✈ 🚊 🚌
ℹ️ Rambla de la Llibertat 1 (972 010
001). 🛒 Tue, Sat. 🎪 Sant Narcís
(29 Oct for a week). 📷
🌐 **girona.cat/turisme**

This handsome town puts on
its best face beside the Riu
Onyar, where tall, pastel-
coloured buildings rise above
the water. Behind them, in the
old town, the Rambla de la
Llibertat is lined with busy
shops and street cafés.
   The houses were built in
the 19th century to replace
sections of the city wall
damaged during a seven-
month siege by French troops
in 1809. Most of the rest of the
ramparts, first raised by the
Romans, are still intact and
have been turned into the
Passeig Arqueològic
(Archaeological Walk), which
runs right round the city.

The walk's starting point is on
the north side of the town,
near the **Església de Sant Pere
de Galligants** (St Peter of the
Cock Crows) *(see p25)*. The
church now houses the city's
archaeological collection.
   From here, a narrow street
goes through the north gate,
where huge Roman foundation
stones are still visible. They mark
the route of the Via Augusta, the
road which once ran from
Tarragona to Rome. The most
popular place of devotion in the
town is the **Església de Sant
Feliu**. The church, begun in the
14th century, was built over
the tombs of St Felix and
St Narcissus, both patrons of the
city. Next to the high altar are
eight Roman sarcophagi.

Despite their name, the nearby
Banys Àrabs (Arab Baths) were
built in the 12th century, 300
years after the Moors had left.

🏛 Museu d'Història
dels Jueus

Carrer de la Força 8. **Tel** 972 21
67 61. **Open** 10am–8pm Mon,
10am–6pm Tue–Sat (to 8pm Jul–Aug),
10am–2pm Sun. **Closed** 1 & 6 Jan,
25 & 26 Dec. 📷 ♿

This centre charts the history of
Jews in Girona. The buildings it
occupies in the maze of
alleyways and steps in the old
town were once part of El Call,
the Jewish ghetto, which was
inhabited by the city's Jews from
the late 9th century until their
expulsion from Spain in 1492.

⛪ Catedral

Pl Catedral s/n. **Tel** 972 42 71 89.
Open Apr–Oct: 10am–8pm daily;
Nov–Mar: 10am–6:30pm daily.
📷 🔇

Girona Cathedral's west face is
pure Catalan Baroque, but the
rest of the building is Gothic.
The single nave, built in 1416
by Guillem Bofill, possesses
the widest Gothic span in the
Christian world. Behind the altar
is a marble throne known as
"Charlemagne's Chair". It is
named after the Frankish king
whose troops took Girona in

Painted houses packed tightly along the bank of the Riu Onyar in Girona

785. In the chancel is a 14th-century jewel-encrusted silver and enamel altarpiece. Among the fine Romanesque paintings and statues in the cathedral's museum are a 10th-century illuminated copy of St Beatus of Liébana's *Commentary on the Apocalypse*, and a 14th-century statue of the Catalan king, Pere the Ceremonious.

The collection's 11th- to 12th-century tapestry, *The Creation*, is decorated with lively figures. The rich colours of this large work are well preserved.

Tapestry of *The Creation*

🏛 **Museu d'Art**
Pujada de la Catedral 12.
Tel 972 20 38 34. **Open** 10am–7pm (to 6pm Oct–Apr) Tue–Sat, 10am–2pm Sun. **Closed** 1 & 6 Jan, 25 & 26 Dec. 🅿 ♿

This gallery holds works from the Romanesque period to the 20th century. The many items from churches ruined by war or neglect tell of the richness of church interiors long ago.

🏛 **Museu del Cinema**
Carrer Sèquia 1. **Tel** 972 412 777.
Open Tue–Sun (Jul–Aug: daily).
Closed 1 & 6 Jan, 25 & 26 Dec. 🅿 free 1st Sun of month. 📷 ♿

Next to Església de Mercadel, this collection includes film and artifacts from the mid-19th century to the present day.

🏛 **Museu d'Història de la Ciutat**
Carrer de la Força 27. **Tel** 972 22 22 29. **Open** Tue–Sun. **Closed** 1 & 6 Jan, 25 & 26 Dec. 🅿 ♿

The city's history museum is in an 18th-century former convent. Recesses where the decomposing bodies of members of the Capuchin Order were placed can still be seen. Exhibits include old *sardana (see p131)* instruments.

🄮 **Figueres**

Girona. 🔼 44,000. 🚍 🚌 ℹ Plaça del Sol (972 50 31 55). 🕗 Thu. 🎉 Santa Creu (3 May), Sant Pere (29 Jun). 📷 🌐 visitfigueres.cat

Figueres is the market town of the Empordà plain. Beside the plane-tree-shaded Rambla is the former Hotel de Paris, now home to the **Museu del Joguet** (Toy Museum). At the bottom of the Rambla is a statue of Narcís Monturiol i Estarriol (1819–95) who, it is said, invented the submarine.

Figueres was the birthplace of Salvador Dalí, who in 1974 turned the town theatre into the **Teatre-Museu Dalí**. Under its glass dome are works by Dalí and other painters. The museum is a monument to Catalonia's most eccentric artist.

Environs
The **Casa-Museu Castell Gala Dalí**, 55 km (35 miles) south of Figueres, is the medieval castle Dalí bought in the 1970s. It contains some of his paintings. East of Figueres is the Romanesque monastery, **Sant Pere de Rodes** *(see p25)*.

Rainy Taxi, a monument in the garden of the Teatre-Museu Dalí

🏛 **Museu del Joguet**
C/ Sant Pere 1. **Tel** 972 50 45 85.
Open Jun–Sep: daily; Oct–May: Tue–Sun. 🅿 ♿ 🌐 mjc.cat

🏛 **Teatre-Museu Dalí**
Pl Gala-Salvador Dalí 5. **Tel** 972 67 75 00. **Open** Jul–Sep: daily; Oct–Jun: Tue–Sun. **Closed** 1 Jan, 25 Dec. 🅿 🌐 salvador-dali.org

🏛 **Casa-Museu Castell Gala Dalí**
C/Gala Dalí, Púbol (La Pera). **Tel** 972 48 86 55. **Open** mid-Mar–Dec: Tue–Sun (mid-Jun–mid-Sep: daily). 🅿 ♿ 📷

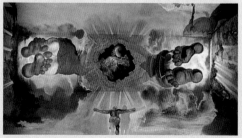

The Art of Dalí

Salvador Dalí i Domènech was born in Figueres in 1904 and mounted his first exhibition at the age of 15. After studying at the Escuela de Bellas Artes in Madrid, and dabbling with Cubism, Futurism and Metaphysical painting, the young artist embraced Surrealism in 1929, becoming the movement's best-known painter. Never far from controversy, the self-publicist Dalí became famous for his hallucinatory images – such as *Woman-Animal Symbiosis* – which he described as "hand-painted dream photographs". Dalí's career also included writing and film-making, and established him as one of the 20th century's greatest artists. He died in his home town in 1989.

Ceiling fresco in the Wind Palace Room, Teatre-Museu Dalí

⓯ Cadaqués

Girona. ⚅ 3,000. 🚌 ℹ️ Carrer Cotxe 1 (972 25 83 15). ⚏ Mon. ⚐ Fiesta major de Verano (first week of Sep), Santa Esperança (18 Dec).
Ⓦ **visitcadaques.org**

This pretty resort is overlooked by the Baroque **Església de Santa Maria**. In the 1960s it was dubbed the "St Tropez of Spain", due to the young crowd that sought out Salvador Dalí in nearby Port Lligat, where he lived for six months of the year, from 1930 until his death in 1989. Today the much modified house, which expanded far beyond the original fisherman's cabin, is known as the **Casa-Museu Salvador Dalí**. Managed by the Gala-Salvador Dalí Foundation, the museum provides a unique interpretation of the artist's life.

🏛 **Casa-Museu Salvador Dalí**
Portlligat. **Tel** 972 25 10 15. **Open** Tue– Sun (daily mid-Jun–mid-Sep). **Closed** 1 Jan, 7 Jan–early Feb, 25 Dec. 🅿
Ⓦ **salvador-dali.org**

⓰ Empúries

Girona. 🚌 L'Escala. **Tel** 972 77 02 08. **Open** Easter, Jun–Sep: 10am–8pm daily; Oct–May: 10am–6pm daily (to 5pm mid-Nov–mid-Feb). **Closed** 1 & 6 Jan, 25 Dec; 15 Nov–15 Feb: Mon. 🦽 ruins; free last Sun of month. 📷 by appt. Ⓦ **mac.cat**

The extensive ruins of this Greco-Roman town *(see p43)* occupy an imposing coastal site. Three settlements were built between the 7th and 3rd centuries BC: the old town (Palaiapolis); the new town (Neapolis); and the

An excavated Roman pillar in the ruins of Empúries

Roman town. The **old town** was founded by the Greeks in 600 BC as a trading port. It was built on what was a small island, and is now the site of the tiny hamlet of Sant Martí de Empúries. In 550 BC this was replaced by a larger new town on the shore which the Greeks named Emporion, meaning "trading place". In 218 BC, the Romans landed at Empúries and built a city next to the new town.
    A nearby museum exhibits some of the site's finds, but the best are in Barcelona's Museu Arqueològic *(see p91)*.

⓱ Peratallada

Girona. ⚅ 400. ℹ️ C/Unió 3, Ajuntament de Forallac, Vulpellac (972 64 55 22). ⚐ Fira de les Herbes (last weekend in Apr), Festa Major (6 & 7 Aug), Medieval Market (first weekend in Oct). Ⓦ **forallac.com**

This tiny village is the most spectacular of the many that lie a short inland trip from the Costa Brava. Together with Pals and Palau Sator it forms part of the "Golden Triangle" of medieval villages. Its mountain-top position gives some dramatic views of the area. A labyrinth of cobbled streets wind up to the well-conserved castle and lookout tower, whose written records date from the 11th century. Peratallada's counts and kings made doubly sure of fending off any attackers by constructing a sturdy wall enclosing the entire village, which even today limits the nucleus from further expansion.

Looking south along the Costa Brava from Tossa de Mar

⓲ Tossa de Mar

Girona. ⚅ 6,000. 🚌 ℹ️ Avinguda Pelegrí 25 (972 34 01 08). ⚏ Thu. ⚐ Festa Major d'Hivern (22 Jan), Festa Major d'Estiu (29 Jun).
Ⓦ **infotossa.com**

At the end of a tortuous corniche, the Roman town of Turissa is one of the prettiest along the Costa Brava. Above the modern town is the **Vila Vella** (old town), a protected national monument. The medieval walls enclose fishermen's cottages, a 14th-century church and countless bars.
    The **Museu Municipal** in the old town exhibits local archaeology and modern art.

🏛 **Museu Municipal**
Plaça Roig i Soler 1. **Tel** 972 34 07 09.

⓳ Blanes

Girona. ⚅ 40,000. 🚆 🚌 ℹ️ Plaça Catalunya (972 33 03 48). ⚏ Mon. ⚐ Santa Ana (26 Jul); Festa Major Petita (21 Aug) Ⓦ **visitblanes.net**

The working port of Blanes has one of the longest beaches on the Costa Brava. The highlight of the town is the **Jardí Botànic Marimurtra**. These gardens, designed by Karl Faust in 1928, are spectacularly sited above cliffs. Their 7,000 species of Mediterranean and tropical plants include African cacti.

🌱 **Jardí Botànic Marimurtra**
Pg Carles Faust 9. **Tel** 972 33 08 26. **Open** daily. **Closed** 1 & 6 Jan, 25 & 26 Dec. 🅿 🚻 ♿ Ⓦ **marimurtra.cat**

◀ The fortified bridge leading into the medieval town of Besalú

The Costa Brava

The Costa Brava ("wild coast") runs for some 200 km (125 miles) from Blanes northwards to the region of Empordà, which borders France. It is a mix of rugged cliffs, pine-backed sandy coves, golden beaches and crowded, modern resorts. The busiest resorts – Lloret de Mar, Tossa de Mar and Platja d'Aro – are to the south. Sant Feliu de Guíxols and Palamós are still working towns behind the summer rush. Just inland there are medieval villages to explore, such as Peralada, Peratallada and Pals. Wine, olives and fishing were the mainstays of the area before the tourists came in the 1960s.

Cadaqués retains an air of seclusion as it is accessible only by a steep road. It has an arty atmosphere and its small, stony beaches are relatively unspoiled and uncrowded.

L'Estartit is a good base for the Illes Medes, a former pirates' lair, which now form a marine reserve with clear waters perfect for skin diving.

Palamós is a working port with modern hotels to the south, and secluded beaches and coves lapped by clear water to the north.

Platja d'Aro's long and sandy beach is lined with modern hotels. It is one of the most popular resorts on the coast.

Tossa de Mar has a golden beach in a small cove beneath the fortified old town.

Roses lies at the head of a sweeping bay. Its sandy beach, the longest on the Costa Brava, has become a mecca for lovers of watersports.

L'Escala is a small resort, popular mainly with local tourists. It has fine beaches and a small port where fishing nets dry in the sun.

Begur is a hilltop town just inland. It has good views of the coast, and small coves are tucked at its feet.

Llafranc, a whitewashed resort, with a promenade leading to neighbouring Calella, is one of the coast's most pleasant resorts.

Lloret de Mar has more hotels than anywhere else on the coast. But there are unspoiled beaches nearby, such as Santa Cristina.

Map labels: Llançà, Port de la Selva, Cap de Creus, Parc Natural del Cap de Creus, Peralada, Cadaqués, Castelló d'Empúries, C260, Roses, N260, Fortià, Empuriabrava, Parc Natural dels Aiguamolls de l'Empordà, C31, L'Escala, Punta del Milà, L'Estartit, Illes Medes, Riu Ter, Torroella de Montgrí, C31, Peratallada, Pals, Begur, C66, Palafrugell, C31, Llafranc, Calella de Palafrugell, Palamós, Llagostera, S'Agaró, Platja d'Aro, C31, Tossa de Mar, Sant Feliu de Guíxols, C35, C63, Tordera, Lloret de Mar, Blanes, Malgrat de Mar

0 kilometres 10
0 miles 5

⑳ Monestir de Montserrat

The "serrated mountain" *(mont serrat)*, its highest peak rising to 1,236 m (4,055 ft), is a superb setting for Catalonia's holiest place, the Monastery of Montserrat, which is surrounded by chapels and hermits' caves. A chapel was first mentioned in the 9th century; the monastery was founded in the 11th century, and in 1409 it became an independent abbey. In 1811, when the French attacked Catalonia in the War of Independence *(see p47)*, the monastery was destroyed. Rebuilt and repopulated in 1844, it was a beacon of Catalan culture during the Franco years. Today Benedictine monks live here. Visitors can hear the Escolania singing the *Salve Regina* and the *Virolai* (the Montserrat hymn) at various times throughout the day except on Saturdays, in July and August and during the Christmas period *(call ahead for details)*.

Plaça de Santa Maria
The focal points of the square are two wings of the Gothic cloister built in 1476. The modern monastery façade is by Francesc Folguera.

KEY

① **Funicular** to the holy site of Santa Cova.

② **The Museum** has a collection of 19th- and 20th-century Catalan paintings and many Italian and French works. It also displays liturgical items from the Holy Land.

③ **Gothic cloister**

④ **The Black Virgin** – La Moreneta – looks down from behind the altar, protected behind glass; her wooden orb protrudes for pilgrims to touch.

⑤ **The rack railway** from Monistrol de Montserrat follows the course of a rail line built in 1880.

⑥ **Cable car** to Aeri de Montserrat station.

View of Montserrat
The complex includes cafés and a hotel. A second funicular transports visitors to nature trails above the monastery.

The Way of the Cross
This path passes 11 statues representing the Stations of the Cross. It begins near the Plaça de l'Abat Oliba.

★ **Basilica Façade**
Agapit and Venanci Vallmitjana sculpted Christ and the Apostles on the basilica's Neo-Renaissance façade. It was built in 1900 to replace the Renaissance façade of the original church, consecrated in 1592.

VISITORS' CHECKLIST

Practical Information
Montserrat (Barcelona province).
Tel 93 877 77 77.
Basilica: **Open** 7am–8pm Mon–Fri, 7am–8:15pm Sat–Sun and throughout Aug. 🕙 11am & noon Mon–Fri; 11am, noon, & 7:30pm Sat; 9:30am, 11am, noon, 1pm & 7:30pm Sun. 🗲
Museum: **Open** 10am– 5:45pm daily. 🗲🗲🗲
w abadiamontserrat.cat

Transport
🚌 Aeri de Montserrat, then cable car; Monistrol-Enllaç, then rack railway. 🚌 from Barcelona.

Basilica Interior
The sanctuary in the domed basilica is adorned by a richly enamelled altar and paintings by Catalan artists.

The Virgin of Montserrat

The small wooden statue of La Moreneta (the dark maiden) is the soul of Montserrat. It is said to have been made by St Luke and brought here by St Peter in AD 50. Centuries later, the statue is believed to have been hidden from the Moors in the nearby Santa Cova (Holy Cave). Carbon dating suggests, however, that the statue was carved around the 12th century. In 1881 Montserrat's Black Virgin became patroness of Catalonia.

The blackened Virgin of Montserrat

Inner Courtyard
On one side of the courtyard is the baptistry (1958), with sculptures by Carles Collet. A door on the right leads towards the Black Virgin.

㉑ Vic

Barcelona. 🗺 40,000. 🚊 🚌 ℹ Plaça del Pes (93 886 20 91). 🅿 Tue & Sat. 🎭 Mercat del Ram (Sat before Easter), Sant Miquel (5–15 Jul), Música Viva (5 days mid-Sep), Mercat medieval (6–10 Dec). 🔗 🌐 **victurisme.cat**

Market days are the best time to visit this small country town. This is when the local sausages *(embotits)*, for which the area is renowned, are piled high in the Gothic Plaça Major, along with other produce from the surrounding plains.

In the 3rd century BC Vic was the capital of an ancient Iberian tribe, the Ausetans. The town was then colonized by the Romans – the remains of a Roman temple survive today. Since the 6th century the town has been a bishop's see. In the 11th century, Abbot Oliva commissioned El Cloquer tower, around which the cathedral was built in the 18th century. The interior is covered with vast murals by Josep-Maria Sert (1876–1945, *see p31*). Painted in reds and golds, they represent Biblical scenes.

Adjacent to the cathedral is the **Museu Episcopal de Vic** *(see p25)*, which has one of the best Romanesque collections in Catalonia. The large display of mainly religious art and relics includes bright, simple murals and wooden carvings from rural churches. Also on display are 11th- and 12th-century frescoes and some superb altar frontals.

Cardona dominating the surrounding area from its hilltop site

🏛 **Museu Episcopal**
Plaça Bisbe Oliba 3. **Tel** 93 886 93 60. **Open** Tue–Sun. **Closed** 1 & 6 Jan, 25 & 26 Dec. 🎭 🔗 📷 free 1st Thu of month.

㉒ Cardona

Barcelona. 🗺 5,000. 🚌 ℹ Avinguda Rastrillo (93 869 27 98). 🅿 Sun. 🎭 Carnival (Feb), Festa major (second weekend of Sep). 🌐 **cardona.cat**

This 13th-century, ruddy-stoned castle of the Dukes of Cardona, constables to the crown of Aragón, was rebuilt in the 18th century and is now a luxurious parador *(see p134)*. Beside the castle is an early 11th-century church, the **Església de Sant Vicenç**.

Set on a hill, the castle gives views of the town and of the Muntanya de Sal (Salt Mountain), a huge salt deposit next to the Riu Cardener which has been mined since Roman times.

12th-century altar frontal, Museu Episcopal de Vic

㉓ Solsona

Lleida. 🗺 9,000. 🚌 ℹ Carretera de Basella 1 (973 48 23 10). 🅿 Tue & Fri. 🎭 Carnival (Feb), Corpus Christi (May/Jun), Festa major (8–11 Sep). 🔗 🌐 **solsonaturisme.com**

Nine towers and three gateways remain of Solsona's fortifications. Inside is an ancient town of noble mansions. The cathedral houses a beautiful black stone Virgin. The **Museu Diocesà i Comarcal** contains Romanesque paintings; a wonderfully preserved ice store, **La Poza de Hielo**, is also worth a visit.

🏛 **Museu Diocesà i Comarcal**
Plaça del Palau 1. **Tel** 973 48 21 01. **Open** Tue–Sun. 🔗 **Closed** 1 Jan, 25 & 26 Dec.

🏛 **La Poza de Hielo**
Portal del Pont s/n. **Tel** 973 48 10 09. **Open** Sat–Sun; daily Jul–Aug and Easter. 🎭 🔗

㉔ Lleida

Lleida. 🗺 138,500. 🚊 🚌 ℹ C / Major 31 (902 25 00 50). 🅿 Thu & Sat. 🎭 Sant Anastasi (11 May), Sant Miquel (29 Sep). 🌐 **turismedelleida.cat**

Dominating Lleida, the capital of Catalonia's only inland province, is **La Suda**, a fort taken from the Moors in 1149. The cathedral, founded in 1203, lies within the fort's walls, above the town. It was transformed into barracks by Felipe V in 1707. Today it is desolate, but remains imposing, with magnificent Gothic windows.

A lift descends from La Seu Vella to the Plaça de Sant Joan

in the busy, pedestrianized shopping street at the foot of the hill. The new cathedral is here, as is the reconstructed 13th-century town hall, the **Paeria**.

㉕ Poblet

See pp128–9.

㉖ Montblanc

Tarragona. 🔼 7,000. 🚉 🚌 🅸
Antigua Església de Sant Francesc (977 86 17 33). 🚌 Tue & Fri. 🎭 Festa Major (8–11 Sep), Festa Medieval (two weeks in Apr). 🗺
Ⓦ **montblancmedieval.cat**

The medieval grandeur of Montblanc lives on within its walls – possibly Catalonia's finest piece of military architecture. At the **Sant Jordi** gate St George allegedly slew the dragon. The **Museu Comarcal de la Conca de Barberà** has displays on local crafts.

🏛 **Museu Comarcal de la Conca de Barberà**
Carrer de Josa 6. **Tel** 977 86 03 49.
Open Tue–Sun & public hols. 🗺

㉗ Santes Creus

Tarragona. 🔼 150. 🚌 🅸 Plaça de Sant Bernat 1 (977 63 81 41). 🚌 Sat & Sun. 🎭 Santa Llúcia (13 Dec).

The tiny village of Santes Creus is home to the prettiest of the "Cistercian triangle" monasteries.

The other two, Vallbona de les Monges and Poblet, are nearby. The **Monestir de Santes Creus** was founded in 1150 by Ramon Berenguer IV *(see p44)* during his reconquest of Catalonia. The Gothic cloisters are decorated with figurative sculptures, a style first permitted by Jaume II, who ruled from 1291 to 1327. His tomb is in the 12th-century church, which features a rose window.

🔝 **Monestir de Santes Creus**
Tel 977 63 83 29. **Open** 10am–7pm (to 5:30pm Oct–May) Tue–Sun & public hols. **Closed** 1 & 6 Jan, 25 & 26 Dec. 🗺 🅿 🗺 by appointment.

㉘ Vilafranca del Penedès

Barcelona. 🔼 39,000. 🚉 🚌 🅸 Carrer Cort 14 (93 892 05 62). 🚌 Sat. 🎭 Fira de Mayo (2nd week of May), Festa major (end Aug). Ⓦ **turisme.vilafranca.com**

This market town is set in the heart of Penedès, the main wine-producing region of Catalonia. The **Vinseum** (Wine Museum) documents the history of the area's wine trade. Local *bodegues* can be visited for wine tasting. **Sant Sadurní d'Anoia**, the capital of Spain's sparkling wine, *cava (see pp34–5)*, is 8 km (5 miles) to the north.

🏛 **Vinseum**
Plaça de Jaume I. **Tel** 93 890 05 82.
Open 10am–2pm, 4–7pm Tue–Sat; 10am–2pm Sun.

Anxaneta climbing to the top of a tower of casteIlers

Human towers

The province of Tarragona is famous for its *casteIler* festivals, in which teams of men stand on each other's shoulders in an effort to build the highest human tower (*castell*). Configurations depend on the number of men who form the base. Teams wear similar colours, and often have names denoting their home town. The small child who has to undertake the perilous climb to the top, where he or she makes the sign of the cross, is called the *anxaneta*. *CasteIlers* assemble in competition for Tarragona province's major festivals throughout the year. In the wine town of Vilafranca del Penedès they turn out for Sant Fèlix (30 August), and in Tarragona city for Santa Tecla, its *festa major* on 23 September. Rival teams in Valls appear on St John's Day (24 June), but strive for their best achievement at the end of the tower-building season on St Ursula's Day (21 October), when teams from all over Catalonia converge on the town square.

Monestir de Santes Creus, surrounded by poplar and hazel trees

㉕ Monestir de Poblet

The monastery of Santa Maria de Poblet is a haven of tranquillity and a resting place of kings. It was the first and most important of three monasteries, known as the "Cistercian triangle" *(see p127)*, that helped to consolidate power in Catalonia after it had been recaptured from the Moors by Ramon Berenguer IV. In 1835, due to the Ecclesiastical Confiscation law, and during the Carlist upheavals, it was plundered and damaged by fire. Restoration of the impressive ruins began in 1930 and monks returned in 1940.

View of Poblet
The abbey, its buildings enclosed by fortified walls that have hardly changed since the Middle Ages, is in an isolated valley near the Riu Francolí's source.

★ Cloisters
The evocative vaulted cloisters were built in the 12th–13th centuries and were the centre of monastic life. The capitals are beautifully decorated with carved scrollwork.

KEY

① **Museum**

② **Royal doorway**

③ **Former kitchen**

④ **Wine cellar**

⑤ **The 12th-century refectory** is a vaulted hall with an octagonal fountain and a pulpit.

⑥ **The dormitory** is reached by stairs from the church. The vast 87-m (285-ft) gallery dates from the 13th century. Half of it is still in use by the monks.

⑦ **Parlour cloister**

⑧ **Sant Esteve cloister**

⑨ **New sacristy**

⑩ **The Abbey Church**, large and unadorned, with three naves, is a typical Cistercian building.

⑪ **Baroque church façade**

Library
The Gothic scriptorium was converted into a library in the 17th century, when the Cardona family donated its book collection.

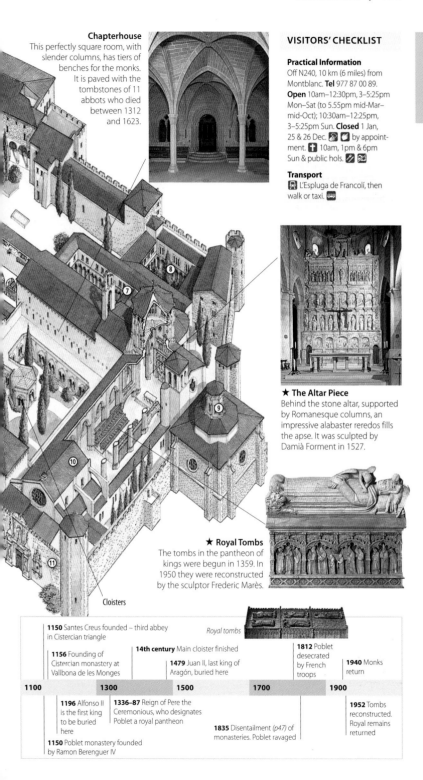

Chapterhouse
This perfectly square room, with slender columns, has tiers of benches for the monks. It is paved with the tombstones of 11 abbots who died between 1312 and 1623.

VISITORS' CHECKLIST

Practical Information
Off N240, 10 km (6 miles) from Montblanc. **Tel** 977 87 00 89. **Open** 10am–12:30pm, 3–5:25pm Mon–Sat (to 5.55pm mid-Mar–mid-Oct); 10:30am–12:25pm, 3–5:25pm Sun. **Closed** 1 Jan, 25 & 26 Dec. 🎫 🅿 by appointment. ⬆ 10am, 1pm & 6pm Sun & public hols. 🅿 ♿

Transport
🚃 L'Espluga de Francolí, then walk or taxi. 🚌

★ The Altar Piece
Behind the stone altar, supported by Romanesque columns, an impressive alabaster reredos fills the apse. It was sculpted by Damià Forment in 1527.

★ Royal Tombs
The tombs in the pantheon of kings were begun in 1359. In 1950 they were reconstructed by the sculptor Frederic Marès.

Cloisters

Royal tombs

1150 Santes Creus founded – third abbey in Cistercian triangle

1156 Founding of Cistercian monastery at Vallbona de les Monges

14th century Main cloister finished

1479 Juan II, last king of Aragón, buried here

1812 Poblet desecrated by French troops

1940 Monks return

1100	1300	1500	1700	1900

1196 Alfonso II is the first king to be buried here

1336–87 Reign of Pere the Ceremonious, who designates Poblet a royal pantheon

1835 Disentailment *(p47)* of monasteries. Poblet ravaged

1952 Tombs reconstructed. Royal remains returned

1150 Poblet monastery founded by Ramon Berenguer IV

Palm trees lining the waterfront at Sitges

㉙ Sitges

Barcelona. 28,000. Plaça Eduard Maristany 2 (93 894 42 51). Thu (in summer). Carnival (Feb/Mar), Festa major (22–27 Aug). **w** sitgestur.cat

Sitges has no less than nine beaches. It has a reputation as a gay resort but is just as popular with Barceloneses. Lively bars and restaurants line its main boulevard, the Passeig Marítim, and there are many examples of Modernista architecture scattered amongst the 1970s apartment blocks. Modernista artist Santiago Rusiñol (see p31) spent much time here and on his death bequeathed his quirky collection of ceramics, sculptures, painting and ornate ironwork to the **Museu Cau Ferrat**. It lies next to Sitges's landmark, the 17th-century church of **Sant Bartomeu i Santa Tecla**.

Museu Cau Ferrat
Carrer Fonollar. **Tel** 93 894 03 64. **Open** Tue–Sun.

㉚ Costa Daurada

Tarragona. Calafell, Sant Vicenç de Calders, Salou. Tarragona (977 23 03 12). **w** costadaurada.info

The long sandy beaches of the Costa Daurada (Golden Coast) run along the shores of Tarragona province. **El Vendrell** is one of the area's active ports. The **Museu Pau Casals** in Sant Salvador (El Vendrell) is dedicated to the famous cellist. **Port Aventura**, south of

Tarragona, is one of Europe's largest theme parks and has many exotically themed attractions, such as Polynesia and Wild West. **Cambrils** and **Salou** to the south are the liveliest resorts – the others are low-key, family holiday spots.

Museu Pau Casals
Avinguda Palfuriana 67. **Tel** 902 10 54 64. **Open** Tue–Sun.

Port Aventura
Autovia Salou–Vila-seca. **Tel** 902 20 22 20. **Open** mid-Mar–6 Jan.

㉛ Tarragona

Tarragona. 134,000. Carrer Major 39 (977 25 07 95). Tue, Thu & Sun. Sant Magí (19 Aug), Santa Tecla (23 Sep). **w** tarragonaturisme.cat

Tarragona is now a major industrial port, but it has preserved many remnants of its Roman past. As the capital of Tarraconensis, the Romans used it as a base for the conquest of the peninsula in the 3rd century BC (see p43).

The avenue of Rambla Nova ends abruptly on the clifftop Balcó de Europa, in sight of the ruins of the **Amfiteatre Romà** and the ruined 12th-century church of **Santa Maria del Miracle**.

Nearby is the Praetorium, a Roman tower that was converted into a palace in medieval times. It now houses the **Pretori i Circ Romans**. This displays Roman and medieval finds, and gives access to the cavernous passageways of the excavated Roman circus, built in the 1st century AD. Next to the Praetorium is the **Museu Nacional Arqueològic**, containing the most important collection of Roman artifacts in Catalonia. It has an extensive collection of bronze tools and beautiful mosaics, including a *Head of Medusa*. Among the most impressive remains are the huge pre-Roman stones on

The remains of the Roman amphitheatre, Tarragona

which the Roman wall is built. An archaeological walk stretches 1 km (half a mile) along the wall.

Behind the wall lies the 12th-century **cathedral**, built on the site of a Roman temple. This evolved over many centuries, as seen from the blend of styles of the exterior. Inside is an alabaster altarpiece of St Tecla, carved by Pere Joan in 1434. The 13th-century cloister has Gothic vaulting, but the doorway is Romanesque (see pp24–5).

In the west of town is a 3rd- to 6th-century Christian cemetery (ask about its opening times in the archaeological museum). Some of the sarcophagi were originally used as pagan tombs.

Environs
The **Aqüeducte de les Ferreres** lies just outside the city, next to the A7 motorway. This 2nd-century aqueduct was built to bring water to the city from the Riu Gaià, 30 km (19 miles) to the north. The **Arc de Berà**, a 1st-century triumphal arch on the Via Augusta, is 20 km (12 miles) northeast on the N340.

The bustling, provincial town of **Reus** lies inland from Tarragona. Although its airport serves the Costa Daurada, it is often overlooked by holiday-makers. However there is some fine Modernista architecture to be seen here, notably some early work by Antoni Gaudí who was born in Reus. The Pere Mata Psychiatric Institute was designed by Domènech i Montaner before his master-piece, the Hospital de la Santa Creu i de Sant Pau (see p81).

🏛 **Museu Nacional Arqueològic de Tarragona**
Plaça del Rei 5. **Tel** 977 23 62 09. **Open** Tue–Sun. 📷 ♿ 🌐 mnat.es

🏛 **Pretori i Circ Romans**
Plaça del Rei. **Tel** 977 23 01 71. **Open** Tue–Sun. 📷 🌐 museutgn.com

❷ Tortosa

Tarragona. 🏔 35,000. 🚹 Pujada Castell de la Suda 1 (977 44 20 05). 📅 Mon. 🎭 Nostra Senyora de la Cinta (1st wk Sep). 🌐 **turismetortosa.com**

A ruined castle and medieval walls are clues to Tortosa's historical importance. Sited at the lowest crossing point on the Riu Ebre, it has been strategically significant since Iberian times. The Moors held the city from the 8th century until 1148. The old Moorish castle, known as La Suda, is all that remains of their defences. It has now been renovated as a parador (see p135). The Moors also built a mosque in Tortosa in 914. Its foundations were used for the present cathedral, on which work began in 1347. Although it was not completed for two centuries, the style is pure Gothic.

Tortosa was badly damaged in 1938–9 during one of the fiercest battles of the Civil War (see p49), when the Ebre formed the front line between the opposing forces.

Ruins of the Palaeo-Christian Necropolis

❸ Delta de L'Ebre

Tarragona. 🚉 Aldea. 🚌 Deltebre, Aldea. 🚹 Deltebre (977 48 96 79). 🌐 **deltebre.net**

The delta of the Riu Ebre is a prosperous rice-growing region and wildlife haven. Some 70 sq km (27 sq miles) have been turned into a nature reserve, the **Parc Natural del Delta de L'Ebre**. In Deltebre there is an information centre and an interesting **Eco-Museu**, with an aquarium containing species found in the delta.

The main towns in the area are **Amposta** and **Sant Carles de la Ràpita**, both of which serve as good bases for exploring the reserve.

The best places to see the variety of wildlife are along the shore, from the Punta del Fangar in the north to the Punta de la Banya in the south. Everywhere is accessible by car except the Illa de Buda. Flamingoes breed on this island and, together with other water birds such as herons and avocets, can be seen from tourist boats that leave from Riumar and Deltebre.

🏛 **Eco-Museu**
Carrer Martí Buera 22. **Tel** 977 48 96 79. **Open** daily. 📷 ♿ 📹

The Sardana

Catalonia's national dance is more complicated than it appears. The dancers must form a circle and accurately count the complicated short- and long-step skips and jumps. Music is provided by a cobla, an 11-person band consisting of a leader playing a three-holed flute (flabiol) and a little drum (tamborí), five woodwind players and five brass players. The sardana is performed during most festes and at special day-long gatherings called aplecs. In Barcelona it is danced on Saturday evenings at 6 in front of the cathedral and usually every Sunday evening at 6 in the Plaça de Sant Jaume.

A group of sardana dancers captured in stone

TRAVELLERS' NEEDS

WHERE TO STAY

Catalonia has an unrivalled variety of accommodation. The Barcelona and Catalonia tourist authorities have complete listings of hotels, country houses and camp sites as well as information on a range of other options. In Barcelona you can stay in the modern luxury of one of Spain's highest skyscrapers, while on the coast you can try a self-catering holiday village with all sorts of entertainments provided. Family-run *cases de pagès*, which are stone-built farm or village houses or country manors, are Catalonia's most distinctive alternative. Some of the best hotels in each price range are listed on pages 136–9.

A hotel in Barcelona's Rambla de Canaletes

Hotel Grading and Facilities

The different types of hotels in Catalonia are denoted by the blue plaques near their doors. These show a star-rating which reflects the number and range of facilities available, rather than quality of service. Hotels (H) and hotel-residències (HR) are graded from one to five stars; motels (M), hostals (H) and hostal-residències (HR) from one to three stars; and pensions (P), with the simplest accommodation, have one or two stars.

Prices and Paying

Spanish law requires all hotels to display their prices at reception and in every room. As a rule, the higher the star rating, the greater the price. Rates are almost invariably quoted per room (but meal prices per person). A double room in a one-star hostal can be as little as €30 a night; one in a five-star hotel will cost more than €180 a night. Prices vary according to region, season, day of the week or a special feature such as a view or balcony. The prices given on pages 136–9 are based on high-season rates. Prices for rooms and meals are usually quoted without VAT (IVA), currently 21 per cent.

Booking and Check-in

Hotels in Barcelona can be very busy during the many trade fairs held all year round, so booking in advance is advisable. In rural Catalonia there is rarely any need to book ahead. Resort hotels often close from autumn to spring. You will not normally be asked for a deposit when you book a room except during peak periods or for a longer stay. Most hotels will honour a booking only until 8pm.

When checking in you will be asked for your passport or identity card to comply with police regulations. It will normally be returned as soon as your details have been copied.

Paradors

There are seven paradors in Catalonia – at Aiguablava, Artíes, Cardona, Seu de Urgell, Vic, Vielha and Tortosa. They form part of Spain's chain of high-quality, government-run hotels in historic buildings or in purpose-built, new buildings in spectacular settings.

Reservations for paradors can be made through the **Central de Reservas**, **PTB Hotels** and **Keytel International**.

Rural Accommodation

Cases de pagès (also called *cases rurales*) are Catalan *masies* (farmhouses) that accept visitors. Some offer bed and breakfast, some an evening meal or full board and many are self-catering. They are listed in the *Guía de Establecimientos de Turismo Rural*, available at the tourist office. You can book directly or through the websites of agencies such as **Rural Catalunya**, **Top Rural** and **Cases Fonda**.

The **Xarxa d'Albergs de Catalunya** runs youth hostels, which also cater for adults and families, and the **Federació d'Entitats Excursionistes de Catalunya** runs mountain refuges for hikers.

A room with a private balcony in Hotel Aiguaclara, Begur *(see p138)*

Solid, stone-built architecture typical of traditional Catalan farmhouses

Recommended Hotels

The hotels listed in this book cover a wide range of price categories and have been selected for their excellent facilities and good value for money. The listings cover a vast variety of accommodation, from simple farmhouses and family-run guesthouses to mountain retreats and extravagant luxury palaces. To make it easier for you to choose your hotel, the establishments have been labelled as boutique, historic, luxury, modern or pensions. Many of the hotels have a good reputation for hospitality and offer a warm welcome to guests.

Among the listings, hotels and pensions that are outstanding in some way have been designated as DK Choice. They have been chosen for their exceptional features, for example they may be set in beautiful surroundings or in a historically important building, offer excellent service, have a romantic atmosphere, be particularly charming, environmentally friendly or have a great spa. Whatever the reason it is a guarantee of a memorable stay.

Self-Catering

Villas and apartments let by the week are plentiful on the Costa Daurada and Costa Brava. *Apart-hotels* (or *hotels-apartament*) and *residències-apartament* are a type of self-catering accommodation. Ranked from one to four stars, each apartment has a kitchen, but each complex also has a restaurant and often a swimming pool and other facilities. Generalitat de Catalunya *(see p174)* tourist offices and most travel agents have details of all types of villas and apartments.

Ciutats de vacances (holiday villages) are similar, but accommodation is in bungalows and includes entertainment and sports facilities.

Gites de Catalunya are superior country houses rented out on a week-by-week basis by **Villas 4 You**. Many *cases de pagès* are also self-catering.

Camp Sites

Catalonia has over 300 camp sites, classified as deluxe (L), one-star, two-star, three-star, or farm (M, *càmpings-masia*). All have basic amenities, guards and a safe. *Catalunya Càmpings*, published by the Generalitat de Catalunya is available from the tourist offices. Many sites in Barcelona are grouped under the **Associació de Càmpings de Barcelona**. Camping is permitted only at official sites.

Sign for a camp site

Disabled Travellers

Few hotels are well equipped for disabled guests, although some youth hostels are. The **Federació ECOM** and Viajes 2000 *(see p175)* will advise on hotels throughout Catalonia for visitors with special needs.

DIRECTORY

Where to Stay

Old Town

Bonic Barcelona €
Pension   Map 5 A3
C/Josep Anselm Clavé 9, 08002
Tel 62 605 34 34
w bonic-barcelona.com
Charming B&B in the Gothic
Quarter. Delightful staff.

Chic & Basic Born €
Boutique   Map 5 C2
C/Princesa 50, 08003
Tel 93 295 46 52
w chicandbasic.com
With its mood lighting and
white-on-white chic, this is a firm
favourite with fashionistas.

Hotel Banys Orientals €
Boutique   Map 5 B3
C/Argenteria 37, 08003
Tel 93 268 84 60
w hotelbanysorientals.com
Stylish and great value accom-
modation in the Born district,
with a choice of rooms or suites.

La Ciudadela Hotel €
Pension   Map 5 C2
Passeig de Lluís Companys 2, 08010
Tel 93 309 95 57
w ciudadelaparc.com
Family-run establishment with
modest rooms and a restaurant.

Montecarlo €
Historic   Map 5 A1
La Rambla 124, 08002
Tel 93 412 04 04
w montecarlobcn.com
Located in the heart of the city.
Rooms are modern, well
appointed and reasonably priced.

Barceló Raval €€
Boutique   Map 5 A1
Rambla del Raval 17, 08001
Tel 93 320 14 90
w barcelo.com
Contemporary hotel in a glassy,
conical building with a
panoramic rooftop terrace.

Casa Camper €€
Boutique   Map 2 F2
C/Elisabets 11, 08001
Tel 93 342 62 80
w casacamper.com
Eco-friendly hotel in the multi-
cultural Raval neighbourhood.

Duquesa de Cardona €€
Boutique   Map 5 A3
Passeig Colom 12, 08002
Tel 93 268 90 90
w hduquesadecardona.com
Stylish place with roof terrace
overlooking Port Vell.

Grand Hotel Central €€
Boutique   Map 5 B1
Via Laietana 30, 08003
Tel 93 295 79 00
w grandhotelcentral.com
Elegant hotel with accommodating
staff. Boasts a fitness centre,
infinity pool and a restaurant
with a Michelin-starred chef.

Hotel Denit €€
Boutique   Map 5 B1
C/Estruc 24–26, 08002
Tel 93 545 40 00
w denit.com
Stylish small hotel in the
Gothic Quarter: great value for
its central location. Rooms are
light, modern and welcoming.

DK Choice

Hotel España €€
Historic   Map 2 E3
C/Sant Pau 9–11, 08001
Tel 93 550 00 00
w hotelespanya.com
This beautifully restored
Modernista gem dates back to
1859, and now combines
contemporary furnishings with
beautiful early 20th-century
details including superb frescoes
by Montaner. There is a
fabulous restaurant, a bar with a
swirling Modernista fireplace,
and a gorgeous roof terrace.

Mesón Castilla €€
Historic   Map 2 F1
C/Valldonzella 5, 08001
Tel 93 318 21 82
w mesoncastilla.com
Old-fashioned, traditional and
welcoming, with comfortable
good-value rooms.

Beautiful Modernista decor in the dining
room of the Hotel España

Musik Boutique Hotel €€
Boutique   Map 5 B2
C/Sant Pere mes Baix 62, 08003
Tel 93 222 55 44
w musikboutiquehotel.com
Welcoming hotel with an 18th-
century façade. Minimalist rooms
have iPod docks and Wi-Fi.

Room Mate Pau €€
Boutique   Map 5 B1
C/Fontanella 7, 08010
Tel 93 314 63 00
w pau.room-matehotels.com
Funky international chain of
designer hotels, this one with
fabulous space-age decor.

Hotel 1898 €€€
Luxury   Map 5 A1
La Rambla 109, 08002
Tel 93 552 95 52
w hotel1898.com
Rooms have colonial decor. Relaxed
atmosphere, central location.

Hotel DO €€€
Boutique   Map 5 A3
Plaça Reial 1, 08002
Tel 93 481 36 66
w hoteldoreial.com
Gourmet hotel featuring three
outstanding restaurants in an
exquisite 19th-century building.

DK Choice

Hotel Mercer €€€
Luxury   Map 5 B3
C/Lledó 7, 08002
Tel 93 310 74 80
w mercerbarcelona.com
Chic, exclusive and intimate, this
ravishing small hotel occupies a
sumptuously restored historic
mansion that incorporates a
section of the ancient Roman
walls. The old façade belies a contemporary interior; there's a roof
terrace with plunge pool, and a
patio shaded by orange trees.

Hotel Neri €€€
Boutique   Map 5 A2
C/Sant Sever 5, 08002
Tel 93 304 06 55
w hotelneri.com
Enchanting hideaway in an 18th-
century palace with a superb
restaurant and plush interiors.
Situated in the Gothic Quarter.

Le Méridien Barcelona €€€
Luxury Map 5 A1
La Rambla 111, 08002
Tel *93 318 62 00.*
W **lemeridienbarcelona.es**
Offers spectacular suites, a great
restaurant and a spa.

Ohla €€€
Luxury Map 5 B1
Via Laietana 49, 08003
Tel *93 341 50 50*
W **ohlahotel.com**
A flamboyant 5-star option, with
a Michelin-starred restaurant and
award-winning mixologists.

The elegantly decorated interior of Hotel Arts

Eixample

DK Choice

**Close to Passeig de
Gràcia B&B** €
Pension Map 3 A5
C/Diputació 327, 08008
Tel *696 53 14 39*
Named simply for its great
location, this charming, family-run
B&B in an exquisite Modernista
building has four huge rooms
featuring a stylish mix of original
details and contemporary
furnishings. The largest suite has
its own glassed-in gallery and a
fireplace. Guests enjoy breakfast
in the delightful shared kitchen.

Hostal L'Antic Espai €
Pension
*Gran Via de les Corts Catalanes 660,
08010*
Tel *93 304 19 45*
W **anticespai.com**
Breakfast is served on a flower-
filled terrace at this delightful B&B.

Hotel Praktik Rambla €
Boutique Map 3 A3
Rambla de Catalunya 27, 08007
Tel *93 343 66 90*
W **hotelpraktikrambla.com**
Chic contemporary rooms in a
gorgeous Modernista townhouse.

Room Mate Emma €
Boutique Map 3 A3
C/Rosselló 205, 08008
Tel *93 238 56 06*
W **emma.room-matehotels.com**
Futuristic design and small but
stylish rooms. Great value.

Hotel Actual €€
Boutique Map 3 A3
C/Rosselló 238, 08008
Tel *93 552 05 50*
W **hotelactual.com**
Chic, minimalist rooms in mono-
chromatic colourways. Free Wi-Fi.
Close to Gaudí's La Pedrera.

Hotel Casa Fuster €€
Luxury Map 3 A3
Passeig de Gràcia 132, 08008
Tel *93 255 30 00*
W **hotelescenter.es/casafuster**
Beautifully restored Modernista
mansion with lavish rooms and
wonderful old-fashioned service.

Hotel Jazz €€
Modern Map 2 F1
C/Pelai 3, 08001
Tel *93 552 96 96*
W **hoteljazz.com**
One of the best bargains in
the city centre, with spacious,
modern rooms and a rooftop
plunge pool.

Hotel Majestic €€
Luxury Map 3 A3
Passeig de Gràcia 68, 08007
Tel *93 488 17 17*
W **hotelmajestic.es**
Features elegant rooms and a
roof terrace with plunge pool.

Hotel Omm €€
Luxury Map 3 A3
C/Rosselló 265, 08008
Tel *93 445 40 00*
W **hotelomm.es**
Boasting one of the most sought-
after addresses in town, with a
restaurant and spa.

DK Choice

Alma €€€
Boutique Map 3 A4
C/Mallorca 271, 08008
Tel *93 216 44 90*
W **almabarcelona.com**
A fashionably decorated
town house near Gaudí's
La Pedrera, this hotel oozes
understated elegance and is
famed for its excellent service.
Some original 19th-century
details have been preserved,
but the rooms are chic and
minimalist. The glorious secret
courtyard and stylish roof
terrace are ideal for relaxing
after a hard day's sight-seeing.

Hotel El Palace €€€
Luxury
*Gran Via de les Corts Catalanes 668,
08010*
Tel *93 510 11 30*
W **hotelpalacebarcelona.com**
This opulent hotel is the grande
dame of Barcelona's hotel scene.

Mandarin Oriental Hotel €€€
Luxury Map 3 A3
Passeig de Gràcia 38-40, 08007
Tel *93 151 88 88*
W **mandarinoriental.com**
A classy white and gold interior
and a Michelin-starred restaurant.

Further Afield

ABaC €€€
Luxury
Av. Tibidabo 1, 08022
Tel *93 319 66 00*
W **abacbarcelona.com**
Ultra-chic hotel attached to one
of the finest restaurants in Spain.

DK Choice

Hotel Arts €€€
Luxury Map K9
C/Marina 19–21, 08005
Tel *93 221 10 00*
W **hotelartsbarcelona.com**
A stunning hotel in a glassy
skyscraper right on the beach.
Outstanding service and
amenities including a Six Senses
Spa, superb restaurants and
bars, and a fabulous collection
of contemporary art.

Catalonia

BAQUEIRA: Hotel Val de Ruda €
Modern
Urb. Baqueira-Beret Cota 1500, 25598
Tel *973 645 811*
W **hotelvalderudabaqueira.com**
Traditional hotel with rustic rooms
in Spain's poshest ski resort.

For more information on types of hotels *see page 135*

BEGUR: Hotel Aiguaclara €€
Boutique
C/Sant Miquel 2, 17255
Tel 972 62 29 05
W hotelaiguaclara.com
Romantic getaway in a beautiful
village, with just a handful of rooms.

BORREDÀ: Masia Jaume Coll €€
Historic
Carretera C-26, Km. 169, 08619
Tel 938 23 90 95
W masiajaumecoll.com
A mellow, stone masia (farmhouse)
amid stunning countryside.

CADAQUÉS: Hotel Llane Petit €€
Boutique
Platja Llane Petit s/n, 17488
Tel 97 225 10 20
W llanepetit.com
Peaceful, beachfront location
with crisp blue-and-white rooms.

**CAMPRODON: Hotel de
Camprodon** €
Historic
Plaça Doctor Robert 3, 17867
Tel 97 274 00 13
W hotelcamprodon.com
An early 20th-century gem, with
charming Modernista details.

**CANOVES I SAMALUS:
Hotel Can Cuch** €€
Historic
Can Cuch de Muntanya 35, 08445
Tel 93 103 39 80
W cancuch.com
Farmhouse set in the hills of
Montseny, with exquisite guest-
rooms and a fine restaurant.

CARDONA: Hotel Bremon €
Historic
C/Cambres 15, 08261
Tel 938 68 49 02
W hotelbremon.com
Elegantly converted convent, with
a choice of rooms or apartments.

CORCÀ: Casa Matilda B&B €
Pension
C/Major 31, 17121
Tel 661 03 02 57/972 63 03 61
W casamatilda.es
Enchanting little B&B that serves
home-made cakes at breakfast.

DELTEBRE: Delta Hotel €
Pension
Av. del Canal, Camí de la Illeta s/n,
43580
Tel 977 48 00 46
W deltahotel.net
Family-run rural hotel, a great
base for exploring the Ebro delta.

ERILL LA VALL: Hostal La Plaça €
Pension
Plaza Iglesia s/n, 25528
Tel 973 69 60 26
W hostal-laplaza.com
This old-fashioned guesthouse in
the lovely Vall de Boí occupies a
traditional stone building.

FIGUERES: Hotel Duran €
Modern
C/Lasauca 5, 17600
Tel 972 50 12 50
W hotelduran.com
Comfortable rooms, gardens and
a pool. Famous for its restaurant.

FIGUERES: Hotel Los Angeles €
Pension
C/Barceloneta 10, 17600
Tel 972 51 06 61
W hotelangeles.com
Clean, tranquil rooms. A short
walk from the Dalí museum.

GIRONA: Bellmirall €
Historic
C/Bellmirall 3, 17004
Tel 972 20 40 09
W bellmirall.eu
A small number of simple rooms
in an ancient stone building
hidden away in the Call.

GIRONA: Hotel Carlemany €
Modern
Plaça Miquel Santaló s/n, 17002
Tel 97 221 12 12
W carlemany.es
Offers good business facilities and
great restaurants. Contemporary
art is also on display.

**GIRONA: Hotel Ciutat de
Girona** €
Modern
C/Nord 2, 17001
Tel 972 48 30 38
W faderson.com/girona/
Boasts stylish, airy rooms, a great
restaurant and a fabulous central
location. Superb value.

GIRONA: Hotel Peninsular €
Pension
Av. Sant Francesc 6, 17001
Tel 972 20 38 00
W hotel-peninsular.com
Modern hotel with clean and
bright rooms.

**GRANOLLERS: Casa Fonda
Europa** €€
Historic
C/Anselm Clavé 1, 08402
Tel 938 70 03 12
W casafondaeuropa.com
Classic inn with elegant rooms
and a smart restaurant serving
Catalan cuisine.

**LLAFRANC: El Far de Sant
Sebastià** €€
Boutique
Muntanya de Sant Sebastià, 17211
Tel 972 30 16 39
W elfar.net
Charming hotel on a clifftop over-
looking one of the most beautiful
stretches of the Costa Brava.

LLEIDA: Finca Prats Golf & Spa €€
Luxury
N-240, 25198
Tel 902 44 56 66
W fincaprats.com
Five-star hotel with an 18-hole
golf course and impressive spa.

**LLORET DE MAR:
Hotel Maremagnum** €
Pension
C/Areny 29, 17310
Tel 972 36 44 26
W maremagnumlloret.com
Welcoming, family-run budget
option close to the beach, with
simple but comfortable rooms.

**LLORET DE MAR: Hotel Santa
Marta** €€
Luxury
Platja de Santa Cristina, 17310
Tel 972 36 49 04
W hstamarta.com
Sumptuous modern hotel in
an enchanting little bay.

A well-furnished room in the Hotel Aiguaclara, Begur

LLORET DE MAR: Sant Pere del Bosc Hotel & Spa €€€
Luxury
Paratge Sant Pere del Bosc s/n, 17310
Tel *972 36 16 36*
W santperedelboschotel.com
Lavish suites and a spectacular spa in a rural Modernista villa.

MONTBLANC: Fonda Cal Blasi €
Historic
C/Alenyá 11, 43400
Tel *97 786 13 36*
W fondacalblasi.com
Spacious, rustic rooms in a 19th-century building. Wonderful little restaurant.

MONTSERRAT: Abat Cisneros €€
Modern
Plaça de Montserrat s/n, 08199
Tel *938 77 77 01*
W montserratvisita.com
Modest place with comfortable rooms and spectacular mountain and valley views.

OLOT: Les Cols Pavellons €€€
Luxury
Av. de les Cols 2, 17800
Tel *972 26 92 09*
W lescolspavellons.com
Unique contemporary hotel with rooms in glassy cube-shaped pavilions in the garden, and an award-winning restaurant.

PALS: Hotel Restaurante Sa Punta €€
Boutique
Platja de Pals, 17256
Tel *972 63 64 10*
W hotelsapunta.com
In a rural setting near the beach, with an excellent restaurant and lots of luxurious extras.

DK Choice

PLATJA D'ARO: Silken Park Hotel San Jorge €€
Boutique
Av. Andorra 28, 17251
Tel *972 652 311*
W hoteles-silken.com
Friendly and relaxed, this elegant hotel on the Costa Brava has comfortable rooms with balconies overlooking the sea from the hotel's clifftop location. Steps lead down the cliff to a perfect little cove fringed with rocks and pine trees.

RUPIT: Hostal Estrella €
Pension
Plaça Bisbe Font 1, 08569
Tel *938 52 20 05*
W hostalestrella.com
A cosy option in the picture-postcard village of Rupit, with plenty of rustic charm.

The magnificent façade of Sant Pere del Bosc Hotel & Spa, Lloret de Mar

S'AGARÓ: Hostal de la Gavina €€€
Luxury
Plaça de la Rosaleda, 17248
Tel *972 32 11 00*
W lagavina.com
Set on a beautiful peninsula between two coves, this handsome hotel oozes Golden Age glamour.

SANT LLORENÇ DE MORUNYS: El Monegal €
Modern
C/ Monegal s/n, 25282
Tel *973 49 23 69*
W monegal.com
Warm and welcoming country farmhouse with stylish rooms and delicious organic cuisine.

SANTA CRISTINA D'ARO: Mas Tapiolas €€
Boutique
Carretera C-65, Km. 7, Veinat de Solius s/n, 17246
Tel *932 83 70 17*
W hotelmastapiolas.com
Gorgeous accommodation in an 18th-century Catalan farmhouse.

SITGES: Hotel Noucentista €
Historic
Illa de Cuba 21, 08870
Tel *93 811 00 70*
W hotelnoucentista.com
Gay-friendly hotel in a Modernista villa with a garden and a pool.

SITGES: Hotel Galeon €€
Boutique
C/Sant Francesc 46, 08870
Tel *93 894 13 79*
W hotelsitges.com
Offers cozy rooms, many with terraces overlooking the sea, and a small pool.

SITGES: Hotel Platjador €€
Modern
Passeig de la Ribera 35-36, Sitges
Tel *938 94 13 79*
W hotelsitges.com
Airy, spacious rooms on the seafront. The rooftop bar has wonderful views out to sea.

TARRAGONA: Hotel Lauria €
Pension
Rambla Nova 20, 43004
Tel *977 23 67 12*
W dormicumhotels.com
Great value hotel with classically decorated rooms and a pool.

TARRAGONA: Hotel Husa Imperial Tarraco €€
Modern
Passeig Palmeras s/n, 43003
Tel *977 23 30 40*
W hotelhusaimperial.com
Rooms may be a tad dated at this chain hotel, but the panoramic views make it a winner.

TORRENT: Mas de Torrent Hotel & Spa €€€
Historic
Afueras de Torrent s/n, 17123
Tel *972 30 32 92*
W mastorrent.com
A handful of exquisite rooms and an outstanding restaurant in a country *masia*.

TOSSA DE MAR: Hotel Cap d'Or €
Pension
Passeig del Mar 1, 17320
Tel *972 34 00 81*
W hotelcapdor.com
Small hotel in an 18th-century building right on the seafront, with its own bar and waterfront terrace.

TOSSA DE MAR: Hotel Diana €€
Historic
Plaça Espanya 6, 17320 Tossa de Mar
Tel *97 234 18 86*
W hotelesdante.com
Elegant hotel in the town centre, replete with charming Modernista details.

VALLCLARA: Ca L'Estruch €
Pension
Raval de Vimbodí 8, 43439
Tel *616 23 68 07*
Lovely, traditional B&B with rustic rooms, stone walls and tiled floors. Home-cooked food and friendly family owners.

For more information on types of hotels *see page 135*

WHERE TO EAT AND DRINK

Eating out is both an everyday event and one of the convivial joys of life in Catalonia. Catalans are proud of their regional cuisine and expect to eat well in restaurants, not only at celebratory dinners, but also at work-day meal breaks and at family lunches out. Country restaurants in particular are packed on Sundays. Barcelona has an unusually large number of restaurants. From the sophisticated feast to the simple tapa, fresh ingredients are usually in evidence as Catalans tend to despise convenience food. The restaurants and cafés listed on pages 144–53 have been selected for their food and atmosphere. Pages 32–3 and 142–3 illustrate some of Catalonia's best dishes.

Comerç 24, one of Barcelona's most innovative restaurants *(see p147)*

Restaurants and Bars

Barcelona and Catalonia possess some of Spain's best restaurants, testifying to the fine quality of Catalan cooking. But the cheapest and quickest places to eat are the bars and cafés that serve *tapes* (tapas). Some bars, however, especially pubs, do not serve food.

Family-run *bars i restaurants*, *hostals* and *fondes* – old Catalan words for the various types of inn – serve inexpensive, sit-down meals. *Xiringuitos* are beachside bar-restaurants that are open only during the busy summer season.

Most restaurants close on one day a week, some for lunch or dinner only, and many for an annual holiday. They may also close on some public holidays.

Eating Times

Catalans, in common with other Spaniards, often eat a *l'esmorzar* (light breakfast) of biscuits or toast (with butter and jam) and *cafè amb llet* (milky coffee), then follow it up with a second breakfast or snack between 10 and 11am, perhaps in a café. This may consist of a croissant, a slice of the ubiquitous *truita de patates* (potato omelette) or an *entrepà* (sandwich) with sausage, ham or cheese. Fruit juice, coffee or beer are the usual accompaniments.

From about 1pm onwards, people will stop in the bars for a beer or an *aperitivo* with tapas. By 2pm, Catalans have *dinar* (lunch), which is the main meal of the day.

The cafés, *salons de te* (tea rooms) and *pastisseries* (pastry shops) fill up by about 6 or 7pm for *el berenar* (tea) of sandwiches or cakes, with tea, coffee or fruit juice. Snacks such as *xurros* (fried, sugar-coated batter sticks) can also be bought from stalls.

By 7pm, bars are crowded with people having tapas with wine or beer. In Catalonia, *el sopar* (dinner or supper) begins at about 9pm. However, restaurants sometime begin serving earlier for tourists. In summer, however, families and groups of friends often do not sit down to dinner until as late as 11pm.

How to Dress

A jacket and tie are rarely required, but Catalans dress smartly, especially for city restaurants. Day dress is casual in beach resorts, but shorts are frowned on in the evenings.

Reading the Menu

Aside from tapas, perhaps the cheapest eating options in Catalan restaurants are the fixed-price *plats combinats* (meat or fish with vegetables and, usually, fried potatoes) and the *menú del dia*. A *plat combinat* is offered only by cheaper establishments. Most restaurants – but not all – offer an inexpensive, fixed-price *menú del dia*, normally of three courses. This menu is generally offered at lunchtime (on weekdays), and it can be a good opportunity to try out an expensive restaurant at a more reasonable price.

The Catalan word for menu is *la carta*. It starts with *amanides* (salads), *sopes* (soups), *entremesos* (hors d'oeuvres), *ous i truites* (eggs and omelettes) and *verdures i llegums* (vegetable dishes). Main courses are *peix i marisc* (fish and shellfish) and *carns i*

ABaC, holder of two Michelin stars for its contemporary Catalan cuisine *(see p150)*

Tables at Can Culleretes *(see p144)*, Barcelona's oldest restaurant

aus (meat and poultry). Daily specials are chalked on a board or clipped to menus. *Paella* and other rice dishes may be served as the first course. A useful rule is to follow rice with meat, or start with *fuet* or *llonganissa* (two popular types of sausage) or salad and follow with *paella*.

Desserts are called *postres*. All restaurants offer fresh fruit, but otherwise the range of *postres* is often limited – the famous *crema catalana* (crème brûlée), or *flam* (crème caramel) and *natillas* (custard) are most commonly available. Gourmet restaurants have more creative choices.

Vegetarians are generally poorly catered for, although things have improved tremendously at least in Barcelona. Some vegetable, salad and egg dishes will be vegetarian, but may contain pieces of ham or fish, so ask before you order.

All eating places welcome children and will serve small portions if requested.

Tapas with an Asian twist at the dining bar of Dos Palillos *(see p147)*

Wine Choices

Dry *fino* wines are perfect with shellfish, sausage, olives and soups. Main dishes are often accompanied by wines from Penedès or Terra Alta *(see p34)* in Catalonia, or from Rioja, Ribera del Duero and Navarra. *Cava* *(see pp34–5)* is popular for Sunday lunch.

Smoking

Smoking is banned in all public places, including bars and restaurants.

Prices and Paying

If you order from *la carta* in a restaurant, your bill can soar way above the price of the *menú del dia*, especially if you order pricey items such as fresh seafood, fish or *ibèric* ham. Sea bass and other popular fish and shellfish, such as giant prawns, lobster and crab, are generally priced by weight.

El compte (the bill) does not usually include service charges, but may include a small cover charge. Menu prices do not include 21 per cent VAT (IVA), which is usually added when the bill is calculated. Clients rarely tip waiters more than five per cent, often just rounding up the bill.

Cheques are never used in restaurants. Travellers' cheques are rarely accepted. Major credit cards and international debit cards are accepted in most larger restaurants. However, do not expect to pay by credit card in smaller eating or drinking places like tapas bars, village *hostals*, cafés, roadside pubs or *cellers*.

Wheelchair Access

All modern restaurants have disabled access, but since older restaurants were rarely designed for wheelchairs, phone in advance (or ask hotel staff to call) to check on access to tables and toilets.

Recommended Restaurants

The restaurants featured in this guide have been selected for their good value, great food, atmosphere or a combination of these. The listings cover a vast variety of eateries, from simple country café-bars serving a cheap yet tasty set lunch menu to bustling tapas bars, refined restaurants for fine dining and seafront eateries where you can enjoy fish fresh from the boats. Whether you are looking for a great *paella* by the beach, some tasty traditional cooking at a local market, or a spectacular *menú de degustació* (tasting menu) at an award-winning restaurant, the following pages provide plenty of choice.

The recommended restaurants highlighted as DK Choice have been chosen because they offer a special experience – exquisite food with local specialities, an inviting ambience, a beautiful location or are simply excellent value for money. Most are very popular, so it is advisable to book well in advance to guarantee a table.

Interior of 7 Portes restaurant *(see p145)* in the waterside Port Vell area

A Glossary of Typical Dishes

Catalan cuisine at its best, using fresh food, is known as *cuina de mercat* (market cuisine) and there is nowhere better to see produce laid out than at Barcelona's Boqueria market *(see p155)*. Peppers glisten, fish sparkle and no meat is wasted – even cocks' combs are sold for the pot. Olives come in all sorts of varieties. Spring brings *calçot* onions and broad (fava) beans, while strawberries, from Easter onwards, are eaten with *cava*. In autumn 30 varieties of mushroom spill across the stalls.

Tapes (Tapas – Snacks)

Bar-hopping around Barcelona is a delightful way to spend an evening, and a good way to try the many local dishes laid out on the counters.

Anxoves: anchovies.
Bunyols de bacallà: salt cod fritters.
Calamars a la romana: fried squid rings.
Escopinyes: cockles.
Pa amb tomàquet: bread rubbed with tomato, garlic and olive oil – a good filler.
Panadons d'espinacs: small spinach pasties or pies.
Patates braves: potato chunks in spicy tomato sauce.
Peixet fregit: small fried fish.
Pernil: ham – leg of pork seasoned and hung to dry.
Popets: baby octopus.
Truita: omelette.
Truita de patates: traditional potato and onion omelette.

Produce at La Boqueria, Barcelona's huge covered market on La Rambla

Pa amb tomàquet (bread with tomato), often served with ham

Entrants (Starters)

These are often unusual dishes and two may be enough for a meal. Some may appear as main courses.

Amanida catalana: Catalan mixed salad.
Arròs negre: squid-ink rice. Can be a main course.

Cargols a la llauna: snails in a spicy sauce.
Empedrat: salad of salt cod and white beans.
Escalivada: char-grilled or roasted aubergines (eggplant) and peppers, all drizzled with olive oil.
Espinacs a la catalana: spinach with pine nuts, raisins and ham; sometimes made with chard *(bledes)*.
Esqueixada: raw salt cod salad.
Faves a la catalana: a broad (fava) bean stew of black pudding, bacon, onion and garlic.
Fideus: noodles, usually served with fish and meat.
Garotes: raw sea urchins, from the Costa Brava, eaten with bread, garlic or spring onions.
Musclos: mussels.
Ous remenats amb camasecs: scrambled eggs with wild mushrooms.
Pa de fetge: liver pâté.
Sardines escabetxades: pickled sardines.
Xató: salt cod salad with *romesco* sauce.

Sopes (Soups)

Caldereta de llagosta: spiny lobster soup.
Escudella i carn d'olla: the liquid from Catalonia's traditional hotpot; the meat and vegetables *(carn i olla)* are served as a main course.
Gaspatxo: a clear, cold tomato soup with raw vegetables.
Sopa de farigola: thyme soup.
Sopa de bolets: mushroom soup.

Main Dishes

Methods of cooking are: *a la brasa* (over open flames); *bullit* (boiled); *cremat* (crisp fried or caramelized); *estofat* (stewed); *farcit* (stuffed); *al forn* (in the oven); *a la graella/ planxa* (cooked on a griddle, pan-fried or barbecued); *a la pedra* (on a hot stone).

Peix i Mariscos (Fish and Shellfish)

Allipebre d'anguiles: spicy eel stew.
Anfós al forn: baked stuffed grouper.
Calamars farcits: squid stuffed with pork, tomatoes and onions.
Cassola de peix: fish casserole.
Congre amb pèsols: conger eel with peas.
Escamarlans bullits: boiled crayfish.
Gambes a la planxa: prawns cooked on a griddle.
Graellada de peix: mixed seafood grill.
Llagosta a la brasa: lobster cooked over open flames.
Llagostins amb maionesa: king prawns and mayonnaise.
Llobarro al forn: baked sea bass.
Lluç a la planxa: hake cooked on a griddle.
Molls a la brasa: red mullet cooked over open flames.
Orada a la sal: gilthead bream baked in salt, which is removed on serving.
Paella valenciana: paella with chicken and seafood.
Peix amb romesco: seafood with the famous *romesco* sauce. Tarragona's master *romesco* makers compete each summer.
Rap a l'all cremat: angler fish with crisped garlic.
Sarsuela: fish, shellfish and spices, everything goes into the pot that gives its name to a light Spanish opera.

Sèpia amb pèsols: cuttlefish with peas.

Suquet de peix: Catalonia's principal fish stew, made with various fish, tomatoes, peppers, potatoes and almonds.

Verats a la brasa: mackerel cooked over open flames.

Carn (Meat)

Ànec amb naps: duck with turnips, ideally the "black" turnips of the Empordà region; also sometimes served with pears (*ànec amb peres*).

Boles de picolat: meatballs in tomato sauce. Meatballs with cuttlefish (*sèpia*) is classic *mar i muntanya* food.

Botifarra amb mongetes: sausage and beans.

Bou a l'adoba: beef casserole.

Costelles a la brasa amb allioli: flame-roast lamb cutlets with garlic mayonnaise.

Costelles de cabrit rostides: roast goat kid cutlets.

Cuixa de xai al forn: roast leg of lamb.

Estofat de bou: beef stew with sausages, potatoes, herbs and sometimes a little chocolate.

Estofat de quaresma: a filling bean and potato Lenten vegetable stew.

Freginat: calf's liver with onions.

Fricandó: braised veal with wild mushrooms.

Llom de porc: pork chops.

Oca amb peres: goose with pears – traditional village festival fare.

Niu: a huge fish and meat stew from Palafrugell, Costa Brava, with pigeon, cuttlefish, cod tripe, pig's trotters, egg and garlic mayonnaise.

Peus de porc a la llauna: pig's trotters in a spicy sauce.

Pollastre amb samfaina: chicken with *samfaina*.

Pota i tripa: lamb's trotters and tripe.

Tripa a la catalana: tripe in *sofregit* and wine with pine nuts and almonds.

Xai amb pèsols: lamb with peas.

Barcelona's cheese and honey market *(see p155)* in the Plaça del Pi

Caça (Game)

Although the hunting season is from October to February, some game is available all year round, especially rabbit.

Becada amb coc: woodcock in a bread roll.

Civet de llebre: jugged hare.

Conill a la brasa amb allioli: rabbit with garlic mayonnaise.

Conill amb cargols: rabbit with snails.

Conill amb xocolata: rabbit with garlic, liver, almonds, fried bread, chocolate and old wine.

Estofat de porc senglar amb bolets: wild boar casserole with wild mushrooms.

Guatlles amb salsa de magrana: quail in pomegranate sauce.

Perdiu: partridge.

Perdius amb farcellets de col: partridge with cabbage dumplings.

Verdures (Vegetables)

Albergínies: aubergines (eggplant).

Bledes: chard.

Bolets: mushrooms.

Calçots: leek-sized green onions, roasted on an open fire and dipped in a spicy tomato sauce. A spring-time speciality of the Tarragona region.

Carbassó arrebossat: battered courgettes (zucchini).

Carxofes: artichokes.

Julivert: parsley.

Mongetes tendres i patates: French beans and potatoes.

Aubergines (eggplant) and peppers, used in abundance

Pastanagues: carrots.

Pebrots: red peppers.

Postres (Desserts)

Although *pastisseria* (pastries) and *dolços* (sweets) are very popular in Catalonia, desserts in restaurants are generally uneventful. The choice may be simply ice cream or fruit: apple (*poma*), peach (*préssec*), banana (*plàtan*), orange (*taronja*), grapes (*raïm*).

Crema catalana: rich egg custard.

Figues amb aniset: figs in anise.

Flam: crème caramel.

Formatge: cheese. There is little local cheese.

Gelat: ice cream.

Mel i Mató: fresh goat's cheese, eaten with honey.

Menjar blanc: an almond blancmange.

Peres amb vi negre: pears in red wine.

Postre de músic: a bowl of mixed nuts and dried fruit, once given as a reward to itinerant musicians.

Recuit: curdled sheep's (or cow's) milk in a small pot.

Mel i mató – a traditional dessert of soft cheese served with honey

Where to Eat and Drink

Old Town

Betawi €
Indonesian **Map** 5 A1
C/Montsió 6, 08002
Tel 93 412 62 64
Intimate and charming restaurant located in the Barri Gòtic. Serves authentic Indonesian fare including tangy soups, salads and noodle dishes.

Bliss €
Café **Map** 5 B2
Plaça de Sant Just 4, 08002
Tel 93 268 10 22
Wonderful café with a terrace on an enchanting Gothic square. Perfect for light meals, coffee and cake, or just a romantic drink in the evening.

DK Choice

Bodega la Plata €
Tapas bar **Map** 5 A3
C/Mercé 2, 08002
Tel 93 315 10 09
Small, old-fashioned *bodega* that serves wine straight from the barrel. Choose from a good variety of red, white or rosé to have alongside a small selection of tasty tapas. Try the in-house speciality – freshly fried sardines. Ideal for a midday bite.

Café de l'Opera €
Café **Map** 5 A2
La Rambla 74, 08002
Tel 93 317 75 85
A classic café with Modernist-style decor and a terrace on the Rambla. The place hosts frequent live music events and has a Bottle Museum on the premises.

Can Culleretes €
Traditional Catalan **Map** 5 A2
C/Quintana 5, 08002
Tel 93 317 30 22 **Closed** Sun dinner, Mon
Barcelona's oldest restaurant, Can Culleretes dates from 1786. Great for classic dishes such as *botifarra amb seques* (country sausage with beans) and Catalan seafood stew.

Caravelle €
Café **Map** 5 A1
C/Pintor Fortuny 31, El Raval, 08001
Tel 93 317 98 92 **Closed** Mon
Lovely café-restaurant with sleek Scandinavian-style decor. Run and owned by an Australian chef, Caravelle serves delicious dishes. Great Sunday brunch.

Dos Trece €
Mediterranean **Map** 2 F2
C/Carme 40, El Raval, 08001
Tel 93 301 73 06
Relaxed, trendy spot with a small terrace. The menu features an eclectic mix of tasty dishes and cocktails. Try the lamb with pineapple chutney.

El Atril €
Brasserie **Map** 5 C2
C/Carders 23, 08003
Tel 93 310 12 20
Friendly bistro with a stone-walled dining room and outdoor tables. Dishes such as Belgian-style mussels supplement the usual steaks and salads. Good brunch.

El Quim de la Boqueria €
Market counter-bar **Map** 5 A2
La Rambla 91, 08002
Tel 93 301 98 10 **Closed** Sun
This famous counter-bar in the Boqueria food market is a local favourite for classic Catalan dishes. Try the signature *la botifarra amb mongetes i allioli*.

Granja Dulcinea €
Café **Map** 5 A2
C/Petritxol 2, 08002
Tel 93 302 68 24
A delightful little eatery that serves the best classic *xocolata amb xurros* (thick hot chocolate with fried dough strips) in the city. Regular queues here.

Granja M. Viader €
Café **Map** 5 A1
C/Xuclà 4–6, 08001
Tel 93 318 34 86 **Closed** Sun
Enchanting old-fashioned café dating back to 1870. Ideal for chocolate and *xurros* or coffee and cake. Also sells produce such as honey, cheeses and cold meats.

Juicy Jones €
Vegetarian **Map** 5 A2
C/Cardenal Casañas 7, 08001
Tel 93 302 43 30 **Closed** Mon
Funky, colourful restaurant that offers a wide range of freshly squeezed fruit and vegetable juices, as well as vegan meals.

Kasparo €
Café **Map** 2 F1
Plaça Vicenç Martorell 4, 08001
Tel 93 302 20 72 **Closed** Jan
With a terrace overlooking a children's playground, Kasparo is a popular hangout with mothers. Serves drinks and light meals.

Kiosko €
Gourmet burgers **Map** 5 B3
Av. Marquès de l'Argentera 1, 08003
Tel 93 310 73 13
Spectacular hamburgers served with organic bread and fries. Vegetarian options available.

La Báscula €
Vegetarian **Map** 5 C2
C/Flassaders 30, 08003
Tel 93 319 98 66
Charming café in a renovated old chocolate factory. Delicious vegan dishes, cakes and pastries.

La Paradeta €
Seafood **Map** 5 C2
C/Comercial 7, 08009
Tel 93 268 19 39 **Closed** Mon
Fish and chips, Barcelona-style. Choose from a selection of fish and watch it being cooked.

Outdoor tables at the bistro-style El Atril, in the Old Town

La Pineda
Tapas   €   **Map** 5 A2
C/Pi 16, 08002
Tel *93 302 43 93*   **Closed** *Sun*
Delightful little deli with a few tables. Enjoy wafer thin slices of Iberian ham with a glass of wine.

La Vinateria del Call
Tapas bar   €   **Map** 5 A2
C/Sant Domènec del Call 9, 08002
Tel *93 302 60 92*
Located in the city's old Jewish neighbourhood, this gourmet tavern serves delicious Catalan cheeses and charcuterie. Good selection of local wines.

Magnolia
Mediterranean   €   **Map** 5 A2
C/Ciutat 5, 08002
Tel *93 304 23 76*
Fashionable, laid-back restaurant offering exquisite Mediterranean cuisine and tasty tapas. Great value set lunch.

Mamacafé
Mediterranean   €   **Map** 2 F2
C/Doctor Dou 10, El Raval, 08001
Tel *93 301 29 40*   **Closed** *Sun, Mon & Tue eve*
Fun, colourful bistro near the Museu d'Art Contemporani. The menu changes every day, based on available seasonal ingredients. Great place for lunch.

Mesón David
Traditional Catalan   €   **Map** 2 E2
C/Carretes 63, 08001
Tel *93 441 59 34*
Loud, convivial restaurant; serves generous portions of authentic Catalan dishes such as *paella* with mixed meat and seafood.

Milk
Café   €   **Map** 5 A3
C/Gignas 21, 08002
Tel *93 268 09 22*
Trendy bistro and cocktail bar, serving meals with a creative touch at affordable prices. Great brunch.

Mosquito
Tapas   €   **Map** 5 C2
C/Carders 46, 08003
Tel *93 268 75 69*
The menu at Mosquito features a great range of pan-Asian tapas, including Hong Kong dim sum and Chinese dumplings.

Organic
Vegetarian   €   **Map** 2 F3
C/Junta de Comerç 11, 08001
Tel *93 301 09 02*
Friendly, good-value café. Imaginative seasonal menu featuring a range of main course dishes: vegetarian lasagnes, stews and an all-you-can-eat salad bar.

The casual, contemporary cocktail bar area at Milk

Pla de la Garsa
Tapas bar   €   **Map** 5 B2
C/Assaonadors 13, 08003
Tel *93 315 24 13*
Situated in the stone-vaulted stables of a 17th-century palace, this establishment serves cheese and ham platters, along with more elaborate dishes.

Sandwich & Friends
Café   €   **Map** 5 B3
Passeig del Born 27, 08003
Tel *93 310 07 86*   **Closed** *Thu–Sun*
A huge mural by the artist Jordi Labanda dominates the wall of this modern café. Choose from a vast selection of sandwiches.

Taller de Tapas
Tapas bar   €   **Map** 5 B2
C/Argenteria 51, 08003
Tel *93 268 85 59*
This reliable chain restaurant with a contemporary urban feel offers a wide range of freshly made tapas. Sunny outside terrace.

Teresa Carles
Vegetarian   €   **Map** 5 A1
C/Jovellanos 2, 08001
Tel *93 317 18 29*
Elegant family-run place with stylish Scandinavian-style wooden interiors. One of the city's best vegetarian restaurants.

Tlaxcal
Mexican   €   **Map** 5 C3
C/Comerç 27, 08003
Tel *93 268 41 34*   **Closed** *Tue*
Tlaxcal offers a fascinating choice of authentic tacos, soups and other Mexican dishes. Great food, packed with plenty of flavour.

Zim
Tapas   €   **Map** 5 B2
C/Daqueria 20, 08002
Tel *93 412 65 48*   **Closed** *Sun*
Miniature bar offering wines and *cava* by the glass accompanied by simple tapas, with a focus on fine Catalan cheeses.

7 Portes
Traditional Catalan   €€   **Map** 5 B3
Passeig Isabel II 14, 08003
Tel *93 319 30 33*
One of Barcelona's oldest restaurants and still going strong, this long-standing institution is famous for its *paella* and other classic dishes.

Agua
Mediterranean   €€   **Map** 6 D4
Passeig Marítim de la Barceloneta 30, 08003
Tel *93 225 12 72*
Stylish restaurant on the beach with floor-to-ceiling windows and abstract fish sculptures. Perfect for a lazy *paella* lunch in the sun.

Agut
Traditional Catalan   €€   **Map** 5 A3
C/Gignàs 16, 08002
Tel *93 315 17 09*
Enjoy slabs of meat grilled over charcoal and served with wild mushrooms in season.

Bacaro
Italian/Venetian   €€   **Map** 2 E3
C/Jerusalem 6, 08001
Tel *695 796 066*
This delightful eatery, tucked away behind the busy Boqueria market, offers authentic Venetian specialities and wines.

For more information on types of restaurants *see page 141*

Once the haunt of artists, Els Quatre Gats (The Four Cats) is an iconic Barcelona rendezvous

DK Choice

Big Fish   €€
Seafood   **Map** 5 C2
C/Comercial 9, 08003
Tel *93 268 17 28*
Gorgeous, retro-chic interiors
with cleverly mismatched
furnishings. Relish fresh,
beautiful sushi and seafood
prepared in a variety of styles
from Asian to Mediterranean.
Loud music after 11pm, when
trendy locals gather here.

Brasserie Flo   €€
Catalan/French   **Map** 5 B1
C/Jonqueres 10, 08003
Tel *93 319 31 02*   **Closed** *Mon*
Elegant brasserie with *fin-de-siècle*
decor. Serves classic Catalan
cuisine with a French twist and
sumptuous home-made desserts.

Ca l'Isidre   €€
Traditional Catalan   **Map** 2 E3
C/Flors 12, 08001
Tel *93 441 11 39*   **Closed** *Sun*
Family-owned tavern, famous
for classic Catalan dishes
prepared with superb local
produce. Excellent wine cellar.

Cal Pep   €€
Tapas bar   **Map** 5 B3
Plaça des les Olles 8, 08003
Tel *93 310 79 61*   **Closed** *Sat dinner,
Sun, Mon lunch*
Long-established, characterful
bar serving a selection of freshly
made tapas.

Can Majó   €€
Mediterranean   **Map** 5 B5
C/Almirall Aixada 23, 08003
Tel *93 221 54 55*   **Closed** *Sun dinner,
Mon*
Great seafood restaurant in
Barceloneta with consistently

good traditional cuisine; the
paella is fabulous. The terrace
has sea views.

Can Solé   €€
Seafood   **Map** 5 B4
C/Sant Carles 4, 08003
Tel *93 221 50 12*   **Closed** *Sun dinner,
Mon*
Traditional restaurant with a pretty
tiled interior. The menu features
classic rice dishes and stews
featuring a variety of seafood.

Cuines Santa Caterina   €€
Modern Catalan   **Map** 5 B2
Av. Francesc Cambó 16, 08003
Tel *93 268 99 18*
Tasty cuisine prepared with
seasonal ingredients freshly
bought from the adjoining market.
Try the baby squid and bean salad.

El Suquet de l'Almirall   €€
Mediterranean   **Map** 5 B5
Passeig Joan de Borbó 65, 08003
Tel *93 321 62 33*   **Closed** *Sun*
Seafood restaurant offering fresh
fish brought in daily from the
quays near the restaurant.

Els Quatre Gats   €€
Traditional Catalan   **Map** 5 A1
C/Montsió 3 bis, 08002
Tel *93 302 41 40*
Beautifully restored tavern,
decorated with original works of
early 20th-century artists. Young
Picasso held his first show here.
The food is delicious; the pork
cheek with prawn is superb.

Espai Sucre   €€
Desserts   **Map** 5 C2
C/Princesa 53, 08003
Tel *93 268 16 30*   **Closed** *Sun & Mon*
Prestigious cooking school with a
restaurant that has menus
composed entirely of exquisite
sweet and savoury desserts.

Gravin   €€
Italian   **Map** 5 B3
C/Rera Palau 3–5, 08003
Tel *93 268 46 28*
Enjoy sophisticated Italian food
from the Puglia region in an
elegant dining room with
exposed brick walls. Come here
for the *tagliono al limone* (pasta
made with lemon and hake).

DK Choice

Kaiku   €€
Mediterranean   **Map** 5 B5
Plaça del Mar 1, 08003
Tel *93 221 90 82*   **Closed** *Mon*
A deceptively simple-looking
beachfront restaurant, Kaiku
serves fantastic local dishes
prepared with smoked rice and
fresh vegetables grown in their
garden. Enjoy them with a bottle
of chilled rosé on the terrace.
Excellent desserts; you can have
a selection served on a platter.

La Bella Napoli   €€
Italian   **Map** 2 D3
C/Margarit 14, 08004
Tel *93 442 50 56*
Italian-run pizzeria with authentic
pizzas cooked to perfection in a
wood-burning stove. Popular, so
book ahead.

The brightly lit contemporary interior at
Espai Sucre

La Mar Salada
€€
Mediterranean **Map** 2 B5
Passeig Joan Borbó 58–59, 08003
Tel *93 221 21 27* **Closed** *Tue*
Bright, modern seafood restaurant
in Barceloneta with views across
the port. Fantastic set lunch.

Lo de Flor
€€
Mediterranean **Map** 2 E2
C/Carretes 18, 08001
Tel *93 442 38 53*
Romantic, rustic restaurant with
minimalist decor and delicious
Mediterranean fare. Short but
well-chosen wine list.

Mam i Teca
€€
Modern Catalan **Map** 2 F2
C/Lluna 4, 08001
Tel *93 441 33 35* **Closed** *Tue*
Mam i Teca serves fantastic
Catalan dishes prepared with
superb, locally sourced produce.
Excellent wine list and a good
range of Scottish single malts.

Montiel
€€
Modern Catalan **Map** 5 C2
C/Flassaders 19, Born, 08003
Tel *93 268 37 29*
Charming restaurant with dishes
inspired by locally sourced pro-
duce. Do not miss the wonderfully
tender *garrinet* (suckling pig).

Ocaña
€€
Mediterranean **Map** 5 A3
Plaça Reial 13, 08002
Tel *93 676 48 14*
Trendy restaurant set in a huge,
splendidly restored town house,
with a terrace looking over the
lively Plaça Reial. Tapas and
snacks are served all day.

Pez Vela
€€
Mediterranean
Passeig del Mare Nostrum 19, 08039
Tel *93 221 63 17* **Closed** *Sun dinner*
Fashionable spot on the beach
serving a range of cuisine but
strong on fresh salads and rice
dishes. The set *paella* menu is
great value for money.

Pla
€€
Fusion **Map** 2 F2
C/Bellafila 5, 08002
Tel *93 412 65 52*
Hidden down a narrow street in
the Gothic Quarter, this reliable
restaurant offers deftly prepared
fusion cuisine in stylish surroundings. Tasting menu available.

Quimet i Quimet
€€
Tapas bar **Map** 2 E4
C/Poeta Cabanyes 25, 08004
Tel *93 442 31 42* **Closed** *Sun; Aug*
Tiny but charming *bodega* with
bottles displayed up to the ceiling.
Delicious cheeses and canapés.

Rincón de Aragón
€€
Aragonese/Spanish **Map** 5 B2
C/Carme 28, 08001
Tel *93 302 67 89* **Closed** *Mon & Tue*
Traditional restaurant specializing
in the cuisine of the Spanish
region of Aragon. Choose from
delicacies such as roast lamb,
fresh trout and tasty stews.

Senyor Parellada
€€
Mediterranean **Map** S3
C/Argenteria 37, 08003
Tel *93 310 50 94*
Elegant restaurant in a handsome
19th-century townhouse. The
creative menu includes trotters
with cuttlefish and grilled baby
squid pan-fried with chorizo
sausage. Reserve in advance.

DK Choice

Suculent €€
Tapas **Map** 2 F3
Rambla de Raval 43, 08001
Tel *93 443 65 79* **Closed** *Mon,
Sun dinner*
A pretty old *bodega* reinvented
as a trendy gastro bar by a trio
of celebrity chefs. Suculent
offers a range of creative tapas,
platters of carefully selected
cheeses and cured meats, as well
as more substantial fare such as
lamb chops and rice dishes.

Delicious tapas is served at the bar at
Dos Palillos

DK Choice

Café de L'Acadèmia €€€
Modern Catalan **Map** 5 B3
C/Lledó 1, Plaça Sant Just, 08002
Tel *93 319 82 53* **Closed** *Sat, Sun*
A long-established favourite,
Café de L'Acadèmia offers tasty,
modern Catalan cuisine in a cozy
brick-lined dining room. The
menu changes regularly based
on what is freshly available in
the market. Spectacular desserts.
Book a table on the atmospheric,
candle-lit terrace overlooking
the enchanting Gothic square.

Comerç 24
€€€
Modern Catalan **Map** 5 C2
C/Comerç 24, 08003
Tel *93 319 21 02* **Closed** *Sun & Mon*
Tapas bar with daring and
sophisticated gastronomy from
the Catalan chef Carles Abellan.
Reservations necessary.

Dos Palillos
€€€
Tapas/Asian **Map** 2 F2
EC/Iisabets 9, 08001
Tel *93 304 05 13* **Closed** *Sun & Mon*
Ultra-chic yet relaxed restaurant
with a Michelin star. Serves
spectacular Asian fusion tapas.

Koy Shunka
€€€
Japanese **Map** 5 B3
C/Copons 7, 08002
Tel *93 412 79 39* **Closed** *Mon,
Sun dinner*
Widely regarded as the best
Japanese restaurant in the city,
this stylish place features a menu
that ranges from classic dishes to
more inventive fare.

Quo Vadis
€€€
Catalan/French **Map** 2 F2
C/Carme 7, 08001
Tel *93 177 07 16*
Long-established and authentic
French-Catalan restaurant. A
favourite for a pre-opera dinner.
Try the house soup.

The intimate and authentic dining area at Suculent

For more information on types of restaurants *see page 141*

The sleek, modern dining area at the popular Saüc restaurant

Saüc €€€
Mediterranean   Map 5 B3
Via Laietana 49, 08003
Tel *93 321 01 89*
Relish award-winning creative cuisine by the Michelin-starred Chef Xavier Franco in the über-chic surroundings of the Ohla Hotel. Reservations essential.

Eixample

Bar Calders €
Café   Map 2 D2
C/Parlament 25, 08015
Tel *93 329 93 49*
Dedicated to the Catalan writer Pere Calders, this place is a great spot for a vermouth. The menu includes delicious tapas, hummus and salads. Small pretty terrace.

El Filete Ruso €
Gourmet burgers   Map 3 B3
C/Enric Granados 95, 08008
Tel *93 217 13 10*   **Closed** *mid-Aug*
The food here is made with organic and locally sourced produce. The menu features grilled gourmet burgers, including a vegetarian option, and handcrafted desserts.

La Bodegueta €
Tapas   Map 3 A3
Rambla de Catalunya 100, 08008
Tel *93 215 48 94*
A good-value tapas bar with marble-topped tables and wooden cabinets in an antique wine cellar. The menu includes classics such as *patates braves*, Iberian cold cuts and *esqueixada*.

Café Emma €€
French   Map 3 B4
C/Pau Claris 142, 08009
Tel *93 215 12 16*
Fashionable bistro serving classic dishes such as French onion soup and *onglet* (hanger steak) with shallot sauce. Warm and welcoming atmosphere.

Can Ravell €€
Traditional Catalan   Map H4
C/Aragó 313
Tel *93 457 51 14*   **Closed** *Sun*
A delicatessen-cum-restaurant where guests share one huge table under a chandelier and dine on Catalan classics. Well-stocked vintage wine cellar.

Casa Alfonso €€
Traditional Catalan   Map 3 B5
C/Roger de Llúria 6, 08010
Tel *93 301 97 83*   **Closed** *Sun*
This cozy restaurant features hanging hams and checked tablecloths. Try the sumptuous sausages, croquettes and tapas on offer. A great spot for lunch.

Fábrica Moritz €€
Tapas   Map 2 E1
Ronda de Sant Antoni 39, 08011
Tel *93 426 50 00*
Huge restaurant and wine-bar in a beautifully renovated Modernista building that was originally a 19th-century brewery. Sample fresh beer on site.

Ikibana €€
Fusion   Map 2 D2
Av. del Paral.lel 148, 08015
Tel *93 424 4648*
A striking interior and Japanese-Brazilian fusion cuisine have made this one of Barcelona's hottest restaurants. The menu includes a variety of wines and sake.

Monvínic €€
Modern Catalan   Map 3 A5
C/ Diputació 249, 08007
Tel *93 272 61 87*   **Closed** *Sat & Sun*
A staggering selection of wines in the large, stylish wine bar and delicious modern cuisine in the dining room.

Petit Comitè €€
Modern Catalan   Map 3 A3
Passeig de la Concepció 13, 08008
Tel *93 550 06 20*   **Closed** *Mon*
Modern Catalan fare with a dash of French aplomb is on offer here. Excellent wine list.

Tapaç 24 €€
Tapas   Map 3 A5
C/Diputació 269, 08007
Tel *93 488 09 77*   **Closed** *Sun*
Inventive selection of fantastic tapas by chef Carles Abellan. Delicacies such as Bikini Comerç 24 and Mcfoie burger are must-tries here.

Tickets €€
Designer tapas   Map 1 C2
Av. Paral·lel 164, 08015
Tel *93 292 42 53*   **Closed** *Mon & Tue; mid-Aug, late Dec-early Jan*
Imaginative tapas and a colourful, funfair-themed interior combine in this restaurant. It is an unmissable destination for devotees of the cuisine created by the Adrià brothers. Extensive selection of sparkling wines.

Caldeni €€€
Modern Catalan   Map 3 C4
C/València 452, 08013
Tel *93 232 58 11*   **Closed** *Sun & Mon*
Fantastic contemporary cuisine from Dani Lechuga, a rising young chef in Barcelona's culinary scene. Try the "Meat Special Selection" menu, which features dishes prepared with wagyu Kobe and Nebraska Angus beef.

Casa Calvet €€€
Traditional Catalan   Map 3 B5
C/Casp 48, 08010
Tel *93 412 40 12*   **Closed** *Sun*
One of Antoni Gaudí's earliest commissions, this Modernista building now houses a restaurant. Modern cooking executed with panache. Don't miss the white tuna with spicy yogurt.

Cinc Sentits €€€
Modern Catalan   Map 2 F1
C/Aribau 58, 08011
Tel *93 323 94 90*
Exquisite contemporary Catalan cuisine by Michelin-starred chef Jordi Artal. Your dining choices comprise a trio of set menus: *gastronòmic, essència* and *sensaciones*.

Softly lit dining room at Cinc Sentits

Elegant interior of the classy Roca Moo

Fonda Gaig €€€
Modern Catalan
Còrcega 200, 08036
Tel 93 453 20 20
Smart bistro with stylish modern decor, serving sophisticated local cuisine by one of the city's top chefs, Carles Gaig.

L'Olivé €€€
Modern Catalan **Map** 3 A4
Balmes 47, 08007
Tel 93 452 19 90 **Closed** Sun dinner
Classic restaurant offering fine Catalan fare prepared with whatever is freshest at the market. Wide variety of delicious home-made desserts.

Moments €€€
Modern Catalan **Map** 3 A5
Passeig de Gràcia 38–40, 08007
Tel 93 151 87 81
Glamorous restaurant situated in the Mandarin Oriental hotel. The mouth-watering, multi-award-winning menu is created by superchef Carme Ruscalleda.

Roca Moo €€€
Modern Catalan **Map** 3 A3
Rosselló 265, 08008
Tel 93 445 40 00 **Closed** Sun & Mon
This ultra-chic restaurant in Hotel Omm features a menu overseen by the Roca brothers of El Celler de Can Roca (see p152). Try one of the three fine tasting menus with matching wines.

Tragaluz €€€
Mediterranean **Map** 3 A3
Passatge de la Concepció 5, 08008
Tel 93 487 06 21
Chic uptown restaurant with a huge skylight. Offers a wide-ranging menu of Mediterranean fare. The ground floor features an oyster bar and a Japanese natural charcoal barbecue grill.

Windsor €€€
Modern Catalan
C/Còrsega 286, 08080
Tel 93 237 75 88 **Closed** Sun
Contemporary Catalan haute cuisine is served here. The menu is based on seasonal local produce. Dine in elegant surroundings with chandeliers. There's also a pretty garden for alfresco dining.

Further Afield

DK Choice

1a de Santa Teresa €
Café **Map** 3 B2
C/Santa Teresa 1, Gràcia, 08012
Tel 93 186 83 17
This cozy and inviting restaurant is well off the beaten tourist track. Come to 1a de Santa Teresa for the delicious tapas including fabulous home-made croquetas (croquettes) or the equally good coffee and cakes. Relax over an excellent lunch or enjoy a refreshing cocktail at the end of a long day's sightseeing.

Anònim €
Tapas **Map** 3 A2
Riera de Sant Miquel 19, 08006
Tel 61 967 72 03
Sophisticated tapas and raciones from an award-winning young chef are on offer at this stylish modern restaurant.

Café Adonis 1940 €
Café **Map** 3 C3
C/Bailèn 188, Gràcia, 08037
Tel 93 459 12 92
Wonderfully old-fashioned, split-level café-bar with a simple menu featuring great burgers, salads and sandwiches.

Café Pagès €
Café **Map** 3 C2
C/Torrent de l'Olla 27, 08012
Tel 93 368 09 58
A Gràcia favourite with retro-style decor, Café Pagès offers a tasty and affordable set lunch menu. Come here for great home-made cakes and coffee.

Café Salombó €
Café **Map** 3 C2
C/Torrijos 51, 08012
Tel 93 218 69 66
This large, split-level café with pool tables is a popular neighbourhood haunt. Serves everything from a good daily set lunch to cocktails in the evening. Regular live music.

Cal Boter €
Traditional Catalan **Map** 3 C2
C/Tordera 62, 08012
Tel 93 204 85 18 **Closed** Sun dinner, Mon
An excellent place for Catalan comfort food. The menu includes traditional carns a la brasa (grilled meats) and local sausages. Fantastic set lunch.

Kathmandú €
Nepalese **Map** 3 C3
C/Còrsega 421, 08037
Tel 93 459 37 69
Sample tasty, aromatic Nepalese dishes including barbecued meat, thalis, tandoori specialities and spicy curries. Great value lunch menu.

Abou Khalil €€
Lebanese
C/Santaló 88, 08021
Tel 93 201 88 30
Barcelona's first Lebanese restaurant is also its best, serving delicious eastern Mediterranean dishes. Live music and dance some nights.

The simple dining area at Tragaluz, chic restaurant in Eixample

For more information on types of restaurants see page 141

Atmosphère €€
Mediterranean **Map** 3 B2
C/Venus 1–3, 08012
Tel 93 458 20 44
Cozy and charming, Atmosphère serves imaginative cuisine with a French twist. Try the cod tartare with orange and fennel and their speciality, *tarte Tatin*.

Casa de Tapes Cañota €€
Tapas **Map** 1 B2
C/Lleida 7, 08004
Tel 93 325 91 71 **Closed** Sun dinner, Mon
The big and bustling Casa de Tapes Cañota near Montjuïc serves freshly made gourmet tapas such as succulent beef with garlic and a seafood basket.

Envalira €€
Mediterranean **Map** 3 B1
Plaça del Sol 13, 08012
Tel 93 218 58 13 **Closed** Sun dinner, Mon; Aug
A family-run restaurant with a laidback ambience. The menu includes delicious Mediterranean rice dishes and Galician shellfish. Attentive service.

La Lluna Bistro €€
Bistro
C/Moià 1, 08006
Tel 93 414 70 67
Stylish uptown eatery with a club feel; offers a simple menu of dishes ranging from burgers to *yakisoba* (Japanese noodles).

La Venta €€
Catalan
Plaça del Doctor Andreu s/n, 08035
Tel 93 212 64 55 **Closed** Sun dinner
Enjoy flavourful local cuisine with stunning panoramic views of the city. This restaurant is housed in a 19th-century Modernista building on the slopes of Tibidabo.

The cool, vaulted dining space of Michelin-starred ABaC

Tram-Tram €€
Modern Catalan
C/Major de Sarrià 121, 08017
Tel 93 204 85 18 **Closed** Sun dinner, Mon (except Mon dinner in Jul), Easter, late Aug & Christmas
A smart, welcoming interior and a delightful terrace are the setting for classic Catalan favourites prepared with a modern twist by young chef Isidre Soler.

Wagokoro €€
Japanese **Map** 3 A1
C/Regàs 35, 08006
Tel 93 501 93 40 **Closed** Sun & Mon
Fantastic, authentic Japanese food, and beverages such as *nihonshu* (sake), *shochu* (spirit) and *umeshu* (fruit liqueur), served in a simple dining room by a charming couple.

ABaC €€€
Modern Catalan
Av. Tibidabo 1, 08022
Tel 93 319 66 00 **Closed** Sun & Mon
Outstanding cuisine from young chef Jordi Cruz, which has earned him two Michelin stars. Enjoy delicacies such as smoked steak tartare and veil of mustard and pepper bread brittle.

Alkimia €€€
Modern Catalan **Map** 3 C2
C/Indústria 79, 08025
Tel 93 207 61 15 **Closed** Sat, Sun, Easter, 3 weeks in Aug & Christmas
This small designer restaurant offers an unforgettable culinary experience from one of the city's most sophisticated chefs, Jordi Vilà. Feast on dishes such as noras rice with saffron and fresh langoustine.

Botafumeiro €€€
Seafood **Map** 3 A2
C/Gran de Gràcia 81, 08012
Tel 93 218 42 30
Large, traditional restaurant with white-aproned waiters bearing platters of ultra-fresh fish to the crowded tables. Try the tender *pulpo Gallego* (Galician octopus).

Con Gracia €€€
European **Map** 3 B2
C/Martínez de la Rosa 8, 08012
Tel 93 238 02 01 **Closed** Sat dinner, Sun & Mon; Christmas
Creative cuisine based on fresh market produce served in a series of sophisticated set menus. Try the wine tasting menu, where each course is paired with a wine.

Els Pescadors €€€
Seafood
Plaça de Prim 1, 08005
Tel 93 225 20 18
Elegant fish restaurant in Poble Nou. Reserve a table on the charming terrace, which overlooks a picturesque square and tuck into beautifully fresh seafood and classic Catalan rice dishes.

Hisop €€€
Modern Catalan
Passatge de Marimon 9, 08021
Tel 93 241 32 33 **Closed** Sat lunch, Sun; early Jan & early Aug
Minimalist natural wood decor ensures the focus is firmly on food at Hisop where the experimental cuisine is always a treat. Excellent wine list with Catalan and Spanish vintages.

La Balsa €€€
Mediterranean
C/Infanta Isabel 4, 08022
Tel 93 211 50 48 **Closed** Sun dinner, Mon lunch
Escape the hustle of the city at this relaxed garden oasis. Sample fresh Mediterranean cuisine on a leafy, plant-filled terrace.

Roig Robí €€€
Modern Catalan **Map** 3 A2
C/Sèneca 20, 08006
Tel 93 218 92 22 **Closed** Sat lunch, Sun; late Aug
Enjoy exquisite Catalan cuisine in elegant surroundings. Good selection of *bacalà* (salt-cod) dishes. Romantic garden terrace for summer dining.

Minimalist but intimate dining room at Wagokoro

Catalonia

ANGLÈS: L'Aliança D'Anglès €€
Modern Catalan
C/Jacint Verdaguer 3, 17160
Tel 972 42 01 56 **Closed** Sun–Wed
dinner, Mon lunch
Fantastic, creative cuisine in an
early 20th-century villa,
surrounded by gardens. Superb
selection of Spanish wines.

ARTIES: Casa Irene €€€
Traditional Catalan
C/Major 3, 25599
Tel 973 64 43 64 **Closed** Mon
Elegant stone-built hotel and
restaurant, which serves an
exquisite menu. A perfect place
to dine after a day on the nearby
ski slopes.

BANYOLES: Ca L'Arpa €€€
Modern Catalan
Passeig Industria 5, 17820
Tel 972 57 23 53
Excellent Michelin-starred rest-
aurant within a chic hotel in the
historic Banyoles quarter. Patrons
can see their food being prepared.

BEGUR: Fonda Caner €€
Traditional Catalan
C/Pi i Ralló 10, Costa Brava, 17255
Tel 972 62 23 91
Traditional restaurant with
old-fashioned charm tucked
away in Begur's old quarter.
Serves seasonal cuisine. Enjoy the
mixed seafood stew.

BEGUR: Restaurant Rostei €€
Mediterranean
C/Concepció Pi 8, Costa Brava, 17255
Tel 972 62 42 15 **Closed** Jun–
Sep: Mon, Dec–mid Jan
Romantic, family-run restaurant
that serves tasty seafood and
fantastic desserts.

BESALÚ: Cúria Reial €€
Traditional Catalan
Plaça de la Llibertat 14, 17850
Tel 972 59 02 63
Delicious food is served in a
beautiful historic building under
stone vaults. Try the duck with
foie gras and coca d'escalivada.

CALDES D'ESTRAC: Marola €€
Seafood
Passeig dels Anglesos 6, 08393
Tel 93 791 32 00 **Closed** Tue
Modest yet charming beachfront
restaurant in Caldes d'Estrac. The
ideal setting to enjoy fresh
seafood and paella.

CAMBRILS: Can Bosch €€€
Seafood
Rambla Jaume I 19, 43850
Tel 977 36 00 19 **Closed** Sun dinner,
Mon; late Dec–late Jan
Smart restaurant overlooking the
port. Great seafood prepared with
a contemporary twist. Patrons
rave about the arroz negro (rice
cooked in squid ink).

ESCUNHAU: El Niu €€
Traditional Catalan
Deth Pònt 1, 25539
Tel 973 64 14 06
Traditional mountain inn in
picturesque Escunhau. The menu
features classic local cuisine,
especially grilled meats. Open
fireplace in winter.

FALSET: El Celler de l'Aspic €€
Traditional Catalan
C/Miquel Barceló 31, 43730
Tel 977 83 12 46 **Closed** Sun dinner,
Wed
Charming, rustic restaurant
with delicious dishes made
using locally sourced organic
produce. The menu changes
seasonally. Extensive selection
of regional wines.

Elegant interior of the Hotel Emporada's
El Motel restaurant in Figueres

FIGUERES: El Motel €€€
Traditional Catalan
Av. Salvador Dalí 170, 17600
Tel 972 50 05 62
Located in the Hotel Emporada,
this elegant restaurant enjoys a
fine reputation for serving classic
regional cuisine. Great wine list.
Excellent fixed-price menu.

GARRAF: La Cúpula €€
Seafood
Platja de Garraf, 08871
Tel 936 32 00 15 **Closed** Mon & Tue
With a splendid clifftop setting
overlooking the pretty Garraf
beach, La Cúpula is a great place
for a fish lunch. There is also an
inexpensive xiringuito next door.

GIRONA: Divinum €€
Tapas
C/Albereda 7, 17004
Tel 872 08 02 18 **Closed** Sun,
Mon dinner
Chic, contemporary restaurant
serving inventive tapas,
accompanied by an excellent
selection of wines.

The brightly lit simple dining area at El Celler de l'Aspic in Falset

For more information on types of restaurants see page 141

DK Choice

GIRONA: El Celler de Can Roca   €€€
Modern Catalan
C/Can Sunyer 48, 17007
Tel 972 22 21 57   **Closed** Sun, Mon, Easter, mid-Aug & Christmas
Voted regularly as one of the world's top restaurants, El Celler de Can Roca is a temple to molecular gastronomy and boasts three Michelin stars. The place is run by the three Roca brothers: Joan is head chef, Jordi is dessert chef and Josep is the sommelier. Expect innovative dishes such as caramelized olives served on a bonsai tree and oysters with champagne.

HORTA DE SANT JOAN: Venta del Romer   €
Traditional Catalan
C/Valderrobres a Tortosa 5, 43596
Tel 977 43 54 70
Rustic country inn with home-cooked food. Famous for its *calçots* (a barbecued leek-like vegetable dipped in nutty romesco sauce) in spring.

L'AMETLLA DE MAR: L'Alguer   €€
Seafood
C/Trafalgar 21, 43860
Tel 977 45 61 24   **Closed** Mon; mid Dec–mid Jan
Enjoy fresh seafood with magnificent sea views in this stunning waterfront dining room with door-to-ceiling glass windows. Great value set lunch menu.

L'ESPLUGA DE FRANCOLÍ: Hostal del Senglar   €€
Traditional Catalan
Plaça Montserrat Canals 1, 43440
Tel 977 87 04 11
Excellent hotel-restaurant near the Monestir de Poblet. Great for flame-grilled meats and hearty country dishes.

LLAGOSTERA: Els Tinars   €€€
Modern Catalan
Ctra de Sant Feliu a Girona, 17240
Tel 972 83 06 26   **Closed** Sun dinner, Mon
Superb contemporary cuisine by an award-winning young chef in an elegant dining room and shaded terrace. Good set menus.

LLEIDA: La Huerta   €€
Traditional Catalan
Av. Tortosa 7, 25005
Tel 973 24 24 13
Delicious local dishes such as fine winter stews, grilled fresh fish and wild mushrooms in season. Warm and friendly service.

Diners can watch their food being prepared at La Huerta in Lleida

MONTSENY: Can Barrina   €€
Traditional Catalan
Carretera Palautordera al Montseny, Km. 12, 08469
Tel 93 867 91 44
Beautiful country restaurant and hotel located in the Montseny Natural Park. Wonderful food.

PERELADA: Cal Sacristà   €€
Traditional Catalan
C/Rodona 2, 17491
Tel 972 53 83 01
Scrumptious Catalan cuisine served in a restored old convent. Save room for dessert.

RIPOLL: Reccapolis   €€
Traditional Catalan
C/Sant Joan 68, 17500
Tel 972 70 21 06   **Closed** Sun–Thu dinner, Wed lunch
Enjoy savoury country favourites

in a handsome 20th-century house with a garden. Excellent set lunch and takeaway menu. Efficient and attentive service.

ROSES: Rafa's   €€€
Seafood
C/Sant Sebastià 56, 17480
Tel 972 25 40 03
Informal, convivial and immensely popular seafood restaurant. A favourite with the chef Ferran Adrià of El Bulli fame. The menu changes daily.

SANT CARLES DE LA RÀPITA: Miami Ca Pons   €€
Seafood
Passeig Marítim 18–20, 43540
Tel 977 74 05 51
Classic seafront restaurant in the Hotel Miami Mar offering great value and quality seafood. Good base for exploring the Ebro delta.

SANT CELONI: Can Fabes   €€€
Modern Catalan
C/Sant Joan 6, 08470
Tel 93 867 28 51   **Closed** Sun dinner, Mon & Tue
Expect truly stellar cuisine from Xavier Pellicer at this outstanding Michelin-starred restaurant. The seasonal menu is based on local fare such as truffles from Osona and rice from the Ebro delta.

SANT FELIU DE GUÍXOLS: Bahía   €€
Seafood
Passeig del Mar 17–19, 17320
Tel 972 32 02 19
Beachfront restaurant serving local specialities from this region of the Costa Brava, such as *brandada de bacallà* (cod puréed with olive oil) and *cim-i-tomba* (fish stew).

The picture-perfect traditional interior of Can Fabes in Sant Celoni

SANT FELIU DE GUÍXOLS:
Cau Del Pescador   €€
Seafood
C/Sant Doménec 11, 17220
Tel *972 32 40 52*
Smart, family-run fish restaurant
with rustic decor set in an old
fisherman's cottage. Do not miss
the famous *suquet* (seafood stew).

SANT FELIU DE GUÍXOLS:
Villa Más   €€€
Traditional Catalan
Passeig de Sant Pol 95, 17220
Tel *972 82 25 26* **Closed** *Mon except
Jun–Aug; early Dec–early Jan*
Enchanting 19th-century villa
overlooking the Sant Pol beach.
Serves outstanding Catalan cuisine
and a fine selection of wines.

SANT FRUITÓS DE BAGES:
L'Angle de Món Sant Benet €€€
Modern Catalan
*Camí de Sant Benet de Bages s/n,
08272*
Tel *93 875 94 29* **Closed** *mid-Aug*
Minimalist dining room housed
in a medieval monastery. Dine on
tasty, memorable contemporary
Catalan cuisine by the Michelin-
starred chef, Jordi Cruz.

SANT JOAN DE LES ABADESSES:
Casa Rudes   €
Traditional Catalan
C/Major 10, 17860
Tel *972 72 01 15*
Established in 1893 and still a
popular local favourite for classic
Catalan dishes. A children's menu
is available.

SANT POL DE MAR: Sant Pau €€€
Modern Catalan
C/Nou 10, 08395
Tel *93 760 06 62* **Closed** *Sun, Mon,
Thu lunch; also first three weeks of
May & Nov*
Top chef Carme Ruscalleda works
her magic at one of Spain's best

Warm dining area at Sant Pau in Sant
Pol de Mar

restaurants. Marvel at wonderful
dishes created from delicate
courgette flowers, wild boar and
espardenyes (sea cucumber).

SANT SADURNÍ D'ANOIA:
La Cava d'en Sergi   €€
Modern Catalan
C/València 17, 08770
Tel *93 891 16 16* **Closed** *Mon, last
Sun of the month; 1 Jan, Easter, first
three weeks of Aug & Christmas.*
Stylish restaurant serving
modernized versions of Catalan
classics. Wonderful range of local
wines. Friendly service.

SITGES: Cinnamon   €
Fusion
*Passeig de Pujades 2, Vallpineda,
08750*
Tel *93 894 71 66* **Closed** *Sun–Thu
dinner, Tue lunch*
Delicious Asian fusion cuisine in
an enchanting old farmhouse. All
dishes are bursting with flavour,
but start with the *tabbouleh*
(Middle Eastern salad). Hosts DJ
sessions and other music events.

SITGES: El Pou   €
Gourmet tapas
C/Sant Pau 5, 08770
Tel *93 128 99 21* **Closed** *Tue*
Located in the old centre of the
city, this restaurant has a relaxed
vibe and offers a good selection
of classic and modern tapas. Try
the speciality wagyu beef burgers,
steak tartare and carpaccio.

TARRAGONA: La Cuineta   €
Mediterranean
C/Nou del Patriarca 2, 43003
Tel *977 22 61 01*
A delightful little restaurant in
the historic quarter, La Cuineta
serves fresh Mediterranean
dishes. The sea bream with
vegetables is superb. Great value
lunch menu.

Outdoor seating in rustic surroundings at Cinnamon in Sitges

TARRAGONA: Aq   €€
Modern Catalan
C/Les Coques 7, 43003
Tel *977 21 59 54* **Closed** *Sun & Mon*
Exciting contemporary cuisine
is executed here by chef Ana
Ruiz and served in a classy
dining room. Perfect for a
special occasion.

TARRAGONA: Les Coques €€
Traditional Catalan
C/Sant Llorenç 15, 43003
Tel *977 22 83 00*
Long-established, charming
restaurant in the old city serving
sophisticated regional dishes and
scrumptious desserts. Great value
set menus.

TARRAGONA: Sol-Ric   €€
Mediterranean
Av. Via Augusta 227, 43007
Tel *977 23 20 32*
This restaurant offers divine
seafood and other regional fare in
an elegant setting. Enjoy dishes
such as *romesco de terragona* (nut
and red pepper sauce) and *arròs
con caneja* (rice with rabbit) on
a lovely summer terrace.

TORTOSA: Sant Carles   €
Traditional Catalan
Rambla de Felip Pedrell 13, 43500
Tel *977 44 10 48* **Closed** *Sun*
Family-run restaurant with hearty,
Catalan cuisine. The emphasis is
on seafood with clam and shrimp
dishes and fish *suquet* (stew).
Friendly atmosphere.

**VIC: Denominació de
Origen Vic**   €€
Modern Catalan
C/Sant Miquel de Sants 16, 08500
Tel *93 883 23 96*
Located in the heart of the city,
this small, minimalist restaurant
serves outstanding Catalan
cuisine with a creative touch.

For more information on types of restaurants *see page 141*

SHOPPING IN BARCELONA

Barcelona is sophisticated, stylish and neatly divided into distinctive shopping districts – Passeig de Gràcia for chi-chi designer stores, the Barri Gòtic for more eclectic antiques and boutiques, El Born for serious fashion divas, and El Raval for markets and museum shops. Though these rules are by no means fixed, they do provide a useful rule of thumb and help define the city, when time is limited. All shops are closed on Sunday. There are food markets as well – 44 in all – for every *barrio*, and a scattering of flea markets such as the Parisian-style Els Encants and the antiques fair in Sant Cugat, which has a more Provençal flavour. A convenient way to tour Barcelona's shops and markets is by taxi or public transport. Even though there are many car parks in the city, there's little point in hiring a car.

Some of the beautifully displayed confectionery at Escribà

Food and Drink

Barcelona's pastry shops are sights in themselves and, with its displays of chocolate sculptures, no *pastisseria* is more enticing or spectacular than **Escribà**. Other food stores also have a great deal of character, none more so than **Colmado Quílez** in the Eixample. This wonderful old place stocks a huge range of hams, cheeses and preserves, in addition to a comprehensive selection of Spanish and foreign wines and spirits.

Department Stores and "Galeries"

The branch of **El Corte Inglés**, Spain's largest department store chain, on Plaça Catalunya is a Barcelona landmark and a handy place to find everything under one roof, including plug adaptors and services like key-cutting. Other branches are located around the city. Barcelona's hypermarkets also sell a wide range of goods. As they are on the outskirts of the city – south along the Gran Via towards the airport, and on the Avinguda Meridiana to the north – a car is the best way to reach them.

The *galeries* (fashion malls), built mostly during the affluent 1980s, are hugely popular. **Bulevard Rosa** has hundreds of stores selling clothes and accessories. **L'Illa** is a large, lively shopping mall containing chain stores as well as specialist retailers. **Maremagnum** has several shops and restaurants and is open daily including public holidays.

Fashion

International fashion labels are found alongside clothes by young designers on and around the Passeig de Gràcia. **Adolfo Domínguez** stocks classically styled clothes for men and women; **Armand Basi** sells quality leisure and sportswear; and discount designer fashion is available at **Montana Outlet**. Many stores offer traditional, fine-quality tailoring skills and **Calçats Solé**, which is situated in the Old Town, specializes in classic handmade shoes and boots.

Speciality Stores

A walk around Barcelona can reveal a wonderful choice of stores selling traditional craft items and handmade goods that in most places have now been largely replaced by the production line. **La Caixa de Fang** has a good variety of Catalan and Spanish ceramics, among them traditional Catalan cooking pots and colourful tiles. **L'Estanc** has everything for the smoker, including the best Havana cigars. **La Manual Alpargatera** is an old shoe store that specializes in Catalan-style espadrilles. These are handmade on the premises and come in all colours. The city's oldest store, **Cereria Subirà**, sells candles in every imaginable form.

Design, Art and Antiques

If you are interested in modern design, or just looking for gifts,

Menswear department in Adolfo Domínguez

you should pay a visit to **Vinçon**, the city's famous design emporium. Situated in a Modernista townhouse on the Passeig de Gràcia, it has everything for the home, including beautiful fabrics and furniture. Another good place to find contemporary interior design is **Pilma**, which sells furniture, kitchen and bathroom accessories, upholstery, carpets, curtains, paintings and lighting from both local and international designers and architects.

Most of the commercial art and print galleries are found on Carrer Consell de Cent, in the Eixample, while the Barri Gòtic – especially the Carrer de la Palla and Carrer del Pi –

Mouthwatering fruit stalls in La Boqueria market

is the best place to browse around small but fascinating antiques shops. As well as fine furniture and old dolls, **L'Arca de l'Àvia** sells antique silks and lace, all of which are set out in pretty displays.

Books and Newspapers

Most of the city centre newsstands sell English-language newspapers, but the best stocks of foreign papers and magazines are found at FNAC at **L'Illa** in Plaça Catalunya. **Come In** is an English bookshop that also sells a selection of DVDs and board games.

Markets

No one should miss the chance to look around **La Boqueria** on La Rambla, one of the most spectacular food markets in Europe. Antiques are sold in the Plaça Nova on Thursdays, and cheese, honey and sweets in the Plaça del Pi on the last Saturday and Sunday of each month from October to May. On Sunday mornings coin and stamp stalls are set up in the Plaça Reial. The city's traditional flea market, **Encants Vells**, takes place on Mondays, Wednesdays, Fridays and Saturdays just north of the Plaça de les Glòries Catalanes.

The stylishly sparse display of furniture at Vinçon

DIRECTORY

Food and Drink

Colmado Quílez
Rambla de Catalunya 63.
Map 3 A4.
Tel 93 215 23 56.

Escribà Pastisseries
La Rambla 83.
Map 2 F4.
Tel 93 301 60 27.

Gran Via de les Corts
Catalanes 546.
Map 2 E1.
Tel 93 454 75 35.

Department Stores and "Galeries"

Bulevard Rosa
Passeig de Gràcia 55.
Map 3 A4.
Tel 93 215 83 31.

El Corte Inglés
Avinguda Diagonal
617–19. **Tel** 93 366 71 00.
L'Illa
Avinguda Diagonal
545–57. **Tel** 93 444 00 00.
Maremagnum
Moll d'Espanya.
W maremagnum.es

Fashion

Adolfo Domínguez
Passeig de Gràcia 32.
Map 3 A5.
Tel 61 966 02 77.
Armand Basi
Passeig de Gràcia 49.
Map 3 A3.
Tel 93 215 14 21.
Calçats Solé
Carrer Ample 7.
Map 5 A3.
Tel 93 301 69 84.
Montana Outlet
C/ Rec, 58. **Map** 5 C3.

Speciality Stores

La Caixa de Fang
C/ Freneria 1. **Map** 5 B2.
Tel 93 315 17 04.

Cereria Subirà
Bajada Llibreteria 7.
Map 5 B2.
Tel 93 315 26 06.

L'Estanc
Via Laietana 4. **Map** 5 B3.
Tel 93 310 10 34.

La Manual Alpargatera
C/ d'Avinyó 7. **Map** 5 A3.
Tel 93 301 01 72.

Design, Art and Antiques

L'Arca de l'Àvia
Carrer dels Banys Nous 20.
Map 5 A2.
Tel 93 302 15 98.

Pilma
Avinguda Diagonal 403.
Map 3 A2.
Tel 93 416 13 99.

Vinçon
Passeig de Gràcia 96.
Map 3 B3.
Tel 93 215 60 50.

Books and Newspapers

Come In
C/Balmes 129.
Map 3 A3.
Tel 93 453 12 04.

Markets

La Boqueria
La Rambla 101. **Map** 5 A2.

Encants Vells
C/ Dos de Maig, P de les
Glòries. **Map** 4 F5.

Food and Drink

Barcelonans are proud of their culinary heritage and rightly so. The land produces superlative fruit and vegetables, flavourful meats and an astonishing array of cheeses; the bounty of the sea offers daily fresh fish and seafood, and the wine-growing regions of the Penedès and the Priorat make some of the best value vintages in the world. Less well known are the candy-makers, chocolate shops and *patisseries*, all of which add up to a complete and sophisticated cuisine that is fast becoming the envy of the world.

Charcuterie, Cheese and Delicatessens

If you can't join them you can at least take some delicious treats home. Barcelona has several wonderful stores for stocking up on general goodies. The Boqueria, the city's most famous food market on La Rambla, is the obvious place to start, but if you prefer to shop without the hustle and bustle, head for one of the city's many specialist food shops.

Orígens in El Born specialises in strictly Catalan products – jars of small, dusky Arbequina olives, Sant Joan truffle-scented salt, oils and vinegars, home-made preserves and artisan *charcuterie*. Just around the corner, **La Botifarrería de Santa María** is great for artisan *charcuterie* and a lip-smacking array of home-made sausages in many intriguing flavours, such as pork and cuttlefish, beef and beetroot, or lamb and wild mushroom. Then there's **Casa Gispert** for top-grade dried fruit and nuts as well as coffee, which is toasted in-house, and the fabulous **Formatgeria La Seu** (closed in August). This is the only cheese shop in Spain that stocks exclusively Spanish and Catalan cheeses. Prowl around the walk-in dairy and choose from a great seasonal collection of cheeses made by small producers. These range from creamy Catalan goat's cheeses, six-month-old Manchegos to beech-smoked San Simóns that come in the shape of a dunce's cap. A tasting of three cheeses and a tumbler of wine is available for the very reasonable price of €2.80. Formatgeria La Seu's owner, Katherine McLaughlin, also stocks a small range of artisan cheese ice creams.

For more general food products and quintessentially Spanish canned goods (many of which come in wonderful packaging), **Colmado Quílez** is a fascinating old place that stocks just about everything from saffron to ham and sauerkraut. Another interesting store in the Eixample neighbourhood is **Mantequeria Ravell**, Barcelona's first proper delicatessen. Its merchandise isn't strictly Spanish – there are plenty of Italian and French goods as well – but it does boast the best and most expensive of everything, from pink Himalayan salt to explosive pickled *guindilla* peppers from the Basque country. Its restaurant on the first floor, incidentally, is pricey but sublime.

The **Herboristeria del Rei** isn't actually a food store, but it does contain a formidable array of medicinal herbs, teas and honeys. When it opened in 1823, Queen Isabel II decreed that it be supplier to the royal household. The handsome marble fountain that contains a bust of Linneo, the botanist and famous herbalist, was where the leeches were kept.

Chocolate and Candies

Swanky chocolate and cake shops proliferate mainly in the Eixample, with the exception of **Xocoa**, which has branches all over the city, including two in El Born and one in the Barri Gòtic. This is the trendiest of the chocolate-makers in the city, with its retro packaging and fun shapes, including chocolate CDs and giant keys. **Escribà Pastisseries** is more extravagant, sculpting magnificent cakes, pastries and life-size chocolate models of famous personalities. The most gourmet chocolate-maker however, is **Enric Rovira**. Although a little off the beaten path, it is worth the journey and effort to see his amazing chocolate re-creations of Gaudí's trademark *rajoles* paving stones and chocolate gift sets designed by well-known Catalan artists. **Cacao Sampaka** is the sweet shop owned by Albert Adrià (Ferran Adrià's brother) and offers amazing off-the-wall fillings of anchovy, black olive and blue cheese as well as the more traditional herb, spice and floral flavours.

Those looking to take home more traditionally Spanish sweets should try **Caelum** for convent-made sweetmeats such as *yemas* (sweetened egg yolks) and *mazapans* (marzipan treats). Award-winning patissier Carles Mampel creates spectacular cakes, desserts and *petit fours* at **Bubó**. They can be taken away or enjoyed at the adjoining café.

In **Papabubble**, a gorgeous wood-panelled, marble-tiled shop, you can still occasionally see the sweets being made.

Bakeries and Patisseries

Almost every street in the city features its very own *panadería*. Usually open all day, these shops are busiest early in the morning and at around 5pm, snack-time in Spain, when you will often find mothers indulging their kids with after-school treats.

Amongst the best of these shops is **Cusachs**, open since 1963 and still producing the traditional Catalan *coques*. These can either be sweet or savoury and are mostly eaten on 23 June, the Sant Joan festival *(see p37)* and the longest day of the year. Some of the best croissants (especially those filled with mascarpone) and other refined pastries as well as cakes and jams can be found at Pastelería Hofmann.

Another great *panadería* is **Foix de Sarriá** on Major de Sarriá, very well known for its excellent pastries and other baked goods. Amongst its specialities are "royal cake", *sachertorte panellets* (round marzipan cakes), *pasta de té* (fruit biscuits) and *saras* (sponge cake covered with butter cream and almonds).

For the best breads in town, visit **Barcelona Reykjavic**, which sells artisan, organic and wholegrain breads. Delicious homemade cakes and pizzas are also available, and all products are baked on the premises.

Wine and Cigars

On the edge of La Boqueria market is **El Celler de la Boqueria**, a very good shop that stocks a range of about 500 of the very best Spanish and Catalan wines. In the El Born quarter, **Vila Viniteca** sells a formidable range of Spanish and Catalan wines, ranging from cheap, cheerful table wines for around €3 a bottle, to decadently expensive Priorats and Riojas that retail in the region of €300. Last, but by no means least, to leave Barcelona without a bottle of the nation's beloved Catalan champagne *(cava)* would be verging on the sacrilegious. This can be bought everywhere, but for something truly special head for **Xampany**, which specializes in artisan *cava* from the Penedès wine-producing region. The ultimate place for cigar-lovers and pipe-smokers is **Gimeno**. This legendary purveyor of all things tobacco-related also stocks a fine range of Cuban havanas.

DIRECTORY

Charcuterie, Cheese and Delicatessens

La Botifarrería de Santa María
Carrer Santa María 4.
Map 5 B3.
Tel 93 319 91 23.

Casa Gispert
C/Sombrerers 23,
Born.
Map 5 B3.
Tel 93 319 75 35.

Colmado Quílez
Rambla de
Catalunya 63,
Eixample.
Map 3 A3.
Tel 93 215 23 56.

Formatgeria La Seu
C/Dagueria 16,
Barri Gòtic.
Map 5 A2.
Tel 93 412 65 48.

Herboristeria del Rei
C/Vidre 1,
Barri Gòtic.
Map 5 A2.
Tel 93 318 05 12.

Mantequeria Ravell
C/Arago 313.
Map 3 A4.
Tel 93 457 51 14.

Orígens
Passeig del Born 4,
El Born.
Map 5 B3.
Tel 93 295 66 90.

Chocolate and Candies

Bubó
C/Caputxes 10,
Map 5 A3.
Tel 93 268 72 24.

Cacao Sampaka
C/Consell de Cent 292,
Eixample.
Map 3 A4.
Tel 93 272 08 33.

Caelum
C/Palla 8,
Barri Gòtic.
Map 5 A2.
Tel 93 301 69 93.

Enric Rovira
Avinguda Josep
Tarradellas 113,
Eixample.
Tel 93 419 25 47.

Escribà Pastisseries
La Rambla 83,
Barri Gòtic.
Map 5 A1.
Tel 93 301 60 27.

Papabubble
C/Ample 28,
Barri Gòtic.
Map 5 A3.
Tel 93 268 86 25.

Xocoa
C/Vidreria 4,
Born.
Map 5 B2.
Tel 93 319 79 05.

C/Princesa 10,
Born.
Tel 93 319 66 40.

C/Petritxol 11–13.
Tel 93 301 11 97.

Bakeries and Patisseries

Barcelona Reykjavic
Doctor Dou 12.
Map 2 F2.
Tel 93 302 09 21.

C/Astúries 20,
Gràcia.
Map 3 B1.
Tel 93 237 69 18.

C/Princesa 16,
Born.
Map 5 B2.
Tel 93 186 63 36.

Cusachs
Bailén 223,
Eixample
Map 3 C2.
Tel 93 213 77 29.

Foix de Sarriá
Major de Sarriá 57.
Tel 93 203 07 14.

Pastelería Hofmann
C/Flassaders 44,
Born.
Map 5 C3.
Tel 93 268 82 21.

Wines and Cigars

El Celler de la Boqueria
C/Petxina 9,
Raval.
Map 2 F2.
Tel 902 889 263

Gimeno
La Rambla 100.
Map 5 A1.
Tel 93 318 49 47.

Vila Viniteca
C/Agullers 7–9,
Born.
Map 5 B3.
Tel 902 327 777.

Xampany
C/Valencia 200,
Eixample.
Map 3 A4.
Tel 93 453 93 38.

Clothes and Accessories

The streets of Barcelona are paved with clothing outlets and dedicated followers of fashion may be surprised to learn that the city can hold its own against New York, London or Paris. With cutting-edge, home-grown Catalan designers such as Antonio Miró and Custo, high-street fashion chains such as Mango and Zara, and literally thousands of unique boutiques, Spanish fashion is currently among the most exciting in the world.

Jewellery, Bags and Accessories

Bags, jewellery, hats and other baubles are essential for serious style divas and Barcelona has plenty of tiny, Aladdin's Cave-type shops to help create the perfect outfit. **Fet amb Love** (Made with Love) is a tiny shop in the Passeig del Born that sells colourful, handmade jewellery and accessories that the owners Ana and Carmen source from all over the world. They also sell their own designs, which include Japanese silk hairpins and party handbags. **Minu Madhu** makes exquisite embroidered jackets, patch-work scarves, appliqué hand-bags and hand-painted silk kerchiefs in sumptuous fabrics, textures and colours, along with a selection of children's clothes.

Take your own piece of Barcelona streetlife home – literally – with a **Demano** handbag from stockists all over town, such as **Vinçon** (see p155). These innovative designs have been produced in conjunction with designers Marcela Manrique, Liliana Andrade, Eleonora Parachini and the City Hall in an endeavour to reclaim and re-use the polyester PVC banners, placards and billboards produced to announce the cultural events in the city. In addition to one-of-a-kind handbags in various sizes, there are laptop bags, bicycle panniers and handlebar bags, wallets, pencil cases and other small accessories.

Ulleres M. Assumpta, on the Carrer Ramalleres, is a tiny shop selling retro-vintage artisan glasses and sunglasses, with its own designs. Another good bet for unique pieces is **Mô Art**,

a gallery shop housed in a 16th-century building. It has locally handmade jewellery, textiles, bags, accessories and other gifts and art objects.

International and Spanish Designer Labels

Josep Font, one of the most awarded Catalan designers, offers truly unique skirts, dresses and long pants for the elegant female customer. El Born has plenty of stores selling a top range of designer labels, including **M69** for the boys with seasonal collections from Paul Smith, Bikkembergs and Vivienne Westwood among others.

Avenida Diagonal and the Passeig de Gràcia, however, are the true homes of fashionistas, with all the big labels such as **Chanel**, **Carolina Herrera**, **Gucci** and **Yves Saint Laurent** as well as **Loewe** for luxury luggage and **Pelleteria La Sibèria** for prêt-à-porter and custom-made designers in suede, nappa and fur.

Second-Hand and Vintage Fashion

Diminutive Carrer Riera Baixa in El Raval is Barcelona's answer to London's Carnaby Street with its own Saturday market (opening times, however, can be erratic) and several wonderful shops. The theatre-turned-vintage-shop **Lailo** sells anything from collectable costumes from the Liceu opera house and vintage dresses to 1950s bathing suits. Across the road is **Galalith**, which specializes in vintage-inspired and restored

second-hand accessories. Its pendants, scarves, purses and bags have a genuine retro feel.

High Street and Sports Fashion

Ubiquitous Spanish fashion houses **Zara** and **Mango** have stores all over town. Both flagships are on the Passeig de Gràcia and they are great for good value basics, work-wear and fashionable party dresses. Both also offer a decent range of menswear. For slightly more upmarket tastes both **Massimo Dutti** and **Adolfo Domínguez** are reliable suppliers of more classical tailoring, smart casuals and practical items such as ties and belts.

More individual fashion is best sought out in the smaller, independent shops of El Born and the Barri Gòtic. Carrer d'Avinyo in the Old Town inspired the young Picasso to paint and today's hip young things to shop. A lively street with a market ambience, it is particularly good for indepen-dent clothing stores and essential sportswear – Adidas, Puma and Nike. For gorgeous, original women's clothes and footwear by Spanish designers, try **Como Agua de Mayo**. The designs are feminine and floaty yet supremely stylish and contemporary. **Desigual** is good for urban casuals, while **Doshaburi** stocks the largest selection of vintage Levi's in Spain as well as the more quirky Japanese labels. **Custo**, the most famous of Barcelona's local designers, has two shops in the old city; both are piled high with his trademark brightly printed T-shirts and mismatched coats and skirts.

Finally, football fans can head for FC Barcelona's official stores, the **Botiga del Barça**. They stock all kinds of merchandise related to the sport, including stripes, scarves, boots and balls.

Hats and Shoes

Patterned leather shoes and decorative soles from the cult Mallorcan shoe-maker

Camper can be purchased for around 25 per cent less in Barcelona than other places in Spain. **La Manual Alpargatera** is another cult classic, beloved by *sardana* dancers (Catalonia's national dance) and celebrities alike for his exquisite hand-made, individually fitted espadrilles and straw hats.

Another shoe shop, **Casas Sabaters**, has several branches around town, all offering a top quality range of leading Spanish footwear brands. They are also a good destination for last-minute sale items and last season's knock-offs. **Muxart** is a Barcelona-based local footwear brand that only sells at its own stores. Here you will find some of the most amazing, original and pricey shoes, handcrafted from the finest materials and in a wide choice of colours. **Vialis** is another local brand, the first shop opening in El Born in 1998. The shoes are unusual, beautifully made and very comfortable. The collection of trainers is also popular.

On a corner in the Old Town's Barri Gòtic, the old-fashioned hat shop **Sombreria Obach** sells all the classics ranging from Basque berets to stetsons, trilbies and hand-woven Montecristi Panamas.

DIRECTORY

Jewellery, Bags and Accessories

Demano
Pallars 94, 7, 1a.
Map 6 E2.
Tel 93 396 94 50.
w demano.net

Fet amb Love
Passeig del Born 2, Born.
Map 5 B3.
Tel 93 319 66 42.

Minu Madhu
C/Sta. Maria 18, Born.
Map 5 B3.
Tel 93 310 27 85.

Mô Art
C/Montcada 25, Born.
Map 5 B3.
Tel 93 310 31 16.

Ulleres M. Assumpta
C/Ramalleres 3, Born.
Map 2 F2.
Tel 93 318 29 96.

International and Spanish Designer Labels

Carolina Herrera
Passeig de Gràcia 87, Eixample.
Map 3 A3.
Tel 93 272 15 84.

Chanel
Passeig de Gràcia 70, Eixample.
Map 3 A4.
Tel 93 488 29 23.

Gucci
Passeig de Gràcia 76, Eixample.
Map 3 A3.
Tel 93 416 06 20.

Josep Font
C/Provença, 304, Eixample.
Map 3 A3.
Tel 93 487 21 10.

Loewe
Passeig de Gràcia 35.
Map 3 A4.
Tel 93 216 04 00.

M69
C/Rec 28.
Map 5 C3.
Tel 93 310 42 36.
w m69barcelona.com

Pelleteria La Sibèria
Rambla de Catalunya 15, Eixample.
Map 3 A5.
Tel 93 317 05 83.

Yves Saint Laurent
Passeig de Gràcia 102.
Map 3 A3.
Tel 93 200 39 55.

Second-Hand and Vintage Fashion

Galalith
C/Riera Baixa 5, El Raval.
Map 2 F2.
Tel 659 99 70 02.
w galalith.org

Lailo
C/Riera Baixa 20, El Raval.
Map 2 F2.
Tel 93 441 37 49.

High Street and Sports Fashion

Adolfo Domínguez
Passeg de Gràcia 32, Eixample.
Map 3 A5.
Tel 93 487 41 70.

Botiga del Barça
Maremagnum (Moll d'Espanya).
Map 5 A4.
Tel 93 225 80 45.

Como Agua de Mayo
C/Argenteria 43.
Map 5 B3.
Tel 93 310 64 41.

Custo
Plaça de les Olles 7.
Map 5 B3.
Tel 93 268 78 93.

Desigual
C/Argenteria 65, Born.
Map 5 B2.
Tel 93 310 30 15.

Doshaburi
C/Lledó 4-6, Barri Gòtic.
Map 2 F2.
Tel 93 319 96 29.
w doshaburi.com

Mango
Passeig de Gràcia 65.
Map 3 A4.
Tel 93 215 75 30.

Massimo Dutti
Passeig de Gràcia (corner Gran Via), Eixample.
Map 3 A5.
Tel 93 412 01 05.

Zara
Passeig de Gràcia 16, Eixample.
Map 3 A5.
Tel 93 318 76 75.

Hats and Shoes

Camper
Plaça Àngels con C/Elizabets, El Raval.
Map 2 F2.
Tel 93 342 41 41.

Casas Sabaters
C/Portaferrissa 25.
Map 5 A2.
Tel 93 302 11 32.

La Manual Alpargatera
C/D'Avinyó 7, Barri Gòtic.
Map 5 A3.
Tel 93 301 01 72.

Muxart
Rambla de Catalunya 47.
Map 3 A5.
Tel 93 467 74 23.

Sombreria Obach
Carrer del Call 2, Barri Gòtic.
Map 5 A2.
Tel 93 318 40 94.

Vialis
C/Vidreria 15.
Map 5 B3.
Tel 93 313 94 91.

Speciality Stores

Part of the fun of getting to know Barcelona is to meander through the Old Town's rabbit-warren-like streets, or to explore the wide boulevards of the Eixample. Both the areas have a wonderful choice of stores selling traditional crafts and handmade goods that in many places have been replaced by the production line. The endless array of shops are a dazzling sight in themselves and even if you are just window-shopping, it's well worth taking a proper look around to see the merchandise on offer.

Art and Antiques

Antiques aficionados and collectors will be richly rewarded by what Barcelona has to offer. The equivalent of an antiques shopping mall, **Bulevard dels Antiquaris** is home to over 70 shops brimming over with relics from the past. These can range from ancient coins and alabaster statues to tin drums, Regency-period candelabras and assorted bric-à-brac. Carrer del Call, the old Jewish quarter in the Barri Gòtic, is another hub for collectors with plush shops, such as **L'Arca de l'Àvia**, which sells antique lace and linens, old dolls and fine furniture, **Heritage**, a purveyor of semi-precious stone jewellery, antique silks and textiles and the odd mink stole, and **Gemma Povo** for decorative antique iron work. Also check out **Artur Ramon** and **Maria Ubach Antigüedades** on Carrer de la Palla for 18th- and 19th-century glassware and ceramics and paintings dating back to the 14th century. **Tandem** specializes in a wonderful range of tawny, old globes.

Barcelona's oldest and most prestigious art gallery is **Sala Parés**, which exhibits serious Catalan artists, both past and present. For keepsake wall hangings that won't break the bank, try the **Boutique Galería Picasso** for prints, lithographs, posters and postcards by the great Spanish masters, Miró, Picasso and Dalí. **Siesta**, a cross between boutique and art gallery, used to be a haberdashery and displays its locally made, contemporary ceramics, jewellery and glassworks in the original wooden glass cabinets.

Books, Music, DVDs and Stationery

Barcelona is a wonderful city for unearthing intriguing knick-knacks and unique, one-of-a-kind gifts that people will treasure forever. **Papirvm** is an old-fashioned stationery store, piled high with beautiful fountain pens, leather-bound and William Morris print notepads, and even feather quills as well as retro Boqueria waiters pads. **Altaïr** is arguably Spain's finest specialist travel bookshop stocking a stupendous range of armchair reads, maps, travel guides and coffee-table books for anyone who lives and loves to move. But if you're just looking for some holiday reading try the **Casa del Llibre**, Barcelona's biggest bookstore for English language novels, magazines, travel guides, maps and glossy coffee-table books.

Thanks to the wide influence of Barcelona's annual electronic music festival, Sónar *(see p163)*, the city has become a hotspot for music collectors. **Wah Wah Records** and El Raval in general are good for stocking up on the latest club tunes and old vinyl, while **Herrera Guitars** is a safe bet for anyone in the market for a handmade classical Spanish guitar. Commissions are accepted.

Unusual Gifts and Knick-Knacks

El Born and the Barri Gòtic are treasure troves, at once delightful and inspiring. **Sabater Hnos. Fábrica de Jabones** sells home-made soaps, which come in all shapes and smells, from traditional lavender to delicious chocolate. **Natura** is ideal for cheap and chic presents such as groovy candy-striped socks, duvet slippers, Chinese-style notepads and other Oriental toys and trinkets. For the Don Juan in your life, **La Condonería** (the condom emporium) stocks all manner of rubber delights in every shape, size, colour and flavour imaginable. **Cereria Subirà** is a gorgeous shop, and the city's oldest, dating back to 1761. Today, it sells a phenomenal array of decorative and votive candles in numerous shapes and sizes, including some several feet tall for dramatic effect. **El Rei de la Màgia** is another golden-oldie, founded in 1881. It reveals a world of fairytale magic for budding magicians. Nearby, **Arlequí Màscares** creates traditional hand-painted folk masks out of papier-mâché, including Italian Commedia dell'arte masks, glossy French party masks, grotesque Catalan *gigantes* (giant heads used in local festivals), Greek tragedy and Japanese Noh masks.

Lingerie and Perfumes

The French chain **Sephora** stocks a wide selection of brand-name perfumes and cosmetics, often cheaper than those at the airport. **La Galería de Santa María Novella** is the Barcelona outlet of the famous, luxury apothecary in Florence, which has produced artisan perfumes and colognes since 1400. Customers are captivated by the scent of flowers, spices and fruits as they enter the store. The shop also sells cosmetics and herbal remedies. This kind of luxury does not come cheap, however.

Le Boudoir is decked out like an 18th-century love nest, complete with brass bed, gilded mirrors, velvet drapery and love poetry inscribed on the walls. It is also the sexiest shop in Barcelona for lace and silk lingerie, nightgowns, fluffy mules and furry handcuffs as well as tasteful sex toys and aphrodisiacs. For more conventional underwear, the quality Spanish chain **Women's Secret** goes in for a funky line of candy- coloured bra and pants sets, swimwear and hip pyjamas.

Interiors

L'Appartement is an eclectic gallery and shop that exhibits and sells furniture ranging from funky lamps to cool folding armchairs. The Zara brand started **Zara Home** with four basic styles in its collection: classic, ethnic, contemporary and white, all at very reasonable prices. **Wa Was**, on the other hand, is more quirky, stocking neon-coloured lamps, decorative objects and cooking tools. They also sell original postcards of Barcelona. Fans of gizmos and gadgets will enjoy **Vinçon**. This is the mecca of Barcelona's design stores.

Housed in a 1900 upper-class apartment, its vast space is filled with everything from French Le Creuset cookware to Basque *chiquito* straight-edged tumblers, silk bean bags and futons. The old-fashioned clientele is more inclined towards **Coses de Casa**. This is a superb place for handmade patchwork quilts, feminine rosebud prints and Laura Ashley-style floral designs for lovers of chintz.

DIRECTORY

Art and Antiques

L'Arca de L'Àvia
C/Banys Nous 20,
Barri Gòtic.
Map 5 A2.
Tel 93 302 15 98.

Artur Ramon Antiquari
C/Palla 23–25,
Barri Gòtic.
Map 5 A2.
Tel 93 302 59 70.

Artur Ramon Mestres Antics Show Room
C/Palla 10,
Barri Gòtic.
Map 5 A2.
Tel 93 301 16 48.

Boutique Galería Picasso
Tapineria 10.
Map 5 B2.
Tel 93 310 49 57.

Bulevard dels Antiquaris
Passeig de Gràcia 55.
Map 3 A2–A5.
Tel 93 215 44 99.

Gemma Povo
C/Banys Nous 7,
Barri Gòtic
Map 5 A2.
Tel 93 301 34 76.

Heritage
C/Banys Nous 14,
Barri Gòtic.
Map 5 A2.
Tel 93 317 85 15.
W heritagebarcelona.
com

Maria Ubach Antigüedades
C/Palla 10, Barri Gòtic.
Map 5 A2.
Tel 93 302 26 88.

Sala Parés
C/Petritxol 5,
Barri Gòtic.
Map 5 A2.
Tel 93 318 70 20.

Siesta
C/Ferlandina 18.
Map 2 E1.
Tel 93 317 80 41.

Tandem
C/Banys Nous 19,
Barri Gòtic.
Map 5 A2.
Tel 93 317 44 91.

Books, Music, DVDs and Stationery

Altaïr
Gran Via 616,
Eixample.
Tel 93 342 71 71.
W altair.es

Casa del Llibre
Passeig de Gràcia 62,
Eixample.
Map 3 A4.
Tel 93 272 34 80.

Herrera Guitars
C/Marlet 6,
Barri Gòtic.
Map 5 A2.
Tel 93 302 66 66.
W herreraguitars.com

Papirvm
C/Baixada de la Llibreteria
2, Barri Gòtic.
Map 5 A2.
Tel 93 310 52 42.
W papirum-bcn.com

Wah Wah Records
Riera Baixa 14,
El Raval.
Map 2 F2.
Tel 93 442 37 03.

Unusual Gifts and Knick-Knacks

Arlequí Màscares
Plaça Sant Josep Oriol 8.
Map 5 A2.
Tel 93 317 24 29.
W arlequimask.com

Cereria Subirà
Baixada Llibreteria 7.
Map 5 A2.
Tel 93 315 26 06.

La Condonería
Plaça Sant Josep Oriol 7,
Barri Gòtic.
Map 5 A2.
Tel 93 302 77 21.

Natura
C/Argenteria 78,
Born.
Map 5 B2.
Tel 93 268 25 25.

El Rei de la Màgia
Carrer de la Princessa 11.
Map 5 B2.
Tel 93 319 39 20.

Sabater Hnos. Fábrica de Jabones
Pl. Sant Felip Neri 1,
Barri Gòtic.
Map 5 B2.
Tel 93 301 98 32.

Lingerie and Perfumes

Le Boudoir
C/Canuda 21.
Map 5 A1.
Tel 93 302 52 81.
W leboudoir.net

La Galería de Santa María de Novella
C/Espasería 4.
Map 5 B3.
Tel 93 268 02 37.

Sephora
C/Rambla de
Cataluña 121.
Map 3 A3.
Tel 93 368 92 33.

Women's Secret
C/Portaferrissa 7,
Barri Gòtic.
Map 5 A2.
Tel 93 318 92 42.

Interiors

L'Appartement
C/Enric Granados 44.
Map 3 A4.
Tel 93 452 29 04.

Coses de Casa
Plaça Sant Josep Oriol 5,
Barri Gòtic.
Map 2 F2.
Tel 93 302 73 28.

Vinçon
Passeig de Gràcia 96.
Map 3 A3.
Tel 93 215 60 50.

Wa Was
Carders 14,
Born.
Map 5 B3.
Tel 93 319 79 92.

Zara Home
Rambla de Catalunya 71.
Map 3 A4.
Tel 93 487 49 72.

ENTERTAINMENT IN BARCELONA

Barcelona has one of the most colourful and alternative live arts scenes in Europe, offering a smörgasbord of entertainment, from the gilded Liceu opera house and the spectacular Modernista masterpiece Palau de la Música Catalana to small independent theatres hosting obscure Catalan comedies and dark Spanish dramas. But there's also much to be seen simply by walking around. Street performance ranges from the human statues on La Rambla to excellent classical, ragtime and jazz buskers in the plazas. In addition, there are a number of weekend-long musical and arts fiestas that run throughout the year, many of which now attract an international audience of people from all over the world.

The magnificent interior of the Palau de la Música Catalana

Entertainment Guides

The most complete guide to what's going on each month in Barcelona is *enBarcelona*, out every Thursday. The Friday *La Vanguardia* also has a good entertainment supplement, *Què Fem?*, and there is a weekly Catalan edition of *Time Out*.

Seasons and Tickets

Theatre and concert seasons for the main venues run from September to June, with limited programmes at other times. The city's varied menu of entertainment reflects its rich multi-cultural artistic heritage. In summer the city hosts the Grec Festival de Barcelona *(see p37)*, a showcase of international music, theatre and dance, held at open-air venues. There is also a wide variety of concerts to choose from during September's Festa de la Mercè *(see p38)*. The simplest way to get theatre and concert tickets is to buy them at the box office, although tickets for many theatres can also be bought from branches of the Catalunya Caixa and La Caixa savings banks, or from Servi Caixa machines. The Ticket Ramblas central point in the Virreina Palace (Rambla 99) also offers 50 per cent discounted theatre tickets from 3 hours before the show. Grec festival tickets are sold at tourist offices.

Film and Theatre

The **Mercat de les Flors** *(see p164)* is an exciting theatre which focuses on contemporary dance and theatre. The adjoining **Teatre Lliure** presents high-quality productions of classic and modern plays in Catalan. The new **Teatre Nacional de Catalunya** *(see p101)*, next to the Auditori de Barcelona, is another fine showcase for Catalan drama. The main venue for classical ballet is the **Liceu** opera house.

Music

Barcelona's Modernista **Palau de la Música Catalana** *(see p65)* is one of the world's most beautiful concert halls, with its stunning interior decor and world-renowned acoustic. Also inspiring is the **L'Auditori de Barcelona** *(see p166)*, which gives the city two modern halls for large-scale and chamber concerts. Its reputation was considerably bolstered when it became the home of the Orquestra Simfònica de Barcelona.

The Liceu opera house, known for operatic excellence, came back from a fire that destroyed the building in 1994 and has been operating at full-octave level ever since.

Big names like David Byrne and Paul McCartney have performed at **Razzmatazz** *(see p166)*. Jazz venues include the **Harlem Jazz Club** *(see p166)* and **Jamboree** *(see p166)*, and salsa fans will enjoy a quick slink down to **Antilla Barcelona**.

Outrageous stage show at one of Barcelona's many clubs

Auditorium of the Teatre Nacional de Catalunya

Nightlife

Among Barcelona's most famous modern sights are the hi-tech designer bars built in the prosperous 1980s, for example the **Mirablau**, overlooking the city. **Otto Zutz** has regular DJs and the less chic but still fun **Apolo** has live music. **Elephant** is located in a beautiful Modernista villa and attracts a fashionable crowd.

Two of the best-known bars are in the old city: **Boadas** for cocktails and **El Xampanyet** for sparkling wine and tapas. **El Bosc de les Fades** is the café of the wax museum and is imaginatively decorated like a fairy's woodland grotto. **The One Barcelona** in the Poble Espanyol is a large nightclub that plays techno music.

Festivals

During the summer, the streets are alive with outdoor festivals, performances and music. The **Festival del Sónar**, in June, began in an experimental manner as a place to showcase the latest musical talents of Southern European youth using new technologies. The **Classics als Parcs**, in June–July, is a good bet for a more serene entertainment.

Amusement Park

In summer, Barcelona's giant amusement park on the summit of **Tibidabo** (see p100) is usually open till the early hours at weekends, but also busy on other days. It is even more fun if you travel there by tram, funicular or cable car.

Sports

The undoubted kings of sport in Catalonia are **FC Barcelona**, known as Barça. They have the largest football stadium in Europe, Camp Nou, and a fanatical following (see p97). Barcelona also has a high-ranking basketball team.

Packed house at the gigantic Camp Nou stadium

DIRECTORY

Film and Theatre

Liceu
La Rambla 51–59.
Map 2 F3.
Tel 93 485 99 00.

Teatre Lliure
Passeig de Santa Madrona, 40–46.
Map 1 B3.
Tel 93 289 27 70.

Teatre Nacional de Catalunya
Plaça de les Arts 1.
Map 4 F5.
Tel 93 306 57 00.

Music

Antilla Barcelona
Carrer de Aragó 141–143.
Tel 93 451 45 64.
W antillasalsa.com

L'Auditori de Barcelona
Carrer de Lepant 150.
Map 6 E1.
Tel 93 247 93 00.

Palau de la Música Catalana
C/Palau de la Música 4.
Map 5 B1.
Tel 90 244 28 82.

Nightlife

Apolo
Carrer Nou de la Rambla 113.
Map 2 E3.
Tel 93 441 40 01.
W sala-apolo.com

Boadas
Carrer dels Tallers 1.
Map 5 A1.
Tel 93 318 95 92.

El Bosc de les Fades
Pasatge de la Banca.
Tel 93 317 26 49.

Elephant
Passeig dels Til.lers 1,
Tibidabo.
Tel 93 334 02 58.
W elephantbcn.com

Mirablau
Plaça Doctor Andreu.
Tel 93 418 58 79.

The One Barcelona
Av de Francesc Ferrer i Guàrdia 13–27.
Map 1 A1.
Tel 90 290 92 89.

Otto Zutz
Carrer de Lincoln 15.
Map 3 A1.
Tel 93 238 07 22.

El Xampanyet
Carrer Montcada 22.
Map 5 B2.
Tel 93 319 70 03.

Festivals

Classics als Parcs
Information Parcs i Jardins
Tel 010 (from Barcelona).

Festival del Sónar
Palau de la Virreina.
W sonar.es

Grec Festival de Barcelona
W grec.bcn.cat

ServiCaixa
Tel 90 215 00 25.
W ticketmaster.es

Telentrada
Tel 90 210 12 12.
W telentrada.com

Amusement Park

Tibidabo
Tel 93 211 79 42.
W tibidabo.cat

Sports

FC Barcelona
Avinguda Aristides Maillol.
Tel 93 496 36 00.
W fcbarcelona.com

Film and Theatre

Large, multiscreen complexes as well as smaller, more intimate venues today screen a variety of films, catering to all tastes. As a result, Barcelona now hosts several film festivals through the year. Theatre, on the other hand, dates back to medieval times and the city's productions have evolved to become the most cutting-edge in Spain. Although language may be a problem, it's well worth seeing a theatrical production. If not, there are always many dinner-shows to interest non-purists.

Film

Directors such as Alejandro Amenábar (The Others), Catalan writer and director Isabel Coixet (My Life Without You) and, of course, Spain's bad boy of film, Pedro Almodóvar (All About My Mother, Bad Education, Volver) have revitalised Spanish cinema. Today Barcelona itself has become the venue for independent film festivals and the biggest event of the year is the **Festival Internacional de Cinema de Catalunya**, held in Sitges in October.

Most Spanish cinemas dub films into Spanish or Catalan, but there are an increasing number of VO (original version) venues that screen not only Hollywood blockbusters, but also film noir and independent art-house movies. The **Centre de Cultura Contemporània de Barcelona (CCCB)** has provided a focal point for modern Barcelona since its opening in 1995, and, has played an integral part in the rejuvenation of El Raval. The CCCB serves as a crossroads of contemporary culture with cutting-edge art exhibits, lectures and film screenings.

Icària Yelmo Cineplex is the town's biggest multiscreen VO complex, built around an American-style mall with a number of fast-food eateries on the ground floor and shops on the first. One of Barcelona's oldest and most popular cinemas is **Comedia**. All films here are shown in Spanish only, regardless of the original language. At the heart of the city, the imposing building it occupies was a former private palace,

then a theatre and now a five-auditorium cinema. Or, try the **Renoir Floridablanca**, a relatively new cinema on the edge of El Raval and the Eixample. It screens a range of European and international movies (subtitles are usually in Spanish or Catalan). In Gràcia, **Verdi** and **Verdi Park** are also good for more independent movie-making as well as an interesting selection of foreign films. They also occasionally have small, themed film festivals that include shorts by new local talent. During the summer, both the **Castell de Montjuïc** (see p93) and the **Piscina Bernat Picornell**, the Olympic swimming pool in Montjuïc, host a number of open-air cinema screenings.

The Catalan government's repertory cinema, the **Filmoteca de la Generalitat de Catalunya** (closed August), screens an excellent range of films over a period of two or three weeks before the schedule changes. The line-up encompasses anything from obscure, bleak Eastern European epics to upbeat modern musicals such as Baz Luhrmann's Moulin Rouge. The two-screen **Méliès** is a gem offering art-house movies, Holly-wood classics, B&W horrors and anything by Fellini or Hitchcock.

Two film festivals held in the city are the **Festival de Cine Documental Musical In-Edit**, combining music with film and usually scheduled for the end of October–early November, and the **Festival Internacional de Cine de Autor**, which is organised by the Filmoteca at the end of April–early May.

There are also an increasing number of small "bar-cinemas", where, for the price of a beer, you can watch a film on a small screen on a hardbacked school playground chair. For children, there is the **IMAX Port Vell**, which shows the usual 3-D roller-coaster knuckle-biters, Everest expeditions and squid-entangled journeys to the bottom of the sea.

It's worth knowing that all cinemas have a dia de l'espectador, usually Monday night, when tickets are reduced. Weekend matinées are also usually cheaper.

Theatre and Dance

Although English-language productions are still in short supply, there are some rather good independent groups that perform at the **Teatre Llantiol** in El Raval. However, many Catalan and Spanish productions are well worth seeing, regardless of the language constraints. Theatre groups Els Comediants and La Cubana, in particular, offer a thrilling mélange of theatre, music, mime and elements from traditional Mediterranean fiestas. The tiny Llantiol stages a repertoire, that changes weekly, of alternative shows, comedy, magic and other off-the-cuff performances designed to attract a mixed crowd from the city's growing expatriate community to local arts lovers. Similarly, the **L'Antic Teatre**, on the other side of town, is a cultural centre and bar with a scruffy but pleasant summer roof-terrace and small vegetarian restaurant that hosts a number of alternative production companies, such as the Argentinian Company 4D Òptic. Also good for avant-garde performances and music is the **Mercat de les Flors**, a converted flower market in the Montjuïc. It is also host to a handful of different themed film festivals including a cele-bration of Asian film in autumn.

La Rambla and Paral.lel are the main hubs of the city's bigger, more mainstream theatres. The

Teatre Tívoli is a gargantuan theatre where high-quality productions, dance and musical recitals by Catalan, Spanish and international stars are held. The Teatre Poliorama on La Rambla meanwhile goes more for musicals, occasional operas and flamenco performances three times a week. For serious theatre-lovers however, the Teatre Nacional de Catalunya (TNC) is an imposing columned affair designed by the Catalan architect Ricard Bofill, with state-of-the-art facilities and a weighty line-up of Spanish and Catalan directors. The Teatre Apolo is good for big-bang musicals such as Queen's

We Will Rock You and ABBA's Mamma Mia!. Modern dance is much loved in Barcelona and there's no shortage of productions, often staged at the city's main theatres. The Teatre Victòria on Avinguda del Paral.lel is a reasonable bet for ballet and more classical dance productions, as is the Liceu opera house (see p166).

Visitors who want to see flamenco (see p167) while in Barcelona can experience reasonably authentic renditions of the sexy, foot- stomping excitement of the peñas (folk bars) of Andalusia. However, if you do get a chance to see the Catalan flamenco singer

Mayte Martín, it's well worth snapping up tickets.

There are also a handful of places that put on a reasonable dinner and show for non-purists including El Tablao de Carmen (see p167). Los Tarantos in Plaça Reial has daily flamenco concerts at affordable prices (usually less than €10).

Salsa, merengue and other sizzling Caribbean moves have a solid following with various clubs playing host to big-name bands from New York, Puerto Rico and Cuba. Join the party (and take part in regular, free dance lessons) at Antilla BCN Latin Club, or at the Mojito Club in Eixample.

DIRECTORY

Film

CCCB
C/Montalegre 5.
Map 2 F2.
Tel 93 306 41 00.
W cccb.org

Cine Comedia
Passeig de Gràcia 13,
Eixample.
Map 3 A5.
Tel 93 301 35 58.
W cinescomedia.com

Festival de Cine Documental Musical In-Edit
W in-edit.beefeater.es

Festival Internacional de Cine de Autor
W cinemadautor.cat

Festival Internacional de Cinema de Catalunya
Sitges.
Tel 938 94 99 90.
W cinemasitges.com

Filmoteca de la Generalitat de Catalunya
Plaça Salvador Segui 1–9,
Raval.
Tel 93 567 10 70.

Icària Yelmo Cineplex
C/Salvador Espriu 61,
vila Olímpica.
Map 6 E4.
Tel 902 22 09 22.
W yelmocines.es

IMAX Port Vell
Moll d'Espanya,
Port Vell. **Map** 5 A4.
Tel 93 225 11 11.
W imaxportvell.com

Méliès
C/Villarroel 102,
Eixample. **Map** 2 E1.
Tel 93 451 00 51.

Piscina Bernat Picornell
Av. de l'Estadi 30–38.
Map 1 A3.
Tel 93 423 40 41.
W picornell.cat

Renoir Floridablanca
C/Floridablanca 135,
Eixample.
Map 1 C1.
Tel 93 426 33 37.
W cinesrenoir.com

Verdi
C/Verdi 32, Gràcia.
Map 3 B1.
Tel 93 238 79 90.
W cines-verdi.com

Verdi Park
C/Torrijos 49, Gràcia.
Map 3 C2.
Tel 93 238 79 90.

Theatre and Dance

L'Antic Teatre
C/Verdaguer i Callís 12,
La Ribera.
Map 5 A1.
Tel 93 315 23 54.
W anticteatre.com

Antilla BCN Latin Club
C/Aragó 141,
Eixample.
Map 3 A4.
Tel 93 451 45 64.
W antillasalsa.com

Gran Teatre del Liceu (Opera House)
La Rambla 51–59.
Map 5 A1.
Tel 93 485 99 00.
W liceubarcelona.com

Mercat de les Flors
C/de Lleida 59.
Map 1 B2.
Tel 93 426 18 75.
W mercatflors.org

Mojito Club
C/Rosello 217,
Eixample.
Map 3 A3.
Tel 93 237 65 28.
W mojitobcn.com

Los Tarantos
Plaça Reial 17.
Map 5 A3.
Tel 93 319 17 89.
W masimas.com/
tarantos

Teatre Apolo
Av del Paral.lel 59.
Map 1 B1.
Tel 93 441 90 07.

Teatre Llantiol
C/Riereta 7, El Raval.
Map 2 E2.
Tel 93 329 90 09.
W llantiol.com

Teatre Nacional de Catalunya (TNC)
Plaça de les Arts 1.
Map 6 F1.
Tel 93 306 57 00.
W tnc.cat

Teatre Poliorama
La Rambla 115,
Barri Gòtic.
Map 5 A1.
Tel 93 317 75 99.
W teatrepoliorama.com

Teatre Tívoli
C/Casp 8–10,
Eixample.
Map 3 B5.
Tel 902 33 22 11.

Teatre Victòria
Av del Paral.lel 67–69.
Map 1 B1.
Tel 93 329 91 89.
W teatrevictoria.com

Music

Few cities in the world can match the eclectic range of Barcelona's music scene. Stunning world-class venues such as Palau de la Música and L'Auditori de Barcelona play host to mega-stars, while smaller jazz rooms attract smouldering songsters. Then there are also the underground dives for the best in experimental electronica as well as the dusty, dimly lit flamenco folk clubs. Traditional Catalan music and dancing (sardanes) can be heard in the Cathedral square most weekends.

Opera and Classical Music

Opera and classical music are beloved by Catalans who lap it up with near religious reverence. Indeed, many of the great artists of the 20th century were locals, including the cellist Pablo Casals and opera singers José Carreras and Montserrat Caballé, who performed Barcelona, the dramatic operatic duet with the late Freddy Mercury.

The city is also home to some of the most spectacular venues in the world, including the glamorous, gilded **Gran Teatre del Liceu**, which first opened its doors in 1847. The opera house has been a continuing beacon of Catalan arts for more than a century and a half, with a rich and dramatic history of fire and bomb attacks. It burned down for the third time in 1994, but careful renovations have restored it to its former glory. Despite its misfortunes, it has sustained a stellar line-up of the greatest composers in the world, among them Puccini, Tchaikovsky and Diaghilev's Russian Ballets, as well as Catalan composers such as Pedrell, Vives and Enric Granados.

The whimsical fancy of the **Palau de la Música** is another of Barcelona's architectural triumphs. A jewel-bright vision by the Modernista master Lluís Domènech i Montaner, this sublime concert hall has a dedicated public, and performers who vie to play here. The Palau is the main venue for the city's jazz and guitar festivals and national and international symphony orchestras perform

here regularly. Both of these venues can be visited on daytime guided tours, but booking tickets for a production is the best way to experience the atmosphere.

Modern, but no less important as a shrine to the Catalan arts scene, **L'Auditori de Barcelona** was built to accommodate growing demand for better facilities and to attract ever greater numbers of world-class musicians. It began primarily as a place for classical concerts and orchestral recitals, but has since begun to embrace giants of jazz, pop and rock. It is also worth keeping your eyes peeled for regular choral music being performed at the city's churches and cathedrals, most notably the Iglesia Santa Maria del Pi, the main cathedral on Plaça del Pi, and the Iglesia Santa Maria del Mar, particularly around Christmas time and Easter.

Live Music: Rock, Jazz and Blues

In terms of popular music Barcelona may not have the endless clubs, pubs, stadiums and music emporiums that make London the best place on the planet for live music, but it doesn't do too badly considering its size. The city attracts a star-studded cast that ranges from pop stars such as Kylie Minogue and Madonna to contemporary jazz prodigies such as the Brad Mehldau Quartet, hip-hoppers, rappers and world-groove mixers, country and good old-fashioned rock'n'roll.

Barcelona still has a clutch of tiny, intimate venues. **Jamboree**,

a cellar-like venue on Plaça Reial, attracts a number of jazz heavyweights as well as more experimental outfits and solo artists such as the saxophonist Billy McHenry. Another good bet is the **JazzSí Club Taller de Músics**, a more obscure destination but much beloved by aficionados of the genre. It doubles up as a jam session space for students from the nearby music school. The famous Cova del Drac closed down in 2004 and reopened a couple of years later as **La Cova del Drac – Jazz Room**. It functions largely as a dance club but there are usually a couple of live gigs every month. **Heligogàbal**, a small underground bar in Gràcia, also hosts jazz concerts.

Concerts are generally free, or very cheap. The **Harlem Jazz Club** is narrow, crowded and smoky but it's one of the city's longest surviving clubs for alternative and lesser-known jazz troupes. **Little Italy** is a boon for those who like the tinkle of the piano keyboard and the soft pluck of the double bass. Enjoy an eclectic mix of blues, jazz and bossa nova over dinner on Wednesdays and Thursdays. The most formal of the jazz venues, however, is Barcelona's "free" theatre – the **Teatre Lliure** in Montjuïc is an excellent source for contemporary jazz masters, modern orchestras and experimental grooves, playing host to a diverse number of musicians from Eric Mingus to The Sun Ra Arkestra directed by Marshall Allen. For lovers of the genre, this is the best of the lot.

One of the two major players for pop and rock maestros is **Bikini**, Barcelona's very own Studio 54 – in fact, it opened in 1953, preceding the New York icon by a year. This veteran of the scene, which opens from midnight onwards, is still going strong with a robust line-up of big-name bands and a cocktail of different club nights. The other, **Razzmatazz**, arguably the city's most important live music venue, plays host to the likes of Róisín Murphy, Arctic

Monkeys, Air and Jarvis Cocker. Club sessions go until dawn in Lolita, The Loft and three other clubs next door. The Loft is a trendy club that also holds rock and jazz concerts several nights a week.

For a touch of unbeatable glam **Luz de Gas** is a glitzy ballroom that oozes old-fashioned atmosphere with its lamp-lit tables, chandeliers and a programme of bands and shows that enjoyed their heyday in the 1970s and '80s. The biggest international stars – including Madonna, Beyoncé, Eric Clapton, and Coldplay – take over the huge arenas on Montjuïc, the **Estadi Olímpic** and the **Palau Sant Jordi** *(see p91)*.

If your taste is for the small and subtle, the **Bar Pastis** is a minuscule bar, decorated with dusty bottles and yellowing posters from French musicals. Live French love ballads, tango and coplas can be heard here most nights of the week.

Flamenco

Although flamenco is traditionally an Andalusian artform, originally created by the gypsies of Southern Spain to depict their sufferings and hardship, it has for many years been a popular form of entertainment in Barcelona and throughout Spain. One of the best places to see a live show is **El Tablao de Carmen**, a stylish

restaurant serving both Catalan and Andalucian dishes in the Poble Espanyol. The venue is named after Carmen Amaya, a famous dancer who performed for King Alfonso XIII in 1929, in the very spot where it now stands. Various dinner/show packages are available.

For a less formal ambience, **Los Tarantos**, situated in the Plaça Reial, is a lively atmospheric nightspot with live flamenco and Latin music every night of the week. Although it caters to the tourist trade, the performances are very reasonably priced.

JazzSí Club Taller de Músics *(see p166)* offers traditional flamenco concerts on Fridays, often accompanied by well-known guest musicians.

DIRECTORY

Opera and Classical Music

L'Auditori de Barcelona
C/Lepant 150,
Eixample.
Map 4 E1.
Tel 93 247 93 00.
W auditori.cat

Gran Teatre del Liceu
La Rambla 51,
Barri Gòtic.
Map 5 A1.
Tel 93 485 99 00.
W liceubarcelona.com

Palau de la Música Catalana
C/Palau de la
Música 4,
La Ribera.
Map 5 B1.
Tel 902 442 882.
W palaumusica.cat

Live Music: Rock, Jazz and Blues

Bar Pastis
C/Santa Mònica 4,
El Raval.
Map 2 F4.
Tel 634 93 84 22.
W barpastis.com

Bikini
Deu I Mata 105,
LesCorts.
Tel 93 322 08 00.
W bikinibcn.com

La Cova del Drac – Jazz Room
C/Vallmajor 33.
Tel 93 319 17 89.
W masimas.com

Harlem Jazz Club
C/Comtessa de
Sobradiel 8,
Barri Gòtic.
Tel 93 310 07 55.
W harlemjazzclub.es

Heliogàbal
Ramón y Cajal 80,
Gràcia.
Map 3 C2.
W heliogabal.com

Jamboree
Plaça Reial 17,
Barri Gòtic.
Map 5 A3.
Tel 93 319 17 89.
W masimas.com

JazzSí Club Taller de Músics
C/Requesens 2,
El Raval.
Tel 93 329 00 20.
W tallerdemusics.com

Little Italy
C/Rec 30,
Born.
Map 5 C3.
Tel 93 319 79 73.

Luz de Gas
C/Muntaner 246.
Map 2 F1.
Tel 93 209 77 11.
W luzdegas.com

Razzmatazz
C/Pamplona 88,
Poblenou.
Map 4 F5.
Tel 93 320 82 00.
W salarazzmatazz.com

Teatre Lliure
Plaça Marigida Xirgu 1.
Tel 93 289 27 70.
W teatrelliure.com

Flamenco

El Tablao de Carmen
Arcs, 9.
Poble Espanyol.
Map 1 B1
Tel 933 25 68 95.
W tablaodecarmen.com

Los Tarantos
Plaça Reial 17.
Map 5 A3.
Tel 933 19 17 89.
W masimas.com/tarantos

Concert Venues

L'Auditori
C/Lepant 150.
Tel 93 247 93 00.
W auditori.com

Teatre Lliure
Plaça Margarida Xirgu 1,
Montjuïc.
Tel 93 289 27 70.
W teatrelliure.com

Sala Fabià Puigserver
Passeig Santa
Madrona 40-46,
Montjuïc.
Map 1 B3.
Tel 93 289 27 70.

Nightlife

If New York is the city that never sleeps, then Barcelona is the one that never goes to bed and those with energy can party around the clock, all week. It has one of the most varied scenes, with something for everybody. Old-fashioned dance halls rub shoulders with underground drum and bass clubs and trashy techno discos, and club-goers are either glammed-up or grunged-out. Each *barrio* (neighbourhood) offers a different flavour.

Nightlife

In the summer the beaches become party havens when the *xiringuitos* (beach bars) spring back into life. Wander from Platja de Sant Sebastià in Barceloneta, all the way to Bogatell (a few kilometres beyond the Hotel Arts) and you'll find people dancing barefoot on the sand to the tune of Barcelona's innumerable DJs. Way uptown (above the Diagonal), the city's most glamorous terraces morph into social hubs while the Barri Gòtic – lively at the best of times – becomes one massive street party throughout the summer. If you want to hang with the locals, the demolition of some of El Raval's less salubrious streets has meant that the neighbourhood has become much safer and easier to move about. The underground vibe, however, remains steadfastly intact with tiny hole-in-the-wall-style bars where folks drink and boogie till the early hours. Similarly, Gràcia has a bohemian, studenty ambience. If it's an alternative scene you seek Poble Sec has a handful of "ring-to-enter" joints and the city's only serious drum and bass club, **Plataforma**. The city also has a thriving and friendly gay scene, most notably within the Eixample Esquerra, also known as the Gay Eixample, boasting numerous late-night drinking holes, discothèques, saunas and cabarets.

Barri Gòtic

The Plaça Reial is overrun with tourists banging on tin drums and whooping it up, but if you're looking for more grown-up fun, check out the **Fantástico Club**. Pop and electro music combined with candy-coloured decor make this club a hit with the fashionable crowd. Underground and cosmopolitan are words that best describe the atmosphere and clientele of **Club Fellini**, where eccentricity merges into the freakishly original. It has three rooms with different music and decor in each. The nightclub **New York**, in contrast, has come over all loungey and these days is inclined towards more commercially gratifying tunes. The vibe here is more disco.

El Raval

Designer clubs proliferate in Barcelona these days, but check out the old-school ambience of **Marsella**, founded in 1820 and still famous for its wicked green absinthe *(absenta)*. The likes of Picasso, Hemingway and Miró are said to have drunk here and the 19th-century-styled interior, with marble tables, chandeliers and battered old mirrors evokes a bygone era. Equally historic is **Bar Almirall**, founded in 1860; head for the back of the room, where deep sofas, strong cocktails and smooth sounds create an intimate atmosphere in the early hours.

With its red, black and white decor and a specially designed underlit bar, **Zentraus** is one of the best looking clubs in the neighbourhood. Doubling up as a restaurant until midnight or so, the tables are cleared away once the DJ sessions get underway. For the more adventurous, **Moog** is more extreme with blaring, heart-pumping techno for aficionados of the genre. The stark industrial interior gives it the character of a New York nightclub in the mid-1990s. Likewise, the state-of-the-art sound system ensures a thumping, ear-bleedingly good night out.

Port Vell and Port Olímpic

Beach parties aside, this area continues to be a hub for creatures of the night. The Port Olímpic itself is nothing but bars and boats, while the leisure and shopping complex **Maremagnum** *(see p155)* has a clutch of elegant clubs. Under the Hotel Arts, **Catwalk** is still one of the only places in the city for hip hop and R'n'B. **C.D.L.C.** and nearby restaurant and lounge bar **Shôko**, in front of the Hotel Arts, however, still manage to draw the celebrities staying nearby.

Eixample

One of the city's best loved discos, **City Hall** is a multiple space and terrace, where you can pick and choose your groove according to your mood. It has different themes every night from Saturday night-fever discos to Sunday chill-outs. **Luz de Gaz** *(see p167)* is theatrically stylish, with retro sounds from the 1970s and '80s. For a more laid-back atmosphere, **Opium** is a beach club on the Barceloneta beach with a pleasant terrace. **Dow Jones** has a unique "Stock Exchange" system for setting the prices of drinks, which rise and fall with demand. For sports fans they also offer Sky coverage.

Poble Sec

The most alternative night-life has come to roost in the "dry village", though in name only. The bars are wet and the music is happening. **Apolo** is another old-fashioned music hall, though it attracts a more independent breed of DJ and performer. Expect anything here, from soulful gypsy folk singers from Marseille, to the legendary purveyor of deep funk, Keb Darge.

Further into the village, **Mau Mau** is an alternative club and cultural centre with a firm eye on what's new and happening. This could mean local DJs, Japanese musicians such as the cultish Cinema Dub Monks, alternative cinema and multimedia art installations. If it's of the here and now, chances are Mau Mau's on it. For the seriously hardcore and lovers of high-speed garage, **Plataforma** is Barcelona's only serious drum and bass club, hosting DJs from far and wide in a huge concrete warehouse.

Gràcia and Tibidabo

Tiny and always packed, the **Mond Bar** attracts music-lovers from all over wishing to dip into tunes from the past. The resident DJs delight a 20-something crowd with 1970s sessions of northern soul and Motown. And high up above the rest, **Elephant** offers the best in mansion-house clubbing experiences, with chill-out lounges, two dance floors, a VIP area, sprawling terraces and prices to suit the altitude.

Out of Town

The mega-clubs are located well away from the city centre and from anyone trying to sleep, and most of them are only open on Friday and Saturday nights. The big boys are based in Poble Espanyol, where folks can party until the sunrise. **La Terrrazza,** is only open in the summer, but is well-known for its all-night rave parties under the stars, and takes its name from the giant terrace it occupies. Nearby, on Plaça Espanya, the Ibiza-style **Privilege** hosts some of the best parties in town with top national and international DJs. It is also possible to book a table in the VIP area.

Further out of town you will find **Up and Down**, the most sophisticated and innovative night club in the area. It also houses a restaurant and a lounge terrace, with an exquisite design. It tries to reproduce the Ibiza spirit. Alternatively, **Liquid** is the city's only summer club with a swimming pool. The only drawback is that should you wish to leave before the party's over, finding a taxi back into town can be a big problem.

DIRECTORY

Barri Gòtic

Club Fellini
La Rambla 27, Barri Gòtic.
Map 2 F3.
Tel 93 272 49 80.
🇼 clubfellini.com

Fantástico Club
Passatge Escudellers 3,
Barri Gòtic.
Map 5 A3.
Tel 93 317 54 11.

New York
C/Escudellers 5,
Barri Gòtic.
Map 5 A3.
Tel 93 318 87 30.

El Raval

Bar Almirall
C/Joaquin Costa 33,
El Raval.
Map 2 F2.
Tel 93 318 99 17.

Marsella
C/Sant Pau 65
El Raval.
Map 2 F3.
Tel 93 442 72 63.

Moog
C/Arc del Teatre 3,
El Raval.
Map 2 F4.
Tel 93 319 17 89.
🇼 moog-barcelona.es

Zentraus
Rambla de Raval 41,
El Raval.
Map 2 F3.
Tel 93 443 80 78.
🇼 zentraus.cat

Port Vell and Port Olímpic

Catwalk
Ramon Trias Fargas 2–4,
Port Olímpic.
Map 6 E4.
Tel 93 221 61 61.
🇼 clubcatwalk.net

C.D.L.C.
Passeig Marítim 32,
Port Olímpic.
Map 6 E4.
Tel 93 224 04 70.
🇼 cdlcbarcelona.com

Shôko
Passeig Marítim 36,
Port Olímpic.
Map 6 E4.
Tel 93 225 92 00.
🇼 shoko.biz

Eixample

City Hall
Rambla Catalunya 2–4,
Eixample. **Map** 3 A3.
Tel 93 233 33 33.
🇼 cityhallbarcelona.
com

Dow Jones ·
Bruc 97, Eixample.
Map 3 B4.
Tel 93 420 35 48.

Luz de Gas
C/ Muntaner 246.
Tel 93 209 77 11.
🇼 luzdegas.com

Opium
Passeig Marítim de la
Barceloneta 34.
Tel 902 26 74 86.
🇼 opiummar.com

Poble Sec

Apolo
C/Nou de la Rambla 113,
Poble Sec.
Map 2 D4.
Tel 93 441 40 01.
🇼 sala-apolo.com

Mau Mau
C/Fontrodona 33,
Poble Sec.
Map 2 D3.
Tel 93 441 80 15.
🇼 maumauunder
ground.com

Plataforma
C/Nou de la Rambla 145,
Poble Sec.
Map 2 D4.
Tel 93 329 00 29.

Gràcia and Tibidabo

Elephant
Passeig dels Til.lers 1,
Tibidabo.
Tel 93 334 02 58.
🇼 elephantbcn.com

Mond Bar
Plaza del Sol 21,
Gràcia.
Map 3 B1.
Tel 93 272 09 10.

Out of Town

Liquid
(summer only) Complex
Esportiu Hospitalet Nord,
Av Manuel Azaña,
Hospitalet.
Privilege C/Tarragona 141.
Tel 63 444 99 66.
🇼 privilege barcelona.
com

La Terrrazza
Poble Espanyol, Av de
Francesc Ferrer i Guàrdia.
Map 1 B1.
Tel 687 96 98 25.
🇼 laterrrazza.com

Up and Down
Av. Doctor Marañón 17.
Tel 93 448 61 15.
🇼 upanddown
barcelona.com

Sports and Outdoor Activities

From the mountains to the sea, Catalonia provides all manner of terrain for enjoying the outdoor life. The hot summer months can be filled with water activities, from fishing to white-water rafting, while skiers head for the hills with the first snowfalls of winter. Nature lovers will find spectacular wildlife habitats, while Barcelona city offers beaches and numerous sports facilities.

City Facilities

Barcelona has around 30 municipal pools (*piscines municipales*), including the **Piscines Bernat Picornell** next to the **Estadi Olímpic** and **Palau Sant Jordi** sports stadia on Montjuïc. The pools were the venue for the 1992 Olympic swimming events. The Estadi Olímpic is an athletics stadium and is often used for concerts. The Palau Sant Jordi is used for indoor sports, as well as musical and recreational activities. Tennis fans are well provided for and the **Centre Municipal de Tennis Vall d'Hebron** caters for younger players too. Ice-skating can be fun and the **Pista de Gel del FC Barcelona** offers skate rental and runs an ice-hockey school. Golf courses within easy reach of Barcelona are **Golf Sant Cugat** and **Golf El Prat**. There are several riding stables, and the **Escola Hípica** at Sant Cugat allows day outings over the Collserola hills. Cycle shops hire by the hour, half day and full day. **Bike Tours Barcelona** organizes cycle tours around Barcelona.

Airborne Activities

Catalonia has several small airports where planes can be hired and parachute jumps made. One of the best known flying clubs is **Aeroclub** in Sabadell. Paragliding is popular from any high spot and **Club Elements** offers all kinds of adventure sports, including bungee jumping and ballooning, as an exciting alternative way to see the sights.

Bird Watching

Bird life in Catalonia is a huge attraction for dedicated bird-watchers. Northern European visitors in particular will be thrilled by the sight of hoopoes, bee-eaters, golden orioles and pratincoles. Two major wetland areas, where migratory birds include flamingoes, are **Delta de l'Ebre** (*see p131*), south of Tarragona, with a visitor centre in Deltebre, and **Aiguamolls de l'Empordà** around Sant Pere Pescador in the Bay of Roses. Both are easy to get to, and their visitor centres supply binoculars and guide services. The best times to visit

Griffon vulture

are early morning and evening. The Pyrenees are home to many raptors, including short-toed, golden and Bonelli eagles, and Egyptian, griffon and bearded vultures. The **Parc Natural del Cadí-Moixeró** (*see p116*), in the foothills of the Pyrenees, has a visitor centre in Bagà. Look out for alpine choughs, wallcreepers and peregrine falcons, as well as black woodpeckers in the wooded areas.

An angler's paradise – fishing for trout amid spectacular scenery

Field Sports

Sea fishing is free, but a permit (*un permís*) is required for river fishing. Permits can usually be obtained through local tourist offices.

The Noguera Pallaresa and Segre are fine trout-fishing rivers and the season runs from mid-March to the end of August. The game-hunting season is generally from October to March. Short leases and permits can be obtained from the **Federació Catalana de Caça** in Barcelona or from a local hunting association (*associació de caça*). Travel agents specializing in hunting and fishing breaks will also readily organise licences.

Hiking

All the national parks and reserves publish maps and walking suggestions. Good areas close to Barcelona are the Collserola hills and the chestnut woods of Montseny. Long-distance GR (*Gran Recorrido*) footpaths criss-cross Catalonia and the walking possibilities

Paragliding above the Vall d'Aran in the eastern Pyrenees

Shooting the rapids on the white waters of the Noguera Pallaresa

in the **Parc Nacional d'Aigües-tortes** *(see p115)* and the Pyrenees are particularly good, with mountain refuges *(see p135)* for serious hikers. Walkers can obtain information from the **Centre Excursionista de Catalunya** *(see p135)*. The **Llibreria Quera**, in Carrer de Petritxol (No. 2) in Barcelona's Barri Gòtic, is the best bookshop for maps and guide books.

All the usual rules apply to those setting off to explore the wilderness – check weather forecasts, wear appropriate clothing, take adequate provisions and let someone know where you are going.

Watersports

There are around 40 marinas along Catalonia's 580 km (360 miles) of coast, and a very wide range of watersports and activities is available. In Barcelona itself, the **Centre Municipal de Vela Port Olímpic** gives sailing lessons and has a variety of craft. The Costa Brava has long been a good spot for

scuba diving. The best place is around the protected Illes Medes *(see p123)*, from the resort of L'Estartit. There are also diving schools around Cadaqués and Cap Begur, notably at Calella de Palafrugell, launching point for the Illes Ullastres.

The town of Sort on the Riu Noguera Pallaresa is a centre for exciting water-sports such as white-water rafting, canoeing, kayaking and cave diving. Bookings for these and other adventure activities can be made through **Yetiemotions**.

Winter Sports

The Pyrenees offer great winter skiing just 2–3 hours' drive from Barcelona, and at weekends the resorts fill up with city crowds. There are some 20 ski areas. La Molina is good for beginners and Baqueira-Beret *(see p115)* is where Spain's royal family skis. Puigcerdà *(see p116)* in the Cerdanya is a good base for downhill and nordic skiing within reach of 15 ski stations in Catalonia, Andorra and France. The **Associació Catalana d'Estacions d'Esquí i Activitats de Muntanya (ACEM)** supplies resort details, while **Teletiempo**, a weather hotline, provides information on current weather conditions. In Barcelona, a dry ski slope has been installed beside the Piscines Bernat Picornell on Montjuïc.

Skiing at one of the many ski stations in the Pyrenees within easy reach of Barcelona

DIRECTORY

ACEM
Tel 93 416 01 94.
[W] catneu.net

Aeroclub de Sabadell
Tel 93 710 19 52.
[W] aeroclub.es

Aiguamolls de l'Empordà
Tel 972 45 42 22.
[W] aiguamolls.org

Bike Tours Barcelona
Tel 93 268 21 05.
[W] bicicletabarcelona.com

Centre Excursionista de Catalunya
Tel 93 315 23 11.
[W] cec.cat

Centre Municipal de Tennis Vall d'Hebron
Tel 93 427 65 00.

Centre Municipal de Vela Port Olímpic
Tel 93 225 79 40.
[W] velabarcelona.com

Club Elements
Tel 90 219 65 59.
[W] clubelements.com

Delta de l'Ebre
Tel 977 48 21 81.

Escola Hípica
Tel 93 553 11 83.
[W] hipicacancaldes.com

Estadi Olímpic/ Palau Sant Jordi
Tel 93 426 20 89.

Federació Catalana de Caça
Tel 93 319 10 66.
[W] federcat.com

Golf El Prat
Tel 93 728 1000.
[W] rcgep.com

Golf Sant Cugat
Tel 93 674 39 08.
[W] golfsantcugat.com

Llibreria Quera
Tel 93 318 07 43.

Parc Nacional d'Aigüestortes
Tel 973 69 61 89.

Parc Natural del Cadí-Moixeró
Tel 93 824 41 51.

Piscines Bernat Picornell
Tel 93 423 40 41.
[W] picornell.cat

Pista de Gel del FC Barcelona
Tel 93 496 36 30.

Teletiempo
Tel 807 17 03 65 (Spain).
[W] aemet.es

Yetiemotions
Tel 97 362 22 01.
[W] yetiemotions.com

SURVIVAL
GUIDE

PRACTICAL INFORMATION

Catalonia has an excellent tourist infrastructure and offers visitors a wealth of options, from soaking in the sun on a sandy beach to hiking on a remote mountain trail. There are tourist offices in every town, which can assist in finding accommodation, restaurants and activities. Larger offices usually have leaflets in several different languages. Be aware that August is Spain's main vacation month, and some businesses close for the whole month. Try to find out in advance if your visit coincides with local *festes* (fiestas), as these can entail widespread closures.

Visas and Passports

Spain is part of the Schengen common European border treaty. Visas are not currently required for citizens of the EU, Iceland, Liechtenstein, Norway, the USA, Canada, Australia or New Zealand. However it is best to check visa requirements before travelling. Spanish embassies supply a list of other countries in the non-visa category. Tourists from these countries may stay for 90 days within a continuous 180-day period. The *Oficina d'estrangers de Barcelona*, a local government office, handles visa extensions.

Tax-Free Goods and Customs Information

Non-EU residents can reclaim IVA (VAT) on single items worth over €90 bought in shops displaying a "Tax-free Shopping" sign, within six months of purchase. (Food, drink, cars, motorbikes, tobacco and medicines are exempt.) You pay the full price and ask the sales assistant for a tax-free cheque, which you then present to customs to be stamped as you leave Spain (do this before checking your bags). The refund is issued either on your credit card or in cash at La Caixa bank branches at Terminals 1 and 2B of Barcelona airport.

Tourist Information

Barcelona has three main *oficines de turisme* providing information on the city, its attractions, transport and places to stay and eat, all run by **Turisme de Barcelona**. A fourth office, in the Passeig de Gràcia and run by **Turisme de**

Catalunya, a department of the Generalitat (Catalonia's government), provides information on the rest of the region. Other major towns have their own tourist offices providing information published by the Generalitat and the province's local administration (*patronat*). There are Spanish National Tourist Offices in the following English-speaking cities: New York, Chicago, Miami, Los Angeles, London and Toronto.

In Barcelona during the summer, pairs of young information officers, known as Red Jackets and generally English-speaking, provide tourist information in the streets of the Barri Gòtic, La Rambla and the Passeig de Gràcia.

Tourists consulting a map in Barcelona

Language

Though Catalan is the language spoken by native Catalans, Catalonia is a bilingual country where people also speak *Castellano* (Spanish). If you respond in Spanish to a question or greeting made in Catalan, the speaker will usually switch to Spanish. Official signs and documents are in both

languages. However, as Barcelona in particular regards itself as truly cosmopolitan, most tourist literature is also in English and French.

Opening Hours

Most museums and monuments close on Mondays. On other days they generally open from 10am to 2pm and, usually reopen from 4 or 5pm to 8pm. It is worth checking specific opening times in advance as larger museums often stay open throughout the day. Churches may only be opened for services. In smaller towns it is common for churches, castles and other sights to be kept locked. The key (*la clau*), available on request, will be with a caretaker, kept at the town hall (*ajuntament*), or perhaps at the local bar. Admission is charged for most museums and monuments, although museums are often free on some specific days and on certain national holidays.

Travelling on a Budget

Nearly all restaurants offer a three-course midday *Menú del día* with wine for as little as €9. You may have to ask to see it.

There are three official types of accommodation, with a *hostal* or a *pensión* being much cheaper than a *hotel*. The quality varies so ask to see a room before booking.

Holders of the International Student Identity Card (ISIC) can get discounts on travel and entrance fees to museums and galleries. **Viatgeteca** sells these as well as youth hostel cards. **Unlimited Youth Student Travel** specializes in student travel.

Many museums offer free or discounted entry to retired visitors. Be prepared to show your passport to prove your age.

Tourist offices sell the €30 articketBCN, which allows entry to six museums for three months from the first visit: the Centre de Cultura Contemporània de Barcelona; Museu Nacional d'Art de Catalunya; Museu d'Art Contemporani; Museu Picasso; Fundació Joan Miró; and Fundació Antoni Tàpies. It can also be bought at the participating museums and at www.telentrada.com.

MACBA *(see p64)* offers reduced admission to students

Travellers with Special Needs

Catalonia's association for the disabled, the Federació ECOM *(see p135)*, has hotel lists and travel advice for the whole region. **Disabled Accessible Travel** can organize tours and excursions, and will also give free advice on accessible hotels in the city. Tourist

Sign for disabled access

offices and the social services departments of town halls supply information on local facilities. A travel agency, **Viajes 2000**, specializes in vacations for disabled people.

Travelling with Children

Barcelona is one of the most child-friendly major cities in Europe, given its numerous parks, play areas, beaches and activities. As in the rest of Spain, people in Catalonia are very family oriented and children are generally welcome in all restaurants and bars until late in

the evening. It is also usual for people to try to interact with your children, offering them sweets in shops or striking up a conversation with them.

All children under 1.35 m (4 ft 5 inches) are required by law to use a specially adapted car seat, except when travelling by taxi. Children under the age of four travel for free on the Metro and on trains there is a reduced fare for those aged between 4 and 13.

Gay and Lesbian Travellers

Barcelona is a famously tolerant and open-minded city. The gay centre of Barcelona is in the Eixample district (sometimes referred to as "Gayxample"), where most of the gay bars, hotels, restaurants and shops are concentrated. The busy gay beach resort of Sitges is a short journey by train or car, but there are smaller beaches within Barcelona: Platja Mar Bella has a gay beach, and Platja de Sant Sebastià has a mixed, clothing optional, nude beach at the end of the Barceloneta district.

Electrical Adaptors

Spain's electricity supply is 220 volts. Plugs have two round pins. A three-tier standard travel converter enables you to use appliances from abroad. You can also find adaptors in department stores *(see p154)* and in hardware stores *(ferreteries)*.

Spanish Time

Spain is 1 hour ahead of Greenwich Mean Time (GMT) in winter *(l'hivern)* and 2 hours in summer *(l'estiu)*, and uses the 24-hour clock. *La matinada* is the small hours, *el matís* (morning) lasts until about 1pm, while *migdia* (midday) is from 1 to 4pm. *La tarda* is the afternoon, *el vespre* the evening and *la nit* the night.

Responsible Tourism

There has been a growth in sustainable tourism in Catalonia over recent years, concentrated

on the excellent network of *Casas rurales*. These are small, traditional, family-owned farmhouses that offer room and board in traditional, rural areas. ASETUR is the association of rural tourism in Spain and has substantial information on its website.

There are also many local green tourism initiatives and activities in different regions; information can be found through local tourist offices. Catalonia still has many small shops selling local produce and it is possible to support the local economies through shopping in these rather than in chain stores.

DIRECTORY

Tourist Information

Turisme de Barcelona
Plaça de Catalunya 17, subterrani.
Map 5 A1.
Tel 93 285 38 34.
C/Ciutat 2 (Ajuntament).
Map 5 A2.
Tel 93 285 38 34.
Estació Sants, Pl Països Catalans.
Tel 93 285 38 34.
w barcelonaturisme.com

Turisme de Catalunya
Palau Robert, Pg de Gràcia 107.
Map 3 A3.
Tel 93 238 80 91/2/3.

Travelling on a Budget

Unlimited Youth Student Travel & Viatgeteca
Carrer Calàbria 147.
Map 2 D1.
Tel 93 483 83 84.

Travellers with Special Needs

Disabled Accessible Travel
Tel 60 591 87 69.
w disabledaccessibletravel.com

Viajes 2000
C/Aribau 123.
Map 2 F1.
Tel 93 323 96 60.
w viajes2000.com

Responsible Tourism

ASETUR
Travessera de les Corts 131–159.
Tel 93 402 29 66.
w ecoturismorural.com

Personal Security and Health

In Catalonia, as in most parts of Western Europe, rural areas are quite safe, while towns and cities warrant more care. Keep cards and money in a belt, don't leave valuables in your car and avoid poorly lit areas at night. If you feel ill, there will always be a local *farmàcia* (pharmacy) open. In Spain, pharmacists can prescribe some drugs as well as advise. Report lost documents to your consulate *(see p177)* and to the *Mossos d'Esquadra* at the local *comissaria* (police station). Emergency numbers are listed opposite.

Police in Catalonia

In Catalonia, police services are organized into three forces. The *Guàrdia Civil* (paramilitary Civil Guard), dressed in olive-green, polices only borders and airports. In black and red uniforms, the *Mossos d'Escuadra*, the autonomous government's police service, deals with major crime in larger towns and national security, as well as immigration. The *Guàrdia Urbana*, dressed in blue, deals with traffic regulation and the policing of local communities.

If you are a victim of crime, report to the local *comissaria*. There are several dotted around the city, including at Carrer Nou de la Rambla 76–8 (between Montjuïc and the Old Town), at Vía Laietana 43 (in the Barri Gòtic) and at Carrer de l'Almirall Cervera 34 (in Barceloneta). There is also a small office located in Plaça Catalunya.

Mosso
d'Esquadra

Guàrdia
Urbana

Crowds strolling on the busy street of La Rambla

What to be Aware of

As in most European cities, pickpocketing in Barcelona is common so it is wise to take sensible precautions when out and about, especially if travelling during peak season. Always be vigilant with handbags, wallets and cameras, especially in crowds, at major tourist attractions, and cafés and bars. In particular, keep an eye on your bag at outdoor cafés, as possessions have been known to disappear.

The more common tricks include someone distracting your attention by alerting you to a "stain" on your clothing (this happens a lot in the Metro) or carnation sellers who deftly empty your wallet when you are trying to pay them.

Never leave valuables in your car and be aware of people hanging around ATMs since credit card frauds are also on the increase, especially along the coast.

Barcelona is generally safe for walking, although it is advisable to avoid the Barri Xinès area at night. It should be remembered, however, that violent crime and muggings in Barcelona are rare.

Always take care when using pedestrian crossings, particularly those without lights. Wait until there is a large enough gap to cross safely.

In an Emergency

The national telephone number throughout Spain for all emergency services is 112. After dialling, ask for *policia* (police), *bombers* (fire brigade) or *ambulància* (ambulance). There are also local numbers for the individual emergency services *(opposite)*.

Outside of Barcelona, the largely voluntary *Creu Roja* (Red Cross) often responds to 112 emergency calls for ambulances.

Ambulances transport patients straight to hospital *urgències* (accident and emergency departments).

Creu Roja

Red Cross ambulance sign

URGÈNCIES

Accident and Emergency sign

Lost and Stolen Property

Report a loss or theft straight away to the *Guàrdia Urbana*, as many insurance companies give you only 24 hours to make the report. You must make a *denúncia* (written statement) to the police and get a copy for your insurers.

Your consulate can replace a missing passport or issue you with an emergency passport to return to your country of residence, but cannot provide financial assistance, even in emergencies.

Outdoor Hazards

Catalonia's hot summers create the prime conditions for forest fires; extinguish cigarettes and take empty bottles away with you as sun shining on the glass can cause flames. If you go climbing or hill-walking, be properly equipped and let someone know your route. Do not enter a *vedat de caça* (hunting reserve) or *camí particular* (private driveway).

In late spring and throughout the summer, make sure you have some good insect repellent with you to deal with Tiger Mosquitoes, a more virulent strain of irritating, biting insects from Asia that have become prevalent in the area surrounding Barcelona.

Legal Assistance

If you are arrested, you have the right to telephone your consulate which can provide a list of bilingual lawyers. The *Collegi d'Advocats* (Lawyers' Association) can guide you on getting legal advice or representation.

Some holiday insurance policies cover legal costs and provide a helpline you can call for assistance.

The most common incidents where the law is broken involve alcohol or drugs. It is illegal to drink alcohol in the street, or to purchase alcohol from unlicensed street vendors. If you are caught you may incur a large fine. Driving offences such as speeding and drink driving also result in heavy fines and the possible loss of your licence.

Front of a high-street *farmàcia* (pharmacy) in Catalonia

Medical Treatment

Any EU national who falls ill in Spain is entitled to social security cover. The Spanish health service is generally efficient and care is of a high standard. To claim medical treatment, UK citizens must apply for a European Health Insurance Card online or at a post office prior to travelling. All basic and emergency treatments are covered by the card at public hospitals, but additional medical insurance is needed for treatment in private hospitals.

For private medical care in Spain ask at a tourist office, or at your consulate or hotel for the name of a doctor. Visitors from the US should make sure their insurance covers medical care abroad. If payment is needed at the time of treatment, ask for an itemized bill. Some insurance companies will ask for an official translation.

For non-emergencies, a *farmacèutic* (pharmacist) can advise and, at times, prescribe without a doctor's consultation for minor infections, but if you have a fever they will direct you to *urgències* (emergencies) at a hospital or, in smaller towns, to an *ambulatori* (medical centre). The sign for a *farmàcia* is an illuminated red or green cross. The addresses of those open at night or at weekends are listed in all pharmacy windows.

Public Conveniences

There are a number of pay-per-use automatic public toilets in the city centre. If you can't find one, simply walk into a bar, café, department store or hotel and ask for *els serveis* or *el lavabo* (in Catalan), or *los servicios* or *los aseos* (in Spanish). On motorways, there are toilets at service stations. Women may have to request *la clau* (the key).

Patrol car of the *Guàrdia Urbana*

Ambulance displaying the Barcelona 061 emergency number

Fire engine displaying the national emergency number

DIRECTORY

In an Emergency

Police (Policia)
Fire Brigade (Bombers)
Ambulance (Ambulància)
Tel 112 (national number).

Police
Policia Nacional
Tel 091.
Guàrdia Urbana
Tel 092.
Mossos d'Esquadra
Tel 088.

Fire Brigade (local numbers)
Tel 080 (Barcelona),
085 (Lleida, Girona, Tarragona).

Ambulance (local numbers)
Tel 061 (Barcelona), use 112 (national number) elsewhere.

Consulates

Canada
Plaça de Catalunya 9, 1°–2°,
08002 Barcelona.
Tel 93 270 36 14.

United Kingdom
Avinguda Diagonal 477, 13°
08036 Barcelona.
Tel 902 109 356.

United States
Passeig de la Reina Elisenda 23,
08034 Barcelona.
Tel 93 280 22 27.

Banking and Currency

You may enter Spain with an unlimited amount of money, but if you intend to export more than €6,000, you should declare it. Traveller's cheques may be exchanged at banks, bureaux de change (*canvi* in Catalan, *cambio* in Spanish), some hotels and some shops. Banks generally offer the best exchange rates. The cheapest exchange rate may be offered on your credit or direct debit card, which may be used in cash dispensers displaying the appropriate sign.

A branch of La Caixa, the largest savings bank in Spain

Banks and Bureaux de Change

As a rule of thumb, banks in Catalonia are open from 8am to 2pm on weekdays. Some open until 1pm on Saturdays, but most are closed on Saturdays from July through September. Branches of some of the larger banks in the centre of Barcelona are beginning to extend their weekday opening hours, but this is not yet a widespread practice.

Some city-centre banks have a foreign exchange desk signed *Canvi/Cambio* or *Moneda estrangera/ extranjera*. Always take your passport as proof of ID to effect any transaction.

You can draw cash on major credit and debit cards at a bank. Several US and UK banks have branches in Barcelona, including **Citibank**, **Barclays** and **Lloyds TSB**. If you bank with them, you can cash a cheque there.

A bureau de change, which is indicated by the sign *Canvi/ Cambio*, or the sign "Change", will invariably charge a higher rate of commission than a bank, but will often remain open after hours. *Caixes d'estalvi/ Cajas de ahorro* (savings banks) also exchange money. They open from 8:30am to 2pm on weekdays, and also on Thursdays from 4:30 to 7:45pm.

ATMs

If your card is linked to your home bank account, you can use it with your PIN to withdraw money from cash dispensers/ ATMs. All dispensers take **VISA** or **MasterCard**. Cards with a Cirrus or Maestro logo can also be widely used to withdraw

money from cash machines. Before you enter your PIN, instructions are displayed in Catalan, Spanish, English, French and German. Many dispensers are inside buildings these days, and to gain access customers must run their cards through a door- entry system.

ServiCaixa cash dispensers can also be used to purchase theatre, concert and cinema tickets, a convenient way to beat the queues for the most popular shows. Credit for mobile phones can also be topped up using one of these dispensers.

Credit and Debit Cards

The most widely accepted cards in Spain are **VISA** and **MasterCard**. **American Express** is also taken in some parts of the city. Credit cards are usually the cheapest method of payment, as you are not charged commission and are given the official rate of the day. You can also use prepaid VISA, MasterCard cards and Travel Money Cards, which work like debit cards in shops and restaurants.

All cash dispensers accept most foreign cards, although the commission charged depends on your bank. You may be given the choice to pay the commission in euro or in your home currency. More and more cash machines are closed at night, particularly in the old city, due to crime.

Before you leave home, it is a good idea to phone your credit card provider and your bank to inform them that you will be travelling abroad, otherwise you may find that your credit card

gets blocked by the bank's fraud prevention system when you start using it in Barcelona.

When you pay with a card, cashiers will usually pass it through a card reading machine. In shops you will always be asked for additional photo ID or to key in your PIN. As leaving your passport in the hotel safe is preferable, make sure that you have an alternative original document on hand (photocopies will rarely do) such as a driver's licence. Cards are not readily accepted in many smaller bars and restaurants, so it is advisable to check first or carry some cash with you.

DIRECTORY

Banks

Barclays Bank
Passeig de Gràcia 45.
Map 3 A4.
Tel 901 14 14 14.

Citibank
Rambla de Catalunya 12.
Map 3 A4.
Tel 93 344 17 38.

Lloyds TSB Bank
Rambla de Catalunya 123
& Avinguda Diagonal 550.
Tel 902 02 43 65.

Lost Cards

American Express
Tel 900 81 45 00.

Diners Club
Tel 902 40 11 12.

MasterCard
Tel 900 97 12 31 (toll free).

VISA
Tel 900 99 11 24 (toll free).

The Euro

The euro (€) is the common currency of the European Union. It went into general circulation on 1 January 2002, initially for 12 participating countries. Spain was one of those countries, with the Spanish peseta phased out in 2002. EU members using the euro as sole official currency are known as the eurozone. Several EU members have opted out of joining this common currency.

Euro notes are identical throughout the eurozone countries, each one including designs of fictional architectural structures and monuments. The coins, however, have one side identical (the value side), and one side with an image unique to each country. Notes and coins are exchangeable in all participating countries.

Euro Banknotes

Euro banknotes have seven denominations. The €5 note (grey in colour) is the smallest, followed by the €10 note (pink), €20 note (blue), €50 note (orange), €100 note (green), €200 note (yellow) and €500 note (purple).

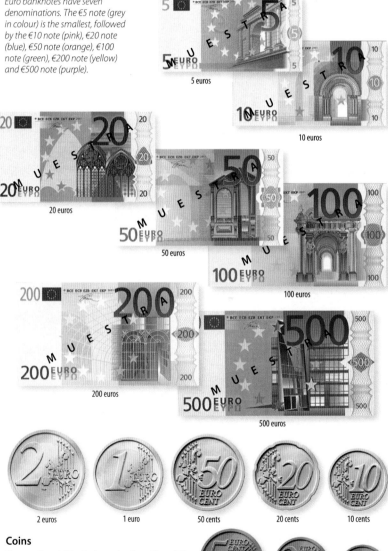

5 euros

10 euros

20 euros

50 euros

100 euros

200 euros

500 euros

Coins

The euro has eight coin denominations: €1 and €2; 50 cents, 20 cents, 10 cents, 5 cents, 2 cents and 1 cent. The €2 and €1 coins are both silver and gold in colour. The 50-, 20- and 10-cent coins are gold. The 5-, 2- and 1-cent coins are bronze.

2 euros 1 euro 50 cents 20 cents 10 cents

5 cents

2 cents

1 cent

Communications and Media

Public telephones, run by the Spanish telecommunications company Movistar, are easy to find and operate with a card or coins, but international calls have a high charge. Depending on your service provider, you may find it is cheaper to use your mobile phone at roaming rates. The postal service, Correos, is identified by a crown insignia in blue or white on a yellow background. Registered mail can be sent from all Correos offices. These also sell stamps, but it is more usual, and quicker, to buy them from *estancs* (tobacconists). There are a number of Internet cafés based in the city centre.

Logo of the Spanish telecom system

When using a mobile phone in Spain, remember to dial 00 followed by your national dialling code (44 for the UK, 1 for the USA) before the number. Most mobile phone operators will charge you to receive calls when using the service outside of your home country.

International and Local Telephone Calls

Public telephone boxes *(cabines)* are available throughout the city, and payphones can also be found in some bars and post offices. Both types take coins. There is a high minimum connection charge, especially for international calls, so it is best to ensure that you have plenty of change ready.

Phonecards are a more convenient option and can be bought at *estancs* and newsstands. Some phones have electronic multilingual instruction displays.

Calls can also be made from *locutoris* (public telephone offices) and paid for afterwards. The cheapest offices are those away from the city centre. Private ones, which are often located in shops, are usually much pricier.

The charges for international calls are divided into four bands: EU countries; non-EU European countries and Northwest Africa; North and South America; and rest of the world. With the exception of local calls, using the phone system can be expensive. Calls from a hotel may also incur a high surcharge.

Reversed-charge (collect) calls made to EU countries may be dialled directly, but most others must be made through the operator.

Spain abolished provincial area codes in 1998, so the full number, including the initial 9, must always be dialled, even from within the area.

Mobile Phones

Spain has several mobile phone operators; the main ones are Movistar, Vodafone, Orange and Yoigo. Roaming rates vary widely depending on agreements between your service provider and the local Spanish provider. Some operators offer special deals for travelling in EU countries. Check with your service provider before leaving. If you plan to make a lot of calls, another good option is to buy a Spanish top-up phone with SIM card and number. A basic phone can be bought for about €30 and SIM cards are sold at most El Corte Inglés and FNAC stores.

Internet

All hotels, airports and many bars in the centre have Internet hotspots, but often they will charge you a small fee for access and you will usually need to ask for a password. Barcelona has a free, non-user registration Wi-Fi service with 185 municipal hotspots in civic centres, museums, sports clubs and libraries. A full list of municipal hotspots is at www.bcn. cat/barcelonawifi/en. Internet

Sign for an Internet hotspot

Useful Spanish Dialling Codes

- When calling within a city, within a province, or to call another province, dial the entire number. The province is indicated by the initial digits: Barcelona numbers start with 93, Lleida 973, Girona 972 and Tarragona 977.
- To make an international call, dial 00, followed by the country code, the area code and the number.
- Country codes are: UK 44; Eire 353; France 33; US and Canada 1; Australia 61; New Zealand 64. When dialling overseas numbers it may be necessary to omit the initial digit of the destination's area code.
- For directory service, dial 11888.
- For an international operator, dial 11825 (English- and French-speaking operators).
- To make a reversed-charge (collect) call to the UK only, dial 900 961682 (from a private landline or telephone box) and you will be asked to dial the number required.
- To report technical faults, dial 1002.
- The speaking clock and wake-up calls can be accessed by dialling 1212 (from Movistar landlines only).

cafés are mainly based in the city centre and nearly all hotels have a computer, or computers, for guests to send emails. Phone centres *(locutorios)* also offer Internet access at a cheaper rate.

Postal Service

Correos, Spain's postal service, is rather slow. It is better to send any urgent or important post by *urgente* (express) or *certificado* (registered) mail, or to use a private courier service.

Post can be registered and sent from all Correos offices. However, it is more convenient to buy stamps for postcards and letters from an *estanc* (tobacconists). Postal rates fall into three price bands: Spain, Europe and the rest of the world. Parcels must be weighed and stamped by Correos and must be securely tied with string, or a charge may be made at the counter to have them sealed by a clerk. Smaller packages, like books, can be sent through the yellow post boxes with stamps bought from the *estanc* after weighing.

Main Correos offices open from 8:30am to 8:30pm Monday to Friday and from 9:30am to 2pm on Saturday. Branches in the suburbs and in villages open from 9am to 2pm Monday to Friday and from 9:30am to 1pm on Saturday.

Typical mailbox

Addresses

In Catalan addresses the street name is written first, followed by the building number, the floor number, and the number or letter of the apartment. For example, C/ Mir 7, 5è-A means apartment A on floor 5 of building number 7 in Carrer Mir. *Carrer* is often shortened to C/. Floor designations are: *Baixos* (ground floor), *Entresol*, *Principal*, *1r*, *2n* and so on, meaning that *2n* is in fact the

4th level above the ground. Some newer buildings use the less complicated designation of *Baixos* followed by *1r*, *2n* and so on upwards. The postcodes have five digits; the first two are the province number.

Newspapers and Magazines

Some newsagents and kiosks in the city centre stock periodicals in English. Newspapers in English available on the day of publication are the *International Herald Tribune*, the *Guardian International* and the *Financial Times*. Others can be found a day after publication. Weekly news magazines such as *Time*, *Newsweek* and *The Economist* are readily available. *Catalonia Today*, a monthly newspaper in English, is available at central kiosks and newsstands.

The main Catalan-language newspapers are *El Punt* and *El Periódico*. *La Vanguardia*, in Spanish, is published in Barcelona and is widely respected. The Spanish newspapers *El País*, *El Mundo* and *ABC* are also reliable.

Barcelona's best weekly listings magazine in Spanish is *enBarcelona*. The monthly *Metropolitan* is published in English and can be found in pubs, cinemas and bars. Also available is the Catalan-language *Time Out*.

Television and Radio

Catalans have a choice of watching TV3 in Catalan run by the regional government, or TVE1 and TVE2, Spain's two state television channels. There is a Catalan channel, Canal 33, and five main Spanish independents: Antena 3, Tele-5, Canal+ (Canal Plus), Cuatro and La Sexta. A regular foreign language news service is

A newsstand on La Rambla in Barcelona

provided by Barcelona Televisio (BTV). Most foreign films on television (and in cinemas) are dubbed. Subtitled films are listed as *V.O. (versión original)*. There are a number of good cinemas in Barcelona that show films exclusively in *V.O.* Satellite channels such as CNN, Cinemanía and Eurosport and other European channels are commonly provided in hotels.

The main radio stations are Catalunya Ràdio (102.8FM) and COM Ràdio (100.4FM), the Spanish state Radio Nacional de España (738FM), and the independent stations Radio 2 (93.0FM), broadcasting classical music, and Ser (96.9FM), a Spanish general-interest station

TV3 television station logo

DIRECTORY

Internet

Ciber Virreina
C/Asturies 78 (Gracia).
Map 3 B1.
Tel 93 368 5770.

Work Centers
Ronda Universitat 9.
Map 2 F1.
Tel 93 481 41 48.
Roger de Lluria 2.
Map 5 B1.
Tel 93 390 83 50.
W workcenter.es

Postal Service

Central Post Office
Plaça Antonio López s/n.
Map 5 B3.
Tel 934 868302.

TRAVEL INFORMATION

Catalonia's three main airports – El Prat, Girona and Reus – receive international flights from all over the globe. While Barcelona's El Prat mainly handles scheduled services, Girona and Reus deal with package holiday flights. Rail networks and toll highways radiate from Barcelona to serve the region's major towns. Barcelona has a well-developed ringroad *(ronda)* system, and a tunnel through the Collserola Hills brings the inland highways right into the city. Both its Metro system and suburban train links are good, and most rural areas are served by intermittent bus services. For remote areas, a car may be required.

Green Travel

As a tourist-intensive area, Catalonia faces environmental challenges, especially around the busy coastal areas. Trains offer an easy alternative to flying or taking the car, and international and national services are both efficient and economical *(see p184)*.

The local Catalan train network – called *Rodalies* – provides access to most of the region, although to reach some rural areas without direct links, such as the Montseny, the Pyrenean mountain villages, and La Garrotxa, you may have to arrange a taxi connection.

Barcelona has a number of cycle-hire shops and a growing network of cycle lanes that provide access to all the major sights of the city. *Bicing*, the municipal government-run free cycle service, can be used with a Bicing card and supplies maps of the city's cycle lanes. Though this is currently open to residents only, commercial operators offer rentals to visitors from around €10 for 2 hours, to €60 for a week.

Arriving by Air

Barcelona's El Prat airport is divided into two main terminals: T1 and T2. Most international flights now arrive at T1 (including all flights operated by **Iberia** and **British Airways**). **easyJet** operates from T2. If you need to transfer between terminals, use the free bus shuttle service, which leaves from outside each terminal.

Barcelona is served by many international airlines. The Spanish national carrier, Iberia, offers daily scheduled flights to Barcelona from all west European capitals. It also offers direct flights from several eastern European capitals.

British Airways offers daily flights to Barcelona from Heathrow and London City airports. easyJet flies to Barcelona from Gatwick, Stansted, Luton, London Southend, Bristol, Newcastle and Liverpool. **Ryanair** flies to Barcelona, Girona and Reus airports from Birmingham, Bristol, Durham, Liverpool, Manchester, Newcastle, Leeds, Stansted, Luton, Doncaster, Bournemouth,

East Midlands, Blackpool, Edinburgh, Glasgow and Dublin. **Delta Air Lines** offers direct flights to Barcelona from the US. Iberia operates a full service from both the United States and Canada.

Catalonia's other two airports mainly handle charter flights: Girona serves the Costa Brava, and Reus, near Tarragona, the Costa Daurada. There are regular buses from Reus and Girona to Barcelona. For passengers arriving from Madrid or other Spanish cities, Spain's domestic flights are operated by Iberia and its associated airlines **Air Nostrum** and **Air Europa**. Iberia's low-cost carrier **Vueling** offers a good service from many Spanish and European destinations to Barcelona.

The most frequent shuttle service between Madrid and Barcelona (El Prat only) is Iberia's **Pont Aeri (Puente Aéreo)**. It flies every quarter of an hour at peak times and passengers can buy tickets just 15 minutes in advance using a self-ticketing machine. The flight takes 50 minutes.

Other services between Madrid and Barcelona are less frequent but, on the whole, their prices tend to be lower. The major international car rental companies *(see p187)* have desks at both terminals of El Prat airport. Girona also has some rental companies on site and cars can be delivered to Reus from nearby Tarragona. Local firms offer tempting deals; check the small print carefully.

Getting to Barcelona

Barcelona airport is only 16 km (10 miles) away from the city. There is a regular bus service to

A waiting area in Barcelona's El Prat airport

the city centre from both terminals, operating from 6am until 1:05am and costing about €5. It takes 25–30 mins from T2 and 35 mins from T1. The final stop is in Plaça Catalunya, but there are also stops in Plaça Espanya and along Gran Vía.

The cheapest way to get to the city is by train. There is a train every 30 minutes. A shuttle bus will take you to the airport train station from T1 and it is a 10-minute walk across the pedestrian flyover from T2. The city centre train stops are at Passeig de Gràcia and Sants.

There are plenty of taxis available from outside of both terminals – join the queue at the taxi rank. Taxis to central Barcelona are metered and the journey should cost between €25 and €32, depending on the volume of traffic, the time of day and which terminal you are using. There is a small supplement added for journeys to and from the airport.

A new Metro line, L-9, which is due to open in 2016, will run from Plaça Catalunya to both airport terminals.

Tickets and Fares

Air fares to Barcelona and the coastal resorts vary through the year, depending on demand. They are generally highest during the summer months. Special deals, particularly for weekend city breaks, are often available in the winter and may

include a number of nights at a hotel. Christmas and Easter flights are almost always booked up well in advance.

Charter flights from the UK to Girona and Reus can be very cheap, but tend to be less reliable, and often fly at unsociable hours.

Good deals can be found online to fly to Barcelona from other cities in Spain through Vueling, Air Europa or Iberia.

Sea Travel

Grimaldi Lines has a ferry service between Civitavecchia (near Rome) or Livorno (near Florence) and Barcelona. **Atlas Cruises and Tours** offers transatlantic cruises between the US and Barcelona, as well as cruises around the Mediterranean. **Costa Cruises** offers Mediterranean cruises

starting in Barcelona, while **Thomson Cruises**, in the UK, has cruises calling at Barcelona, but starting out from Mallorca.

Travel to the Balearic Islands

Barcelona is the main city on the Spanish mainland from which to reach the Balearic Islands. Flights are run by Iberia, Air Europa and Vueling. **Balearia** runs a hydrofoil (a kind of catamaran) service to Ibiza, which takes 8 hours. It also goes to Majorca, taking 7 hours, and Menorca, taking 4 hours. They also offer car ferry crossings, which take about 8 hours, by **Acciona Trasmediterránea** to Ibiza, Majorca and Menorca. To travel to Formentera you need to take a ferry service from Ibiza. It is wise to book in advance, especially in summer.

Balearia car ferry to the Balearic Islands

DIRECTORY

Airports

Barcelona El Prat
Tel 902 40 47 04.

Girona
Tel 902 40 47 04.

Reus
Tel 902 40 47 04.

Airlines

Air Europa
Tel 902 401 501 (Spain).
W air-europa.com

British Airways
Tel 902 11 13 33 (Spain).
Tel 0844 493 0787 (UK).
W britishairways.com

Delta Air Lines
Tel 902 810 872 (Spain).
Tel (800) 241 41 41 (US).
W delta.com

easyJet
Tel 902 599 900 (Spain).
Tel 0843 104 5000 (UK).
W easyjet.com

Iberia, Air Nostrum
Tel 902 400 500 (Spain).
Tel 0870 609 0500 (UK).
Tel (800) 772 4642 (US).

Ryanair
Tel 08712 460000 (UK).
W ryanair.com

Vueling
Tel 902 808 005 (Spain).
W vueling.com

Sea Travel

Atlas Cruises & Tours
Tel (800) 942 3301 (US).
W atlastravelweb.com

Costa Cruises
Tel 902 23 12 31 (Spain).
W costacruceros.es

Grimaldi Lines
Tel 902 531 333 (Spain).
W grimaldi-lines.com

Thomson Cruises
Tel 0871 230 2800 (UK).
W thomson.co.uk/cruise.html

Travel to the Balearic Islands

Acciona Trasmediterránea
Tel 902 45 46 45 (Spain).
W transmediterranea.es

Balearia
Tel 902 16 01 80 (Spain).
W balearia.com

Travelling by Train and Metro

There are two providers of rail services in Catalonia. The Spanish national RENFE *(Red Nacional de Ferrocarriles Españoles)* operates Spain's intercity services, including first-class fast Talgo and AVE trains and some of Barcelona's commuter services *(Rodalies)*. The Catalan government's FGC *(Ferrocarrils de la Generalitat de Catalunya)* runs some suburban trains in Barcelona and some special-interest services in Catalonia's provinces. Barcelona also has the Metro, an efficient city-wide network of underground (subway) trains.

Trains on the platform at one of Barcelona's major railway stations

Arriving by Train

There are direct international train services to Barcelona from several European cities including Paris, Montpellier, Geneva, Zurich and Milan. Sleeping compartments can be booked on direct service overnight trains. All trains entering the eastern side of Spain from France go through Port Bou/Cerbère or La Tour de Carol on the Franco-Spanish border. Travelling to Barcelona from departure points not offering a direct service may mean picking up a connection here. International trains arrive at Sants mainline station, located in the centre of Barcelona.

Services from Barcelona to other cities in Spain are fast and frequent. Overnight trains are offered by Estrella (a basic service) to Madrid, and by Trenhotel (a more sophisticated service) to A Coruña and Vigo. AVE runs a high-speed train between Barcelona and Madrid; the journey takes 2, 3 or 5 hours, with around 25 services a day.

renfe

Logo of the Spanish national rail service

Exploring Catalonia by Train

Catalonia has a network of regional trains *(regionals)* covering the whole of Catalunya and run by **RENFE**. There are three types – the *Media Distancia* and Talgo linking the main towns with few stops in between, and the *Regional* trains which take longer and stop frequently. A high-speed Euromed service from Barcelona to Tarragona (continuing south to Castelló, València and Alacant/Alicante) leaves from Estació de Sants. **FGC** *(Ferrocarrils de la Generalitat de Catalunya)* is a network of suburban trains run by the Catalan government in and around Barcelona. FGC also runs some special services, such as the rack railway (cog railroad) from Ribes de Freser *(see inside back cover)* to Núria in the Pyrenees and La Cremallera, which runs up to Montserrat. It also runs the cable cars and funiculars at the Monastery of Montserrat *(see pp124–5)* and at Vallvid-rera, as well as several historic steam trains and an electric train for tourists. Details are available at the FGC station at Plaça de Catalunya or by calling the FGC number listed in the Directory.

Most trains have disabled access – it is worth checking at the time of booking.

Tickets and Reservations

Tickets for Talgo, AVE, Alvia, international trains and all other long-distance travel by train may be bought at any of the major RENFE railway stations from the *taquilla* (ticket office). They are also sold by travel agents, plus a booking fee. Tickets can be purchased on the RENFE website, and long-distance train tickets have a discount if bought online at least 15 days in advance. During the peak months (July to September), many of the most popular intercity routes, particularly to the coasts, are booked up weeks in advance, so it is worth planning ahead. You can also reserve tickets by phone *(see Directory)*. They are held for 48 hours (up to 2 hours before the train leaves) and can be collected at main stations.

Tickets for local and regional services can be purchased from station booking offices. In some larger stations, they can also be bought from ticket machines. Tickets for *Rodalies* (local services) cannot be reserved. A one-way journey in Catalan is *anada* and a round trip is *anada i tornada*.

Train Fares

Fares for rail travel depend on speed and quality. Talgo and

DIRECTORY

Public Transport

FGC Information
Tel 93 205 15 15.
Ⓦ fgc.es

RENFE Information and Credit Card Bookings
Tel 902 320 320.
Ⓦ renfe.es

Secretaria General de Juventud (Young People's Tourist Office)
Carrer de Calàbria, 147.
Tel 93 483 83 84.

TMB Information
Tel 902 075 027.
Ⓦ tmb.cat

Ticket machines in use at one of Barcelona's Metro stations

AVE trains are more expensive than local and regional trains. RENFE offers discounts to children and people over 60, groups of ten and through travel cards on local, regional and long-distance trains; there are also significant discounts when purchasing online.

Interrail tickets are available for people of all ages from EU member states and Switzerland. Eurail tickets are for residents of non-European countries (you will need to prove your residence status to train staff). These tickets offer discounts on rail travel and can be purchased at Estació de Sants and Estació de França stations. Young Person's cards are available through the **Secretaria General de Juventud** and are intended for people under 26, of any nationality. They offer a discount of up to 20 per cent on journeys from any point in Spain to Europe. To purchase these, you will need proof of your age and identity.

The Barcelona Metro

There are nine underground Metro lines in Barcelona, run by TMB (Transports Metropolitans de Barcelona). Lines are identified by number and colour. Platform signs distinguish between trains and their direction by displaying the last station on the line. In the street it is easy to spot a Metro station – look for a sign bearing a red "M" on a white diamond background.

The Metro is usually the quickest way to get around the city, especially as all multi-journey tickets are valid for the Metro and FGC lines (in Zone 1),

as well as on the bus and local RENFE services. A RENFE or FGC sign at a Metro station indicates that it has a RENFE or FGC connection.

Metro trains run from 5am to midnight from Monday to Thursday, to midnight on Sunday and weekday public holidays, from 5am to 2am on Friday and the day before a public holiday, and all night on Saturdays.

Barcelona is in the process of building a new Metro line, the L9, which will eventually reach the airport and pass through the heart of the city. There are currently five new stops on the L9 on the outskirts of the city, with more being added over the coming years. When

A one-way (single) Metro ticket for Barcelona's subway

completed in 2016, the L9 will be the longest Metro line in Europe.

Barcelona Tickets and Travelcards

A range of tickets and money-saving travel cards are available to tourists. Some cover train, bus and Metro. Combined tickets allow travellers to hop from Metro to FGC to bus lines without leaving the station to pay again.

Tickets are as follows: T-dia and T-mes are for unlimited daily and monthly travel respectively; the senzill ticket, for one single journey, can be used on Metro, bus and FGC; the T-10, which can be shared and is the most useful for tourists, allows ten trips and combines journeys on Metro, bus and FGC in one trip (with a time limit of an hour and a half); the T-50/30 is for 50 journeys in 30 days on Metro, bus and FGC.

Details of special tourist travel cards are on the inside back cover of this guide.

There are 2-, 3-, 4- and 5-day travelcards available which offer unlimited journeys on the Metro, FGC and bus.

Using a Metro Ticket Machine

Insert tickets that don't work to make a duplicate.

Press to ask for information.

4 Collect your ticket and change due.

3 c Insert coins.

3 b Insert banknote(s).

3 a Insert credit card.

2 Select ticket: senzill (single trip), T-10 (10 trips), T-50/30 (50 trips in 30 days), then choose the area and quantity.

1 Select language: Catalan/Spanish, English, French.

Travelling by Car and Bus

Driving conditions in Catalonia vary enormously, from the dense road network and heavy traffic in and around Barcelona to almost empty country roads in the provinces, where villages – and in particular petrol (gas) stations – can be far apart. Toll highways *(autopistes)* are fast and free-flowing, but the ordinary main roads along the coast are usually very busy at all times of day. For tourists without private cars, joining an organized bus tour is a good way to visit well-known, but rather more remote, places of interest.

A toll motorway, a popular way of travelling across the region

Arriving by Car

Many people drive to Spain via the French motorways (highways). The most direct routes across the Pyrenees are the motorways through Hendaye in the west and La Jonquera in the east. Port Bou is on a scenic coastal route, while other routes snake over the top, entering Catalonia via the Vall d'Aran, Andorra, and Puigcerdà in the Cerdanya. From the UK, car ferries run from Plymouth to Santander and from Portsmouth to Santander and Bilbao in northern Spain.

Car Rental

International car rental companies, such as **Hertz**, **Avis** and **Europcar**, as well as some Spanish ones, such as **National ATESA**, operate all over Catalonia. You are likely to get better deals with international companies if you arrange a car from home. A hire car is *un cotxe de lloguer*. Catalonia's three main airports *(see p182)* have car rental desks. However, those at Girona and Reus have irregular opening hours, so if you need a car there, it is best to book in advance and they will meet

your requirements. Avis offers deals in chauffeur-driven cars from major cities.

Logo of the National ATESA car-rental company

Taking your own Car

A green card from a car insurance company is needed to extend your comprehensive cover to Spain. In the UK, the RAC, AA and Europ Assistance have rescue and recovery policies with European cover. Vehicle registration, insurance documents and your driver's licence must be carried at all times. Non-EU citizens should obtain an international driver's licence; in the US, these are available through the AAA. You may also be asked to produce a passport or national identity card as extra proof of identification. A country of origin sticker must be displayed on the rear of

foreign vehicles. All drivers must carry a red warning triangle, spare light bulbs, a visibility vest and a first-aid kit. Failure to do so will incur an on-the-spot fine.

Driving in Catalonia

At junctions give way to the right unless directed otherwise. Left turns across the flow of traffic are indicated by a *canvi de sentit* sign.

Speed limits for cars without trailers are: 120 km h (75 mph) on *autopistes* and *autovies* (toll and non-toll motorways/ highways); 90 km h (56 mph) on *carreteres nacionals* (main roads), *carreteres comarcals* (secondary roads); 80 km h (50 mph) on Barcelona's ring roads and 30 or 40 km h (19 or 25 mph) in urban areas. There are on-the-spot speeding fines of up to €520.

The blood alcohol limit is 0.5 g per litre (0.25 mg per litre in a breath test) – tests are frequently given and drivers over the limit are fined. Front and rear seat belts must be worn; children under 1.35 m (4 ft 5 inches) must use a specially adapted car seat *(see p175)*. Ordinary unleaded fuel *(Súper 95)*, superior unleaded fuel *(Súper 98)* and diesel *(gas oil)* are sold by the litre.

Autopistes

On toll motorways *(autopistes)*, tolls are calculated per kilometre driven. Over some stretches near cities a fixed toll is charged. You collect a ticket from the *peagte* (toll booth/ plaza) when you join the *autopiste*, and pay when you leave. You must join one of three channels at the *peatge*: *Automàtic* has machines for credit cards; in *Manual* an attendant takes your ticket and money; for *Teletac* you need an electronic chip on your vehicle's windscreen (windshield).

Autopistes have emergency telephones every 2 km (1.25 miles) and service stations every 40 km (25 miles).

Parking

Central Barcelona has a pay-and-display system from 9am to 2pm and 4 to 8pm Monday to Friday and all day Saturday. You can park in blue spaces for about €2–3 per hour. Tickets are valid for 2 hours but can be renewed. Green spaces are reserved for residents but can be used, if available, at a higher rate and are free at off-peak hours.

At underground car parks (parking lots), *lliure* means there is space, *complet* means full. Most are attended, but in automatic ones, you pay before returning to your car. Do not park where the pavement edge is yellow or where there is a private exit *(gual)*. Blue and red signs saying "1–15" or "16–30" mean that you cannot park in the areas indicated on those dates of the month.

No parking at any time of day

Taxis

Barcelona's taxis are yellow and black, and display a green light when free. All taxis are metered and show a minimum fee at the start of a journey. Rates increase after 10pm and there is a €2 surcharge on Thursday–Sunday nights. The minimum fee stays the same. In unmetered taxis, such as in villages, it is best to negotiate a price before setting off. Supplements are charged for going to and from the airport and the port. **Radio Taxis** have cars adapted for disabled people, which need to be booked a day ahead. They also have some cars that will take up to seven people.

An Alsa long-distance bus

Long-Distance Buses

Spain's largest inter-city bus company, **Alsa**, is an agent for **Eurolines**. This runs regular services from all over Europe to Sants bus station in Barcelona. Buses from towns and cities in Spain arrive at Estació del Nord and Sants.

Several companies run day trips or longer tours to places of interest in Catalonia. **Turisme de Catalunya** *(see p175)* has details of trips to Catalonia; in other towns, tourist offices can usually help with tours in their provinces.

Buses in Barcelona

The main city buses are white and red. You can buy a single ticket on the bus, or a *T-10* ten-trip ticket at Metro stations, valid for bus, Metro and FGC *(see p185)*. Other combined tickets are described inside the back cover. The *Nitbus* runs nightly from around 10pm to 5am, and the *Aerobus* offers a service between Plaça de Catalunya and El Prat airport. A good way to sightsee is by Bus Turístic. It runs all year on three routes from Plaça de Catalunya. A ticket, bought on board, is valid for all three routes and lets you get on and off as you please. **Julià Tours** and **Pullmantur** also offer tours of Barcelona.

A busy taxi rank in Barcelona

BARCELONA STREET FINDER

The map references given with the sights, shops and entertainment venues described in the Barcelona section of the guide refer to the street maps on the following pages. Map references are also given for Barcelona's hotels (see pp136–39) and its restaurants, cafés and bars (see pp144–53). The schematic map below shows the areas of the city covered by the Street Finder. The symbols used on the Street Finder maps to indicate sights, features and services are explained in the key at the foot of the page.

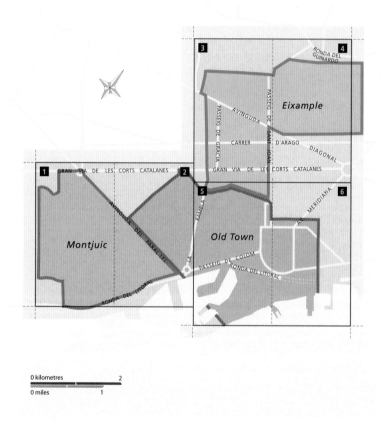

0 kilometres 2
0 miles 1

Key to Street Finder

- ▪ Major sight
- ▪ Place of interest
- ▪ Other building
- ▪ Main train station
- ▪ Local (FGC) train station
- ▪ Metro station
- ▪ Main bus stop
- ▪ Cable car
- ▪ Funicular station
- ▪ Tramway stop

- ℹ Tourist information
- ✚ Hospital with A&E unit
- ▪ Police station
- ✝ Church
- ═ Railway line (railroad)
- ▪ Pedestrianized street
- ▪ Funicular line
- ●—● Cable car line

Scale of Map Pages

0 metres 250
0 yards 250

Street Finder Index

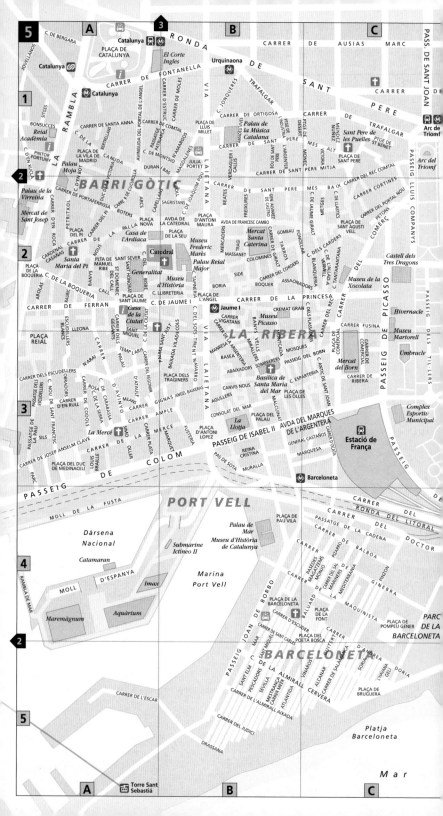

General Index

Acknowledgments

Dorling Kindersley would like to thank the following people whose contributions and assistance have made the preparation of this book possible.

Main Contributor

Roger Williams contributed to the *Eyewitness Travel Guide to Spain* and has written Barcelona and Catalonia titles for Insight Guides. He was also the main contributor to the *Eyewitness Travel Guide to Provence. Lunch with Elizabeth David*, set around the Mediterranean, is his latest novel.

Additional Contributors

Mary Jane Aladren, Pepita Arias, Emma Dent Coad, Sally Davies, Rebecca Doulton, Josefina Fernández, , Mary-Ann Gallagher, Nick Rider, David Stone, Judy Thomson, Clara Villanueva, Suzanne Wales (Word on Spain).

Revisions Team

Louise Abbott, Amaia Allende, Queralt Amella Miró, Gillian Andrews, Imma Espuñes i Amorós, Shruti Bahl, Claire Baranowski, Kate Berens, Marta Bescos, Stuti Tiwari Bhatia, Daniel Campi (Word on Spain), Paula Canal (Word on Spain), Anna Freiberger, Mary-Ann Gallagher, Alrica Green, Swati Gupta, Lydia Halliday, Christine Heilman, Jessica Hughes, Claire Jones, Zafar ul Islam Khan, Juliet Kenny, Elly King, Priya Kukadia, Kathryn Lane, Alison McGill, Caroline Mead, Sam Merrell, Barbara Minton, Jason Mitchell, Sonal Modha, Casper Morris, Vikki Nousiainen, Susie Peachey, Marianne Petrou, Rada Radojicic, Mani Ramaswamy, Lucy Richards, Ellen Root, Collette Sadler, Azeem Siddiqui, Meredith Smith, Susie Smith, Vatsala Srivastava, Alícia Ribas Sos, Helen Townsend, Nikhil Verma, Hugo Wilkinson, Lola Carbonell Zaragoza.

Proofreader

Stewart J Wild, Huw Hennessey.

Indexer

Hilary Bird.

Special Photography

Max Alexander, Departure Lounge/Ella Milroy, D. Murray/J. Selmes, Dave King, Ian O'Leary, Alessandra Santarelli, Susannah Sayler, Clive Streeter

Photography permissions

© Obispado de VIC; © Cabildo de la Catedral de Girona; Teatre Nacional de Catalunya (Barcelona); Institut Mpal. del Paisatge Urba i la Qualitat de Vida, Ajuntament de Barcelona.

Dorling Kindersley would like to thank all the churches, museums, restaurants, hotels, shops, galleries and other sights too numerous to thank individually.

Picture credits

Key: a= above; b = below/bottom; c = centre; f = far; l = left; r = right; t = top.

Works of art have been reproduced with the permission of the following copyright holders:

Salvador Dalí *Rainy Taxi* and *ceiling fresco in the Wind Palace Room, Teatre - Museu Dalí* © Kingdom of Spain, Gala - Salvador Dalí Foundation, DACS, London 2011; George Kolbe *Morning* © DACS, London 2011; IOC/Olympic Museum Collections; Joan Miró *Dona i Ocell* 1983 and Tapestry of the Foundation Joan Miró 1975 © Succession Miró/ADAGP, Paris and DACS, London 2011.

The publisher would like to thank the following individuals, companies and picture libraries for their kind permission to reproduce their photographs:

ABaC Restaurant & Hotel: 140bl, 150tr; **Hotel Aiguaclara:** 134bc, 138bl; **Hotel Arts Barcelona:** 137tr; **AISA, Barcelona:** 16bl, 20br, 25bl, Jaume Huguet *San Jorge* 30cla, 46cb, 48cb, 48bl, 176bl; **Alamy Images:** Douglas Armand 99cr; Jon Arnold Images 78tr; John Barab 18; Andrew Bargery 64br, 78cb; Neil Barks 79tl; Peter Barritt 84tr; Oliver Bee 78crb, 79br; CW Images 50-1; Dalgleish Images 98cl; Danita Delimont 174cb; Iain Davidson Photographic 104cla, 105tl; Chad Ehlers 99tl; Mike Finn-Kelcey 185bc; Richard Foot 98tr; Kevin Foy 185tl; B J Gadie 64tc; Guido 186cla; Platinum GPics 1c; Terry Harris 17c; Chris Hellier 102; Guillem Lopez 40-1; Stephen Saks Photography 70t; Neil Setchfield 62br; Sandro Vannini 84bc; Ruben Vicente 187bl; Ken Welsh 175tl; Alsa Group s.l.l.c. 187tr; **Aquila Photographics:** Adrian Hoskins 114cl; 114bl, 114clb; James Pearce 23bl; **National Atesa:** 186c; **El Atril:** 144br.

Balearia: 183cr; Basilica Sagrada Familia: Pep Daudé 83crb; **Mike Busselle:** 113br, 114tc.

Can Culleretes: 141tl; **Can Fabes:** 152br; **El Celler de l'Aspic:** 151b; **Cinnamon:** 153tr; **Cinc Sentits:** 148 br; **Codorniu:** 35tl, 35ca; **Bruce Coleman Collection:** Erich Crichton 22tr; José Luis González Grande 23tr; Norbert Schwirtz 23tl; Colin Varwdell 23crb; **Comerc24:** 140cla; **Corbis:** 33tl, 33c, Archivio cla; Peter Aprahamian 107br; Carlos Dominguez 11clb; Owen Franken 32cla; Andrea Jemolo 84cla; Ken Kaminesky 76-7; Julian Martin/EPA 12bl; Jose Fuste Raga 11tl; Mark L. Stephenson 85cla; Vanni Archive 85br. **Cover,** Madrid: Pepe Franco 154cla; Matias Nieto 191b.

Dreamstime.com: Bayda127 12tr; Blitzkoenig 92tl; Alexandre Fagundes De Fagundes 93bl; Gurgenb 21t;

Hugera 96b; Mihai-bogdan Lazar 63cb; Lornet 91t; Marlee 110; Carlos Soler Martinez 13tc; Juan Moyano 81tl; Toxawww 10cl, 19b; Yuryz 182bl.

Hotel Empordà: 151tr; Espai Sucre: 146br; L'Estartit Tourist Office: 123cl; European Commission: 179.

Firo Foto: 71cl; Flickr.com: www.flickr.com/photos/del15xavii_xavo/4123975385/177tr; Frieixenet: 34cl, 35br; Fundacion Collection Thyssen-bornemisza: Fra Angelico Madonna of Humility 97t; Fundacio Joan Miro, Barcelona: Joan Miró Flama en l'espai i dona nua 1932 © Succession Miró/ ADAGP, Paris and DACS, London 2011 90tl.

Generalitat de Catalunya: 177cra; Getty Images: Peter Adams 120-1; Danbalboa Fotografo 94; Niko Guido 13br; Hulton Archive/Stringer 8-9; Conor MacNeill 54; Nikada 172-3; JosÃ © Fuste Raga 2-3; Ferran Traite Soler 72; Godo Photo: 126bl, 131t, José Luis Dorada 127t; Grupo Tragaluz: 149br.

Robert Harding Picture Library: 27tr, 61cra, 74cla, 93tr, 91b; La Huerta: 152tc.

The Illustrated London News Picture Library: 49t; Index, Barcelona: CJJ. 21br, 46tl, 49crb; Image Bank: 26bl, 75crb; Images Colour Library: 26clb; AGE Fotostock: 115br, 155tr, 155cl, 170cr; Nick Inman: 22b, 98br.

La Caixa: 178tr; Life File Photographic: Xabier Catalan 27crb; Emma Lee 27cra.

Marka, Milan: Sergio Pitamitz 64tl; Mas Salvanera: Ramón Ruscalleda 135tl; Milk Bar & Bistro: 145tr; Museu Arqueologic: 89cra; Museu de Ciencies Naturals de Barcelona: 68clb; Museu Nacional D'art De Catalunya: Ramon Marti Alsina La Compañia de Santa Barbara 1891 47tl; Museu Picasso: Pablo Ruiz Picasso Auto Retrato 1899–1900 © Succession Picasso/ DACS, London 2011 66bl.

Natural Science Photos: C Dani & I Jeske 170c; Naturpress, Madrid: Oriol Alamany 36cl, 39cra; Walter Kvaternik 39c, 177cra; Carlos Vegas 180tr; Jose A Martinez 111b.

Oronoz, Madrid: 43b, 44tr, 44cl, 47bl, 48tl.

Dos Palillos: 141bl, 147tr; Park Zoologic: 68tr; Photographersdirect.com: Michael Dobson/Echo Imagery 109c, 109br; Fran Fernandez Photography 104bc, 107c, 108tl, 109tl; Jan van der Hoeven, 105br, 106cla, 108br. Francisco Fernandez Prieto:106bc; Prisma, Barcelona: 4tr, 20tl, 47crb, 48cra, 154br, 163c; Carles Aymerich 24bl, 38cra;; Jordi Cami 36br; Ramon Cases Carbo Procession outside Santa María del Mar c. 1898 30tr; Albert Heras 38bl; Kuwenal 45tr, 45bl; Mateu 37cra; Joaquim Mir Trinxet La Catedral de los Pobres 31bl; Isidro Nunell Monturiol Esperando la Sopa 1899 31tl; Santiago Rusiñol y Prats Jardines de Aranjuez 1907 30br; Antoni Tàpies Litografia 1948 © Foundation Tàpies, Barcelona/ADAGP, Paris & DACS, London 2011 31br.

Els Quatre Gats: 146t.

Raimat: 34cb; RENFE: 184cb; Rex Features: 119cb; Roca Moo, Hotel Omm: 149tl.

M Angeles Sanchez: 37bc; Sant Pau: 153bl; Sant Pere del Bosc Hotel & Spa: 139tr; Sauc Restaurant: 148tl; Spectrum Colour Library: 26tr; Stockphotos, Madrid: 170bl; Campillo 171tl; Suculent: 147bl; Superstock: Age Fotostock 184cla; MIVA Stock 86.

TV3 Television de Catalunya: 181cra.

Wagakoro: 150bl.

Map Cover:
Getty Images: Scott Barbour.

Jacket:
Front and Spine - Getty Images: Scott Barbour.

Front End Paper:
Dreamstime.com: Marlee Rcr; Getty Images: Danbalboa Fotografo Rc; Conor MacNeill Lbr; Ferran Traite Soler Rtc; Superstock: MIVA Stock Lbl.

All other images © Dorling Kindersley. For further information see www.DKimages.com.

Special Editions of DK Travel Guides

English–Catalan Phrase Book

In Emergency

Help!	**Auxili!**	ow-**gzee**-lee
Stop!	**Pareu!**	**pah**-reh-oo
Call a doctor!	**Telefoneu un metge!**	teh-leh-fon-**eh**-oo oon meh-**djuh**
Call an ambulance!	**Telefoneu una ambulància!**	teh-leh-fon-**eh**-oo oo-nah ahm-boo-**lahn**-see-ah
Call the police!	**Telefoneu la policia!**	teh-leh-fon-**eh**-oo lah poh-lee-**see**-ah
Call the fire brigade!	**Telefoneu els bombers!**	teh-leh-fon-**eh**-oo uhlz boom-**behs**
Where is the nearest telephone?	**On és el telèfon més proper?**	on-ehs uhl tuh-leh-**fon** mehs proo-**peh**
Where is the nearest hospital?	**On és l'hospital més proper?**	on-ehs looss-pee tahl mehs proo-**peh**

Communication Essentials

Yes	**Sí**	see
No	**No**	noh
Please	**Si us plau**	sees plah-oo
Thank you	**Gràcies**	**grah**-see-uhs
Excuse me	**Perdoni**	puhr-**thoh**-nee
Hello	**Hola**	**oh**-lah
Goodbye	**Adéu**	ah-**they**-oo
Good night	**Bona nit**	**bo**-nah neet
Morning	**El matí**	uhl muh-**tee**
Afternoon	**La tarda**	lah **tahr**-thuh
Evening	**El vespre**	uhl **vehs**-pruh
Yesterday	**Ahir**	ah-**ee**
Today	**Avui**	uh-voo-**ee**
Tomorrow	**Demà**	duh-**mah**
Here	**Aquí**	uh-**kee**
There	**Allà**	uh-**lyah**
What?	**Què?**	keh
When?	**Quan?**	**kwahn**
Why?	**Per què?**	puhr keh
Where?	**On?**	ohn

Useful Phrases

How are you?	**Com està?**	kom uhs-**tah**
Very well, thank you	**Molt bé, gràcies.**	mol **beh grah**-see-uhs
Pleased to meet you.	**Molt de gust.**	mol duh **goost**
See you soon.	**Fins aviat.**	feenz uhv-**yat**
That's fine.	**Està bé.**	uhs-**tah beh**
Where is/are …?	**On és/són?**	ohn ehs/**sohn**
How far is it to …?	**Quants metres/ kilòmetres hi ha d'aquí a …?**	kwahnz meh-truhs/ kee-loh-muh-truhs yah dah-**kee** uh
Which way to …?	**Per on es va a …?**	puhr on uhs **bah** ah
Do you speak English?	**Parla anglès?**	**par**-luh an-**glehs**
I don't understand	**No l'entenc.**	noh luhn-**teng**
Could you speak more slowly, please?	**Pot parlar més a poc a poc, si us plau?**	pot par-**lah** mehs **pok** uh pok sees plah-oo
I'm sorry.	**Ho sento.**	oo **sehn**-too

Useful Words

big	**gran**	gran
small	**petit**	puh-**teet**
hot	**calent**	kah-**len**
cold	**fred**	fred
good	**bo**	boh
bad	**dolent**	doo-**len**
enough	**bastant**	bahs-**tan**
well	**bé**	beh
open	**obert**	oo-**behr**
closed	**tancat**	tan-**kat**
left	**esquerra**	uhs-**kehr**-ruh
right	**dreta**	**dreh**-tuh
straight on	**recte**	**rehk**-tuh
near	**a prop**	uh prop
far	**lluny**	**lyoon**yuh
up/over	**a dalt**	uh **dahl**
down/under	**a baix**	uh **bah**-eeshh
early	**aviat**	uhv-**yat**
late	**tard**	tahrt
entrance	**entrada**	uhn-**trah**-thuh
exit	**sortida**	soor-**tee**-thuh
toilet	**lavabos/ serveis**	luh-**vah**-boos sehr-**beh**-ees

more	**més**	mess
less	**menys**	men-yees

Shopping

How much does this cost?	**Quant costa això?**	kwahn kost ehs-**shoh**
I would like …	**M'agradaria …**	muh-grad-uh-**ree**-ah
Do you have?	**Tenen?**	**tehn**-un
I'm just looking, thank you	**Només estic mirant, gràcies.**	noo-mess ehs-**teek** mee-**rahn grah**-see-uhs
Do you take credit cards?	**Accepten targes de crèdit?**	ak-**sehp**-tuhn tahr-**zhuhs** duh **kreh**-deet
What time do you open?	**A quina hora obren?**	ah **keen**-uh oh-ruh **oh**-bruhn
What time do you close?	**A quina hora tanquen?**	ah **keen**-uh oh-ruh **tan**-kuhn
This one.	**Aquest**	ah-**ket**
That one.	**Aquell**	ah-**kehl**
expensive	**car**	kahr
cheap	**bé de preu/ barat**	beh thuh **preh**-oo/ bah-**rat**
size (clothes)	**talla/mida**	tah-lyah/**mee**-thuh
size (shoes)	**número**	noo-mehr-oo
white	**blanc**	blang
black	**negre**	**neh**-gruh
red	**vermell**	vuhr-**mel**
yellow	**groc**	grok
green	**verd**	behrt
blue	**blau**	**blah**-oo
antique store	**antiquari/botiga d'antiguitats**	an-tee-**kwah**-ree/ boo-tee-gah/dan-tee-ghee-**tats**
bakery	**el forn**	uhl forn
bank	**el banc**	uhl bang
book store	**la llibreria**	lah lyee-bruh-**ree**-ah
butcher's	**la carnisseria**	lah kahr-nee-suh-**ree**-uh
pastry shop	**la pastisseria**	lah pahs-tee-suh-**ree**-uh
chemist's	**la farmàcia**	lah fuhr-**mah**-see-ah
fishmonger's	**la peixateria**	lah peh-shuh-tuh-**ree**-uh
greengrocer's	**la fruiteria**	lah froo-ee-tuh-**ree**-uh
grocer's	**la botiga de queviures**	lah boo-**tee**-guh duh keh-vee-**oo**-ruhs
hairdresser's	**la perruqueria**	lah peh-roo-kuh-**ree**-uh
market	**el mercat**	uhl muhr-**kat**
newsagent's	**el quiosc de premsa**	uhl kee-**ohsk** duh **prem**-suh
post office	**l'oficina de correus**	loo-fee-**see**-nuh duh koo-**reh**-oos
shoe store	**la sabateria**	lah sah-bah-tuh-**ree**-uh
supermarket	**el supermercat**	uhl soo-puhr-muhr-**kat**
tobacconist's	**l'estanc**	luhs-**tang**
travel agency	**l'agència de viatges**	la-**jen**-see-uh duh vee-**ad**-juhs

Sightseeing

art gallery	**la galeria d'art**	lah gah-luh-**ree**-yuh dart
cathedral	**la catedral**	lah kuh-tuh-**thrahl**
church	**l'església la basílica**	luhz-**gleh**-zee-uh lah buh-**zee**-lee-kuh
garden	**el jardí**	uhl zhahr-**dee**
library	**la biblioteca**	lah bee-blee-oo-**teh**-kuh
museum	**el museu**	uhl moo-**seh**-oo
tourist information office	**l'oficina de turisme**	loo-fee-**see**-nuh thuh too-**reez**-muh
town hall	**l'ajuntament**	luh-djoon-tuh-**men**
closed for holiday	**tancat per vacances**	tan-**kat** puh bah-**kan**-suhs
bus station	**l'estació d'autobusos**	luhs-tah-see-**oh** dow-toh-**boo**-zoos
railway station	**l'estació de tren**	luhs-tah-see-**oh** thuh tren

Staying in a Hotel

Do you have a vacant room?	¿Tenen una habitació lliure?	teh-nuhn oo-nuh ah-bee-tuh-see-oh lyuh-ruh
double room with double bed	habitació doble amb llit de matrimoni	ah-bee-tuh-see-oh doh-bluh arn lyeet duh mah-tree-moh-nee
twin room	habitació amb dos llits/ amb llits individuals	ah-bee-tuh-see-oh am dohs lyeets/ am lyeets in-thee-vee-thoo-ahls
single room	habitació individual	ah-bee-tuh-see-oh een-dee-vee-thoo-ahl
room with a bath	habitació amb bany	ah-bee-tuh-see-oh am bah-nyuh
shower	dutxa	doo-chuh
porter	el grum	uhl groom
key	la clau	lah klah-oo
I have a reservation	Tinc una habitació reservada	ting oo-nuh ah-bee-tuh-see-oh reh-sehr-vah-thah

Eating Out

Have you got a table for…	Tenen taula per…?	teh-nuhn tow-luh puhr
I would like to reserve a table	Voldria reservar una taula.	vool-dree-uh reh-sehr-vahr oo-nuh tow-luh
The bill please.	El compte, si us plau.	uhl kohm-tuh sees plah-oo
I am a vegetarian	Sóc vegetarià/ vegetariana	sok buh-zhuh-tuh-ree-ah/buh-zhuh-tuh-ree-ah-nah
waitress	cambrera	kam-breh-ruh
waiter	cambrer	kam-breh
menu	la carta	lah kahr-tuh
fixed-price menu	menú del dia	muh-noo thuhl dee-uh
wine list	la carta de vins	lah kahr-tuh thuh veens
glass of water	un got d'aigua	oon got dah-ee-gwah
glass of wine	una copa de vi	oo-nuh ko-pah thuh vee
bottle	una ampolla	oo-nuh am-pol-yuh
knife	un ganivet	oon gun-ee-veht
fork	una forquilla	oo-nuh foor-keel-yuh
spoon	una cullera	oo-nuh kool-yeh-ruh
breakfast	l'esmorzar	les-moor-sah
lunch	el dinar	uhl dee-nah
dinner	el sopar	uhl soo-pah
main course	el primer plat	uhl pree-meh plat
starters	els entrants	uhlz ehn-tranz
dish of the day	el plat del dia	uhl plat duhl dee-uh
coffee	el cafè	uhl kah-feh
rare	poc fet	pok fet
medium	al punt	ahl poon
well done	molt fet	mol fet

Menu Decoder (see also pp32–33 & 142–3)

l'aigua mineral	lah-ee-gwuh mee-nuh-rahl	mineral water
sense gas/ amb gas	sen-zuh gas/ am gas	still/ sparkling
al forn	ahl forn	baked
l'all	lahlyuh	garlic
l'arròs	lahr-roz	rice
les botifarres	lahs boo-tee-fah-rahs	sausages
la carn	lah karn	meat
la ceba	lah seh-buh	onion
la cervesa	lah-sehr-ve-sah	beer
l'embotit	lum-boo-teet	cold meat
el filet	uhl fee-let	sirloin
el formatge	uhl for-mah-djuh	cheese
fregit	freh-zheet	fried
la fruita	lah froo-ee-tah	fruit
els fruits secs	uhlz froo-eets seks	nuts
les gambes	lahs gam-bus	prawns
el gelat	uhl djuh-lat	ice cream
la llagosta	lah lyah-gos-tah	lobster
la llet	lah lyet	milk
la llimona	lah lyee-moh-nah	lemon
la llimonada	lah lyee-moh-nah-thuh	lemonade
la mantega	lah mahn-teh-gah	butter
el marisc	uhl muh-reesk	seafood
la menestra	lah muh-nehs-truh	vegetable stew
l'oli	loll-ee	oil
les olives	luhs oo-lee-vuhs	olives
l'ou	loh-oo	egg
el pa	uhl pah	bread

el pastís	uhl pahs-tees	pie/cake
les patates	lahs pah-tah-tuhs	potatoes
el pebre	uhl peh-bruh	pepper
el peix	uhl pehsh	fish
el pernil salat serrà	uhl puhr-neel suh-lat sehr-rah	cured ham
el plàtan	uhl plah-tun	banana
el pollastre	uhl poo-lyah-struh	chicken
la poma	la poh-mah	apple
el porc	uhl pohr	pork
les postres	lahs pohs-truhs	dessert
rostit	rohs-teet	roast
la sal	lah sahl	salt
la salsa	lah sahl-suh	sauce
les salsitxes	lahs sahl-see-chuhs	sausages
sec	sehk	dry
la sopa	lah soh-puh	soup
el sucre	uhl-soo-kruh	sugar
la taronja	lah tuh-rohn-djuh	orange
el te	uhl teh	tea
les torrades	lahs too-rah-thuhs	toast
la vedella	lah veh-theh-lyuh	beef
el vi blanc	uhl bee blang	white wine
el vi negre	uhl bee neh-gruh	red wine
el vi rosat	uhl bee roo-zaht	rosé wine
el vinagre	uhl bee-nah-gruh	vinegar
el xai/el be	uhl shahee/uhl beh	lamb
el xerès	uhl shuh-rehs	sherry
la xocolata	lah shoo-koo-lah-tuh	chocolate
el xoriç	uhl shoo-rees	red sausage

Numbers

0	zero	seh-roo
1	un (masc)/una (fem)	oon/oon-uh
2	dos (masc)/dues (fem)	dohs/doo-uhs
3	tres	trehs
4	quatre	kwa-truh
5	cinc	seeng
6	sis	sees
7	set	set
8	vuit	voo-eet
9	nou	noh-oo
10	deu	deh-oo
11	onze	on-zuh
12	doce	doh-dzuh
13	tretze	treh-dzuh
14	catorze	kah-tohr-dzuh
15	quinze	keen-zuh
16	setze	set-zuh
17	disset	dee-set
18	divuit	dee-voo-eet
19	dinou	dee-noh-oo
20	vint	been
21	vint-i-un	been-tee-oon
22	vint-i-dos	been-tee-dohs
30	trenta	tren-tah
31	trenta-un	tren-tah oon
40	quaranta	kwuh-ran-tah
50	cinquanta	seen-kwahn-tah
60	seixanta	seh-ee-shan-tah
70	setanta	seh-tan-tah
80	vuitanta	voo-ee-tan-tah
90	noranta	noh-ran-tah
100	cent	sen
101	cent un	sent oon
102	cent dos	sen dohs
200	dos-cents (masc)	dohs-sens
	dues-centes (fem)	doo-uhs sen-tuhs
300	tres-cents	trehs-senz
400	quatre-cents	kwah-truh-senz
500	cinc-cents	seeng-senz
600	sis-cents	sees-senz
700	set-cents	set-senz
800	vuit-cents	voo-eet-senz
900	nou-cents	noh-oo-cenz
1,000	mil	meel
1,001	mil un	meel oon

Time

one minute	un minut	oon mee-noot
one hour	una hora	oo-nuh oh-ruh
half an hour	mitja hora	mee-juh oh-ruh
Monday	dilluns	dee-lyoonz
Tuesday	dimarts	dee-marts
Wednesday	dimecres	dee-meh-kruhs
Thursday	dijous	dee-zhoh-oos
Friday	divendres	dee-ven-druhs
Saturday	dissabte	dee-sab-tuh
Sunday	diumenge	dee-oo-men-juh

Rail Transport Maps

The main map shows the whole of Barcelona's Metro system, which has nine lines. It also shows the city's FGC suburban lines, funiculars and tram *(see pp184–5)*. Public transport in Barcelona is modern and efficient, and the integrated transport system allows for interchanging between different modes of transport if you have a multi-journey (for example a *T-10)* card. A special ticket for tourists is the *Barcelona Card*, available in one-day to five-day values, which offers unlimited travel on Metro and bus, and discounts at leading sights and museums. The inset map shows Catalonia's mainline rail network, which is run by RENFE, the Spanish state system. The stations selected for inclusion here are those closest to sights described in this guide.

Key

L1   Metro line
O   Interchange station
—   Tram line
+++   Funicular
===   FGC line
—   Renfe line

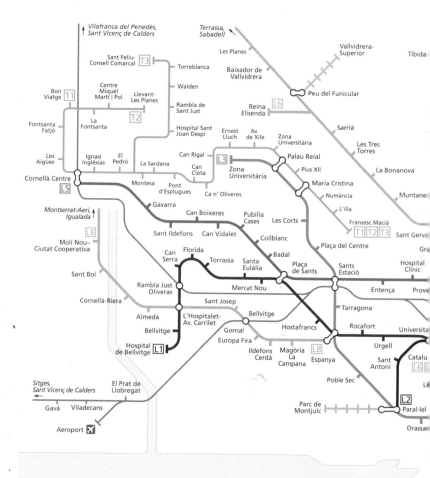